Imagined Homelands

IMAGINED HOMELANDS
British Poetry in the Colonies

Jason R. Rudy

Johns Hopkins University Press
Baltimore

© 2017 Johns Hopkins University Press
All rights reserved. Published 2017
Printed in the United States of America on acid-free paper
2 4 6 8 9 7 5 3 1

Johns Hopkins University Press
2715 North Charles Street
Baltimore, Maryland 21218-4363
www.press.jhu.edu

Library of Congress Cataloging-in-Publication Data

Names: Rudy, Jason R., 1975– author.
Title: Imagined homelands : British poetry in the colonies / Jason R. Rudy.
Description: Baltimore : Johns Hopkins University Press, 2017. |
Includes bibliographical references and index.
Identifiers: LCCN 2017009940| ISBN 9781421423920 (hardback : acid-free paper) | ISBN 9781421423937 (electronic) | ISBN 1421423928 (hardback : acid-free paper) | ISBN1421423936 (electronic)
Subjects: LCSH: Commonwealth poetry (English)—History and criticism. | English poetry—19th century—History and criticism. | Colonies in literature. | National characteristics, English, in literature. | Literature and society—Great Britain—Colonies—History—19th century. | Imperialism in literature. | BISAC: LITERARY CRITICISM / Semiotics & Theory. | LITERARY CRITICISM / European / English, Irish, Scottish, Welsh. | LITERARY CRITICISM / Poetry.
Classification: LCC PR9082 .R83 2017 | DDC 821/.8099171241—dc23
LC record available at https://lccn.loc.gov/2017009940

A catalog record for this book is available from the British Library.

Special discounts are available for bulk purchases of this book.
For more information, please contact Special Sales at 410-516-6936
or specialsales@press.jhu.edu.

Johns Hopkins University Press uses environmentally friendly book materials, including recycled text paper that is composed of at least 30 percent post-consumer waste, whenever possible.

For Scott and Aaron

CONTENTS

Acknowledgments ix

Introduction: Unsettling Colonial Poetry 1

1 Floating Worlds: Poetry and the Voyage Out 19

2 Colonial Authenticity: Circulation, Sentiment, Adaptation 43

3 Sounding Colonial: Dialect, Song, and the Scottish Diaspora 75

4 Native Poetry: Forms of Indigeneity in the Colonies 107

5 Colonial Laureates: Navigating Settler Culture 134

6 The Poetry of Greater Britain:
Race and Nationhood at Century's End 163

Conclusion: Genres of Belonging 189

Appendix A. Colonial Ship Journals 193
Appendix B. Timeline of British Colonial Poetry 195

Notes 197
Bibliography 223
Index 241

ACKNOWLEDGMENTS

This book would not have been possible without the support of friends in many places. When I first arrived in Sydney, Russ Alexander was there to welcome me. I have learned a great deal from him over our many years of friendship. Ben Clark at the State Library of New South Wales introduced me to the emigrant ship journals, the subject of my first chapter, and effectively launched my research into this project. Also in Sydney, I have enjoyed the company of Matthew Hankins, Christian Bonett, Annette Tesoriero, and Kirstin Tranter: good friends, local insiders. My colleague Michael Olmert enabled my first trip to Australia, and I remain grateful for that and for his friendship.

In South Africa I thank Sandra Young, who warmly hosted a research visit to Cape Town; the faculty at the University of Cape Town for their enthusiastic welcome; and the staff at both the National Library of South Africa and the library at the University of Cape Town, in particular Melanie Geustyn and Lesley Hart. In Nova Scotia, I thank Marjorie Stone for welcoming me to Dalhousie University and Karen Smith for so ably helping me navigate the Killam Library's extraordinary special collections. I thank as well the research staffs at the National Library of New Zealand in Wellington, the National Library of Australia in Canberra, the National Maritime Library in Greenwich, England, and the British Library in London. Simon Avery, Emma Mason, and Christina Morris have been fantastic UK hosts and steadfast friends.

Kirstie Blair has for many years been an almost uncanny interlocutor. I remain indebted to her insights, her generosity as a host in Glasgow, and her work in convening a daylong seminar, "Scottish Emigrant Literatures of the Long Nineteenth Century," at the University of Stirling. I presented my earliest work on this project at Yale University, where I was hosted by the late

Linda Peterson; I will remember her warmth and encouragement. Other chapters were shared and workshopped at Indiana University, Princeton University, Temple University, the University of Stony Brook, the University of Warwick, and the City University of New York. I thank the faculty and graduate students at each of those institutions for their engagement with my work, and in particular Ross Forman, Rae Greiner, Ivan Kreilkamp, Peter Logan, Monique Morgan, Pablo Mukherjee, Adrienne Munich, Deborah Nord, and Talia Schaffer.

I am especially grateful for the support of my home institution, the University of Maryland at College Park, both for the travel funds that allowed me to conduct my research and for a semester of leave during which I was able to travel. I thank in particular Kent Cartwright and William Cohen, who, as chairs of the English Department, encouraged my archival wanderings. Yearlong fellowships from the National Endowment for the Humanities and the American Council of Learned Societies gave me the time first to research and then to write: my heartfelt thanks to both of those institutions for their incomparable generosity. This work would not have been completed without the time and financial support provided by those institutions. At Johns Hopkins University Press, I thank Matt McAdam for his early encouragement of this project and Catherine Goldstead for guidance in the final stages. Barbara Lamb copyedited with grace and kindness.

No book is written in isolation, thank goodness, and I have been particularly fortunate in my readers. For commenting on drafts of this project both early and late, I thank Tanya Agathocleous, Michelle Boswell, Andrew Elfenbein, Deborah Jackson, Charles LaPorte, Tricia Lootens, Meredith Martin, Emma Mason, Carla Peterson, Natalie Phillips Hoffmann, Sangeeta Ray, Martha Nell Smith, Laurie Tiemann, Scott Trudell, Carolyn Williams, and David Wyatt. My thinking has benefited from conversations with many friends and colleagues, including especially David Kurnick, Vincent Lankewish, Sebastian Lecourt, Benjamin Morgan, Kate Thomas, and Mary Helen Washington. The participants in the Nineteenth-Century Seminar at the 2016 Dickens Universe, ably led by Tricia Lootens and Sharon Aronofsky Weltman, helped in the very final stages of revision.

The Historical Poetics Working Group has been a source of inspiration for nearly a decade, a community of scholars like none other: Max Cavitch, Michael Cohen, Mary Ellis Gibson, Virginia Jackson, Tricia Lootens, Meredith Martin, Meredith McGill, Yopie Prins, Eliza Richards, Alex Socarides, and Carolyn Williams. Each of the following six chapters developed in relation to our ongoing conversations. I wish especially to thank Meredith Martin, who read the full manuscript and helped shape the final work: Meredith, you have made this a far better book.

Collaborative projects with Tanya Agathocleous, Hester Blum, and Mary Ellis Gibson have been generative for my thinking and heartwarming in their company. I thank in particular Tanya for being my co-conspirator, travel companion, and wonder twin. For their friendship and encouragement I thank as well Elizabeth Bearden, Fatma Daglar, Kevin Jones, Rick Lee, Marilee Lindemann, Patricia Nathanson, Martha Nell Smith, and Bari Trivas-Fore.

My interest in Australia began many years ago, in graduate school at Rutgers, when our Victorian reading group tackled a special issue dedicated to the poetry of nineteenth-century Australia. Kate Flint, Barry Qualls, Jonah Siegel, Carolyn Williams: you were with me at the beginning, and you're with me still.

Finally, I thank my family. My mother, Patricia, accompanied me on several research trips—Sydney, Wellington, Halifax—making those journeys more fun and more meaningful by far. Mom, I'm so happy to have shared those adventures with you. For unfailing support, I thank as well my father, Glenn; my brother, Michael; my sister, Elizabeth; and my new parents-in-law, Laurie and Dale.

This book is dedicated to my son, Aaron, and my partner, Scott, who together have made real the home I long imagined.

An earlier version of chapter 1 appeared as "Floating Worlds: Emigré Poetry and British Culture" in *ELH* (Spring 2014): 325–50; it is reprinted here in expanded form with the permission of Johns Hopkins University Press. Short excerpts from chapters 1 and 6 first appeared in "Manifest Prosody," in *Victorian Poetry* 49 (Summer 2011): 253–66, and a portion of chapter 3 first appeared as "Scottish Sounds in Colonial South Africa: Thomas Pringle, Dialect, and the Overhearing of Ballad" in *Nineteenth-Century Literature* 71 (Sept. 2016): 174–214; I am grateful for permission to reprint from the University of West Virginia Press and the University of California Press. Finally, a very early version of my writing on Richard Hengist Horne and colonial Melbourne, now divided between chapters 2 and 5, was first published online as "Literary Melbourne: Poetry in the Colony, ca. 1854" as part of *BRANCH: Britain, Representation, and Nineteenth-Century History* (general editor, Dino Franco Felluga) at http://branchcollective.org. My thanks to the editors for permission to reprint that material here in revised and expanded form.

Excerpt from "Alabanza: In Praise of Local 100" by Martín Espada from *Alabanza: New and Selected Poems, 1982–2002* (W. W. Norton, 2003), ©2003 by Martín Espada. Reprinted by permission of the author.

I am deeply grateful to Gordon Syron for permission to use his painting *Invasion Day* (2012) on the cover of this book. About this artwork, which comes from a series of paintings of the same title, Mr. Syron has written the following:

> I want to show the negative feelings of the Aboriginal people. The truth is, the way it was, the white master race came and took our land and did not even have the courtesy to ask us or buy it. They said we weren't even human beings when they claimed our land as "terra nullius." British law is alright for the British but Aboriginal law, customs, language, dance, Mimi spirits have been around a lot longer than "British law."
>
> I wanted to make the Aboriginal people in control of the land and when the ships arrived the Aboriginal people were along the shoreline and they told them to go away. Terra Nullius was used as a valid reason to claim Australia and I dispute that claim, using this painting as proof.
>
> Gordon Syron
Redfern, New South Wales, 2012

Imagined Homelands

INTRODUCTION

Unsettling Colonial Poetry

> It yet may be our lot to wander wide
> Through many lands before at last we come
> Unto the gates of our enduring home.
> —William Morris, *The Earthly Paradise* (1868)

The State Library of New South Wales in Australia sits atop one of Sydney's relative high points. From the entry to that sandstone building, the view today takes in first the sprawling botanical gardens and then, after sloping grass lawns, the spectacular harbor into which Arthur Phillip first sailed in January of 1788: "the finest harbour in the world," he wrote, "in which a thousand sail of the line may ride with the most perfect security."[1] From that vantage point, members of the Cadigal people, the original inhabitants of Sydney's lands, may have looked out at Phillip's approaching *murri nowie*, his "strange canoes."[2] The artist Gordon Syron imagines such a perspective in his painting *Invasion Day*. In the bloodied waters of Sydney Harbor and the skeletal faces of the arriving British, Syron aims to show us "the truth . . . the way it was."[3]

We have been told many versions of this historical moment. Most accounts practice what Paul Carter calls "imperial history," an approach that understands history as a dramatic narrative unfolding on a variety of world stages.[4] As spectators of Sydney's historical drama, we look out from the State Library, across the gardens and to the harbor, picturing storylines shaped by our knowledge of the events that followed—events broadly recognizable within the frameworks of British settlement and Indigenous displacement. Imperial history privileges coherent narrative and, as a result, overlooks elements peripheral to the dominant storyline. Carter's own version of history, traced vividly through *The Road to Botany Bay* (1987), relies on letters, journals, and maps to move beyond "cause-and-effect" storytelling structures.[5] Syron's accounting takes the form of dynamic visual tableaux. The present volume turns to poetry.

Poetry was everywhere as nineteenth-century British emigrants ventured out to the lands we now call Australia, New Zealand, Canada, and South Africa: printed in the newspapers of emigrant ships; carried as physical volumes; and transported by memory, internalized by the tens of thousands who annually left Great Britain for colonial shores.[6] These poems worked their way into the everyday lives of emigrants, from the bustling urban centers of Melbourne and Cape Town to the Canadian frontier and the Australian outback. They were recited and sometimes sung at public gatherings, printed in local newspapers, circulated by colonial lending libraries, and eventually rewritten, sometimes parodically, as colonial poetic cultures took root and developed into their own.

As a genre far more prominent in the nineteenth century than in our current day, poetry played a significant, necessary role as emigrants shaped new colonial identities for themselves. In Bendigo, for example, a gold town to the northwest of Melbourne, residents in 1863 might have heard Margaret Aitken recite Tennyson's "The May Queen" at the town's newly constructed Temperance Hall.[7] A popular Scottish actress who toured Australia through the 1860s, Aitken earned praise from the *Sydney Morning Herald* for her performances at the Australian Library.[8] A Melbourne newspaper reported that "she sobs as she gives the history of Tennyson's hapless damsel"—the wild, wayward, and tragically doomed young woman of "The May Queen"— "and her sobs are freely responded to by gentle women and strong men."[9] These scenes of shared public emotion show that the poet laureate's sentimentality resonated in the colonies, helping to bridge cultural divisions between Great Britain and the new homelands emigrants imagined for themselves overseas.

Scenes of public feeling also show that poetry throughout British colonial spaces was fundamentally political. Settler colonialism was communal by nature, as Lorenzo Veracini has argued, and poetry was vital in establishing that sense of community. Though "most of the colonists who moved to the New Worlds did so individually, without a conscious determination to establish a new, ideal, society," nonetheless "ideas about entitlements"— about the rights settlers imagined for themselves in the colonies—proceeded from a "corporate" and "pluralistic" sensibility.[10] Scholars have too often overlooked the role poetry played in this communal dynamic, perhaps because we have taken John Stuart Mill too much at his word in imagining that nineteenth-century British poetry was "overheard" and not "heard": that poetry in effect was something individuals experienced in isolation from their communities.[11]

Mill's notion of overheard poetry reflects a nineteenth-century ideal identified by Virginia Jackson as "lyricization." Within this model, readers after the eighteenth century came to think of poetry as "requir[ing] as its context only the occasion of its reading," to the exclusion of all other frames of reference: historical setting, place of publication, medium, author.[12] To the contrary, as Jackson and others have argued, nineteenth-century poetry was more often shared and public.[13] Within emigrant communities, poetry's enthusiastic circulation helped substantiate the pluralism Veracini identifies. After the Bible and religious texts such as *Pilgrim's Progress*, the most likely shared literary knowledge for British emigrants would have taken poetic form.[14] Poetry in the colonial context resonated as especially political, as nineteenth-century poets and scholars came to understand certain forms of poetry as foundational to culture itself: "the ballad theory of civilization," in Meredith Martin's notable phrase, whereby a nation was thought to arrive at civilized "unity" through the communal experience of poetry.[15]

That colonial poetry has for the most part failed to make its way into our understanding of the period—we generally do not find it on literature syllabi, in scholarly studies, or in modern anthologies of British literature—has kept from our attention an archive that significantly enhances our sense of both the nineteenth-century settler-colonial world and the broader canon of British literature. Indeed, the poems examined in this book offer insight not just into British settler culture and history but into nineteenth-century English-language poetry more generally. Edmund Clarence Stedman included in his 1895 anthology of Victorian poetry a significant "selection from the minstrelsy of Great Britain's colonies."[16] Though he disparaged the "Australian yield" as a whole, he still included fourteen poets in his section on Australasia, plus works by English poets who spent extended time abroad. Twenty-three poets appear under the "Dominion of Canada," and Stedman acknowledges Canada as having produced "a group of lyricists whose merit has made their names familiar" and whose work reflects "the sentiment, the atmosphere, of their northern land." Even in the nineteenth century, then, and at a time generally uncharitable toward colonial poetics, Stedman (an American) understood the need to include poetry of Australia, New Zealand, and Canada in his "Victorian Anthology."

Stedman aside, however, Victorian colonial writing—poetry especially—has historically been understood as second-rate, leaving a vast and diverse body of colonial literature largely unexamined, generally misunderstood, and absent from historical account. Over the course of many archival trips, I became accustomed to the looks of skepticism that greeted me from archivists and friends alike. Both the tone and function of colonial poetry have been especially subject to misunderstanding, in part because scholars have tended to read local verse cultures as necessarily unsophisticated. From this perspective, colonial culture takes the guise of a reproduced, lesser version of British culture. The historian James Belich best represents this approach in arguing that a vast "cloning system" was foundational to nineteenth-century Anglophone settlerism, whereby legal, governmental, and cultural institutions familiar to the British at home were reproduced abroad.[17] David Cannadine has similarly pointed to the "exaggerated regard for British traditions" visible throughout nineteenth-century colonial spaces.[18]

Cultural reproduction was indeed a crucial part of settler colonial culture, and poetry played a necessary role in that process. But in focusing primarily on institutions such as the law and on public exercises like government ceremony, Belich and Cannadine overstate the exactness and pervasiveness of colonial replication while overlooking the many ways settlers distinguished themselves from their British origins—the ways their poetry reveals aspects of colonial culture otherwise difficult to perceive. Literary scholars have too infrequently recognized these counter-narratives because assumptions of aesthetic taste have relegated colonial poetry to the status of "verse." Like the Victorians themselves, then, historical and literary studies have mostly dismissed colonial poetry as unworthy of critical attention: intellectually bereft and aesthetically disappointing.

The chapters that follow approach colonial poetry from a range of perspectives. This volume is not a thorough history of British colonial poetry; it is neither a survey of colonial literature nor an attempt to view colonial poetry as a system from afar, the "distant reading" advocated by Franco Moretti. "If you want to look beyond the canon," argues Moretti, "close reading will not do it."[19] These chapters suggest otherwise. Colonial poetry, long absent from the canon of nineteenth-century British poetry, offers us clear historical, literary, and theoretical payoffs that come in part through the art of close reading. My chapters span a set of texts variously major and minor, published in different media, and composed under diverse circumstances and from manifold environs. I am most concerned with asking how reading British colonial poetry reshapes our understanding of the period, its history, and colonialism more broadly. The answers to these questions are multiple and include a challenge to limited notions of colonial cultural replication, a more robust sense of poetry's political compass, and an accounting of colonial homes and homelands that does not immediately take nationalistic form.

Poetic Homelands

The concept of a homeland, composed of attributes both tangible and intangible, rests at the center of this study. I would like first to distinguish my use of the term *homeland* from that of Salman Rushdie, whose 1982 essay "Imaginary Homelands" considers the notion of homeland from the perspective of writers like Rushdie himself: those who, as "exiles or emigrants or expatriates" from their native homelands, "are haunted by some sense of loss, some urge to reclaim, to look back." *Homeland* in 1982 had yet to achieve its post-9/11 invocation as a space with borders to be defended and governmental departments charged to ensure its security. Rushdie instead writes metaphorically about "reclaiming [not] precisely the thing that was lost . . . not actual cities or villages, but invisible ones, imaginary homelands, Indias of the mind."[20] For Rushdie, the imaginary homeland is the India of the exile's imagination, an imperfectly recollected land from which he has emigrated and to which he will never return, except as temporary visitor.

The "imagined homelands" of the present study, by contrast, are colonial spaces, shores upon which colonizing emigrants arrived throughout the nineteenth century.[21] For these long-voyaging Britons, the imagined homeland was a future "enduring home" like that of William Morris's *Earthly Paradise*: the place of arrival that might become, through hard work and perhaps only after the passing of significant time, a place of genuine belonging. My use of the term contradicts the *Oxford English Dictionary*, which defines "the homeland" as Britain itself, specifically in opposition to "British colonies and territories." Reference to "the homeland," according to the *OED*, is necessarily a reference to Britain, as suggested by an 1862 *All the Year Round* article cited in the definition: "The walls [of my tent] are decorated with such simple keepsakes and souvenirs of the home-land as I carry about with me." The author of the *All the Year Round* essay is a traveler in Persia, and he fills his makeshift canvas tent with mementos of home, including "an English pointer" and "tea-things."[22] In no way does the traveler imagine he might create a homeland for himself in Persia; his "homeland" is a version of Rushdie's, an England of his mind.

If both Rushdie and the traveler in Persia look behind to their own imaginary homelands, the emigrants of this study instead look ahead: they are in the continuous process of imagining homelands on the shores where they have arrived. As settler colonialists, their forward-looking aspirations require the often violent dislocation of others and the brutal transformation of natural landscapes. Imagining home also involved transporting the familiar to foreign shores, remaking forms of Britain in Australia, New Zealand, Canada, and South Africa. This work of remaking took important literary—and specifically poetic—form, sometimes parodic, sometimes imitative, but most often knowingly asserting connections between home and abroad, or between an original home and a new homeland to come.

The chapters of this book propose a range of frameworks for thinking through this imaginative work. In each case, I show poetic genre to be a powerful mechanism supporting the cultural work of British colonialism. I begin with poetry of the voyage out: shipboard poems written in largely parodic registers and demonstrating a playful relationship between popular poetry and the life imagined on colonial frontiers. The four chapters that follow examine facets of colonial literary culture: the replication of canonical poems; the use of dialect to signal particular forms of cultural belonging; the challenges raised by questions of indigeneity; and the public duties of "colonial laureates," or those poets who took upon themselves the role of colonial spokesperson. A final chapter examines the late-century turn to various forms of nationalism in the British colonies and the intersection of poetry with the racial politics of these newly nationalized spaces.

To view colonialism from the perspective of poetry requires understanding that poems have histories and also that the meanings of poems change as they circulate through different communities and across time. When Felicia Hemans first published "The Homes of England" in the April 1827 issue of *Blackwood's Edinburgh Magazine*, she could not have anticipated how that poem would resonate in Sydney in the 1840s, or in Saint John, New Brunswick, in the 1860s. Readings of Hemans's poem evolved as it circulated through Britain's colonial spaces. In the chapters that follow, I question as far as possible the changing meaning of poems, and I examine what those meanings might indicate more broadly for the colonial cultures in which they circulated. This style of reading should be understood as one manifestation of what has been called "historical poetics," a set of methodologies that attend to the situatedness of poetic meaning: the necessary relationship between a poem's readerly contexts and its meaning.[23]

The methods of historical poetics insist, in Yopie Prins's words, that "we cannot separate the practice of reading a poem from the histories and theories of reading that mediate our ideas about poetry."[24] Poems are mediated by the cultural implications of their structure (metrical, rhythmic, and other formal features), by the media of their publication (newspaper, broadside, letter, chapbook, volume), their place of publication, modes of circulation, and a good deal more. Poems also change with time, as they move through physical and temporal space, inhabiting different media and circulating in different spaces among changing sets of readers. I take as axiomatic, then, that the meaning of any one poem is both contingent and malleable.

Poetry offers cultural and theoretical frameworks distinct from those offered by other genres, the novel in particular. Poetry's portability—readily scribbled on a scrap of paper, reprinted in a letter, or fixed in an emigrant's memory—meant it could circulate with ease through Britain's colonies, spaces that at first were not equipped to publish longer works. Less bound by the physical limitations and expenses of printed books, poems could also adapt quickly to new cultural spaces: the particular cultures of emigrant ships, early colonial cities, or miner encampments in the Australian outback, to take just a few examples. Antoinette Burton and Isabel Hofmeyr's notion of a "global imperial commons," a shared literary canon circulating throughout the British Empire, works somewhat differently when considered from the perspective of poetry.[25] Less a core of printed and bound texts radiating out from Britain to colonial peripheries, poetry adapted more quickly to colonial spaces, allowing for more local forms of expression: for example, rewritings of canonical works from colonial perspectives or repurposing of works in new media and with different effects. Burton and Hofmeyr consider printed, physical volumes traversing the globe; this study instead takes as its foundational object the individual poem and its permutations.

Take as just one example the Felicia Hemans poem mentioned above, which in its original form—composed in England, printed in Scotland—reads like a conservative paean to British class structure. An 1868 rewriting of the poem in Saint John, New Brunswick, recycled it a year after Canadian Confederation to celebrate the emerging industrialized Canadian nation, where,

From East to great Pacific's shore,
The Iron Horse shall land,
Stores of great riches gathered up
By many a toil-worn hand.[26]

Part of the Canadian poem's effectiveness came from its resonance with Hemans's lyric, which would have been both familiar and well loved. Equally important were the poem's departures from the original, which allowed the Canadian poet Letitia F. Simson to assert her distance from the conditions of Hemans's original. Most significantly, in Simson's version, the hard-working, "toil-worn" Canadian has access, via the railroad, to the continent's "great riches": a narrative of potential upward mobility unimagined in Hemans's neatly segregated England. (I'll note parenthetically that Simson's class progressivism here rests awkwardly but predictably beside her apparent disregard for the Canadian First Peoples to be displaced by the coming railroad and settler expansion.) Revisions to canonical works such as Simson's appear everywhere in Britain's colonies, assessing and critiquing colonial culture with an immediacy unavailable to most prose publications.

Simson allows us to go even further, to consider the scene of the poem's composition: "Written upon hearing John Boyd, Esquire, recite Mrs. Hemans' beautiful Poem entitled 'The Homes of England,' in the Union Street Congregational Church."[27] Pause for a moment to imagine the scene in the Saint John church, the public recitation of a poem that many would have known by heart. "The merry Homes of England!" wrote Hemans in 1827, "Around their hearths by night, / What gladsome looks of household love / Meet in the ruddy light!"[28] In the original moment of John Boyd's recitation, Hemans's poem no doubt facilitated nostalgic recollections of the English homeland, memories that resonated in a way similar to the feelings Rushdie describes: homelands of the mind, here experienced communally. Simson's revision is no slight adjustment to Hemans's original. Her poem emphatically turns Canadian nostalgia into a forward-looking urgency, with both cultural and political consequences. From the scene of shared feeling, then, emerges a revisionary impulse, bristling with immediacy and the charge of an inspired, colonizing energy: "From East to great Pacific's shore," imagining homelands to come.

Poetry Everywhere

In addition to its portability, poetry also differed from prose in its ubiquity. "Poetry is everywhere," wrote an 1869 newspaper aboard the S. S. *Somersetshire* during a voyage from Plymouth, England, to Melbourne, Australia: "It is circumambient." No matter where one went, there was poetry. "It is found alike on the mountain top, or the deepest valley. In the waves, in their angriest moods, or the gentle ripple of the tide on the pebbly beach."[29] Insofar as it is "circumambient," poetry surrounded British emigrants, journeying from one place to another. Scottish Canadian poet Alexander McLachlin voiced this same sentiment in his 1861 volume *The Emigrant*: "Poetry is every where, / In the common earth and air."[30]

British emigrants carried literary works out with them *to* the colonies, but they also understood poetry to exist around them, waiting to be heard. Charles Harpur (1813–68), son of Australian convicts, suggests as much in "The Voice of the Native Oak," a poem first published 13 September 1851, in Sydney's foremost liberal newspaper, the *Empire*. Harpur instructs his readers to lie under "a lone oak by a lonely stream" and listen to the sounds emanating from it:

> Up in its dusk boughs, down tressing,
>   Like the hair of a giant's head,
> Mournful things beyond our guessing
>   Day and night are utterëd.[31]

The character of these Australian sounds eludes the poet, but Harpur nonetheless testifies to their uncanny presence. In 1851, the poet Judith Wright reminds us, Australia was as yet "largely unexplored, without literature or pride or nationhood, with little to its credit, and seen through European eyes as ugly, barbarous and monotonous."[32] Accordingly, Harpur does not yet know how to describe the sounds of Australian nature; he does not yet know what kind of poetry the continent will produce. He knows only that poetry—unwritten future poems—resides there in one form or another.

Even explorers generally unfamiliar with poetic composition found inspiration in colonial spaces. Such was the case for John Campbell, a Scottish missionary to South Africa who published a volume on his travels in 1815. With just one exception, Campbell wrote in prose; but on a winter's morning in July, he looked out over the South African landscape and realized "that no European eye had ever surveyed these plains, and mountains, and rivers, and that [he] was ten thousand miles from home." In awe of the natural world before him, Campbell discovered poetry. "I snatched a scrap of paper from my pocket, on which I wrote the following lines":

> I'm far from what I call my home,
> In regions where no white men come;
> Where wilds, and wilder men are found,
> Who never heard the gospel sound.

> Indeed they know not that there's one
> Ruling on high, and GOD alone.—
> In days and nights for five months past,
> I've travell'd much; am here at last,
> On banks of stream well named Great,
> To drink its water is a treat.—
> But here to have the living word,
> Enriching treasure! Spirit's sword,
> A favour this that can't be told,
> In worth surpassing finest gold.
> May Bushmen and the Bootchuanas,
> The Namacquaas and the Corannas,
> All soon possess this God-like feast,
> And praise the Lord from west to east.[33]

What strikes me as important here is Campbell's elision between the "living word" of his Christian faith and that of his own poem, which came to him as an inspiration, scrawled on a stray scrap of paper. Campbell's poem makes sense as part of a colonizing narrative—he was, after all, a missionary—but we should also read it as a work of simultaneous discovery: of both Campbell's god and poetry, omnipresent "from west to east"; they are both, according to Campbell, *everywhere*; they are both, the memoir suggests, *circumambient*.

British explorers, colonialists, and emigrants carried poetry within them, in their hearts, their minds, and their blood, importing poetry to spaces where it may not have existed before. But these pioneers also brought with them the capacity to write their own poems, poems that eventually might fall within the long and increasingly wide tradition of British poetics. Campbell's poem, for example, inhabits the South African landscape by way of iambic tetrameter couplets, among the most common structures of British ballad poetry. Words unfamiliar to the average British reader—*Namacquaas, Corannas, Bootchuanas*—seem less strange within Campbell's familiar metrical structure. So too, Fidelia Hill's 1840 poem on the new city of Adelaide, South Australia, part of the first volume of poetry published by a woman in Australia, carries forward into the streets and shops of the colonial outpost her memories of London and the blank verse of Wordsworth's "Tintern Abbey" (see chapter 5). Adam Lindsay Gordon, riding through the Australian outback in the 1850s, hears in the rhythm of his horse's hooves the galloping

Figure 1. John Campbell, frontispiece of *Travels in South Africa* (Andover, MA: Flagg and Gould, 1816 [1815]). Engraved by H. Meyer, drawn by the Reverend W. I. Strait. Campbell towers incongruously over the African landscape. From the collection of the McKeldin Library at the University of Maryland, College Park.

stanzas of Robert Browning's "How They Brought the Good News from Ghent to Aix" (see chapter 2).

These two perspectives on poetry's origins—poetry as existing already in distant places versus poetry carried by travelers to foreign lands—offer a broad framework for this volume. Scholarship on nineteenth-century British poetry has for the most part been limited to works composed and printed in the United Kingdom, primarily England and Scotland. Even studies focused ostensibly on poetry and the British Empire have relied primarily on works composed from within the British Isles—or, at best, continental Europe: Matthew Reynolds' excellent *Realms of Verse* (2001), for example, attends primarily to Alfred Tennyson, Robert Browning, Elizabeth Barrett Browning, and Arthur Hugh Clough, as does Christopher Keirstead's *Victorian Poetry, Europe, and the Challenge of Cosmopolitanism* (2011).

Mary Ellis Gibson's work on English-language poetry in colonial India, *Indian Angles* (2011), offers an important exception, constructing a historical framework for poetry composed on the Indian subcontinent from the eighteenth century to the early twentieth. Gibson's study, which "argues for an understanding of a canon that takes nationalism as a subject of inquiry rather than a criterion for selection," inspires some of my own thinking here.[34] Alison Chapman also looks "away from insular Anglocentrism and towards the transnational, international, and cosmopolitan" in her recent *Networking the Nation* (2015), a study of British and American women poets in Italy during the Risorgimento.[35] The emigrant spaces of Australia, New Zealand, Canada, and South Africa, however, differed significantly from the imperial spaces of India and the internationalist spaces of midcentury Italy, so one's approach to the poetry written there must be different, too. These are spaces long inhabited by historians of the nineteenth century, but for the most part overlooked by scholars of poetry.[36] Those scholars who *have* addressed British colonial poetry have most often narrated its contributions toward nationalist projects, the emergence of literary traditions that eventually took national form.[37] Rarely have we considered colonial poetry in connection with a larger constellation of nineteenth-century British culture and literary history.[38]

This volume looks to the global composition and movement of British poetry, works important both to Britain's domestic literary scene and to Britain's emerging colonies. Nationalism remains as just one among many constitutive terms. The dates of the project envelop the 1832 and 1867 Reform bills, which opened voting rights and pushed Britain closer toward democracy. The period also represents the height of British colonial efforts *and* the onset of skepticism with respect to that global project; by the 1860s, emigrants in Australia and Canada had begun the move toward political independence from Britain. Poetry through the nineteenth century participated actively in Britain's political challenges, at home and abroad, even as it helped settlers negotiate the transition abroad.

I by no means offer a comprehensive study of British colonialism, either from a historical or a literary perspective. India, for example, remains largely absent, as does British Guiana, Sierra Leone, and Hong Kong: territories that were politically and financially significant to the British Empire, but which were not primary destinations for British emigrants. Immigration to the United States is similarly excluded, understood as culturally distinct from settlement in nineteenth-century British colonial spaces, as are poems written in other languages—French poems in Canada, for example, and Dutch poems in South Africa. Focusing on British emigrant poetry has meant that the authors examined, with just one exception, are white, and the absence of nonwhite voices in this body of poetry is a persistent, painful reminder of the iniquities that shaped the British colonial world.[39] I address some of these wrongdoings, specifically in relation to race, in chapters 4 and 6. For the most part, colonial poetry was not a radical political endeavor, and a search there for progressive values will usually turn up short.[40] The political energies of colonial poetry instead tend toward a limited collective rather than the broadly humanitarian, drawing our attention to the immediacy of colonial life rather than distant utopian possibilities.

What follows then is a study of key issues in the history of British settler poetry, problems representative of challenges faced across the British Empire: the transportation and adaptation of British culture; the use of poetry to make foreign spaces seem familiar; and the emergence of new traditions, and ultimately new national identities, in those spaces colonists eventually came to call home.

Reframing Colonial Poetry

My archive of settler poetry allows me to depart significantly from most literary work in British colonial studies. With rare exception, the novel has occupied center stage in calibrating nineteenth-century British engagements with the world. Edward Said's claim at the opening of *Culture and Imperialism* (1993)—that the novel stands as "*the* aesthetic object whose connection to the expanding societies of Britain and France is particularly interesting to study"—continues to reflect the field of Victorian colonial studies more broadly.[41] For example, Lauren Goodlad's compelling study, *The Victorian Geopolitical Aesthetic* (2015), takes the novels of Trollope, Collins, Eliot, and Forster as its primary literary objects of study. Not one of the *Ten Books That Shaped the British Empire* (2014) is a volume of poetry. As a field, literary scholarship has encouraged the devaluing of poetic texts that were signally important to the ways British emigrants thought of themselves and the work of British colonialism.

Scholars outside the nineteenth century have begun addressing global Anglophone poetry, but that work—such as Jahan Ramazani's *A Transnational Poetics* (2009)—has focused almost exclusively on the twentieth and twenty-first centuries, rather than taking account of nineteenth-century global movement and circulation.[42] My book shows the many ways poetry opens significant new perspectives on British colonialism. There could be no genre more interwoven with the everyday lives of nineteenth-century British individuals, from religious hymns to the communal recitation of songs and ballads, the circulation of lyrics in newspapers, the reprinting of poems in anthologies, the memorization of poetry as part of grade-school curricula, and the continued practice of reading poems as part of one's everyday life. In all these ways and more, poetry was built into the lives of British citizens both at home in the United Kingdom and abroad.[43] Poetry, as the author on board the 1869 S. S. *Somersetshire* knew, was "everywhere" in the British colonial world, and we have much to learn from attending to the stories its many forms have to tell.

The chapters that follow propose six distinct frameworks for thinking through British colonial culture. The first chapter, "Floating Worlds: Poetry and the Voyage Out," examines poetry published in newspapers and journals onboard mid-Victorian emigrant ships en route from England to Australia, New Zealand, and South Africa. "Printed at Sea, where the Press is Licensed," as the *Wanderer's Gazette* wryly put it in 1841, these publications, more than sixty of which are now housed at the State Library in Sydney and the National Library of Australia in Canberra (see appendix A), capture the enthusiasms, dreams, and anxieties of British subjects as they moved toward the colonial periphery.[44] They were printed on presses while at sea and distributed to passengers; in many cases they were later bound as keepsakes for subscribers. These poems and the journals in which they were published say much about the experience of mid-Victorian emigration and the ways in which poetry might have helped to shape that experience. I use the shipboard poems to open a larger conversation about imitation, rewriting, and parody, all of which feature prominently in colonial poetry. In rewriting familiar, canonical poems such as Tennyson's *Maud*, Hood's "Song of the Shirt," and Longfellow's *Hiawatha*, emigrant poets heading to the colonies performed a double gesture, looking back toward the literary traditions they were leaving behind while also, through their own innovation and creativity, pointing the way toward a future as colonialists.

Once British emigrants arrived in colonial spaces such as Melbourne, Cape Town, and Halifax, newspapers and literary journals were not long in following, and the poetry of these journals continued the shipboard tradition of parody and revision. My second chapter, "Colonial Authenticity: Circulation, Sentiment, Adaptation," explores the literary culture of those early colonial cities, tackling head-on the assessment that colonial culture was often derivative, if not plagiaristic. Plagiarism, viewed within the specific context of settler publications, was a necessary component of colonial culture. The chapter begins with the first anthology of English-language poetry published in South Africa, *Poetry of the Cape of Good Hope* (1828), which opens with an unattributed poem by the American poet William Cullen Bryant. Significantly, then, the first anthologized South African poem in English was actually written by an America. Subsequent sections of the chapter consider the ways Felicia Hemans's form of sentimental lyricism circulated in colonial Australia and Canada, and the degree to which Adam Lindsay Gordon was an outright plagiarist of Robert Browning. Throughout the chapter, I argue that replication and derivativeness were important first steps toward establishing independent colonial cultures: plagiarism, then, might be reframed in colonial contexts as a sort of virtue.

Chapter 3, "Sounding Colonial: Dialect, Song, and the Scottish Diaspora," uses Scottish dialect poetry to think through the ways poems circulated in emigrant communities. When Thomas Pringle is recognized as founding an English-language poetic tradition in South Africa, we infrequently recognize his Scottish origins, just as we often marginalize the importance of Scottish culture within British colonial culture more broadly. Dialect was a significant feature of colonial poetry, capturing the particular sounds of such localities as the borderlands of Scotland. More than that, dialect signaled an especially communal form of identification, given the long association between dialect and oral culture. Scottish dialect poems in emigrant communities had a special power to invoke a communal consciousness, a sense of being together that arose from having come from the same place. Even into the twentieth century, and in some cases to the present day, Scottish dialect served an important function in the New Zealand and Canadian communities descended from nineteenth-century Scottish settlers. This chapter offers a corrective to narratives of a roughly unified "British" culture that was transported the world over. In fact, diverse cultures from within the United Kingdom were transported and then adapted, and both dialect and song were important markers of those processes. Other chapters of this book might have examined the specific cultures transported from elsewhere in the United Kingdom: from Ireland, for example, or various regions within England; instead, I take the Scottish case as representative of the larger phenomenon.

British settler colonial engagement with Indigenous peoples has been the subject of much important historical and literary work. Chapter 4, "Native Poetry: Forms of Indigeneity in the Colonies," takes up the question of indigeneity from the perspective of the second- and third-generation immigrants who liked to call themselves "native." The chapter looks at the key ways poetry engaged with questions of belonging for colonists born in Australia, New Zealand, Canada, and South Africa who grew up knowing nothing but those colonial spaces and yet living, as Elleke Boehmer writes, "culturally in exile."[45] My focus here examines how colonial perceptions of Indigenous cultures shaped the colonialists' sense of their own belonging, their own culture in exile.[46] British emigrants' cultural identification with Britain was, as Simon Gikandi has noted, always "uneasy": an uneasiness stemming in part from questions of indigeneity and belonging brought into uncomfortable relief by the presence of actual Indigenous peoples throughout British colonial spaces.[47]

Emigrant poets throughout the nineteenth century were expected simultaneously to maintain their roots in the long history of British culture and to be poets recognizably *of the colonies*: to be at once British and indigenous. When in 1862 the *Athenaeum* printed a few poems by the then-unpublished Henry Kendall—born near Ulladulla, in New South Wales, and soon to be among the most important of nineteenth-century Australian poets—the journal echoed a popular sentiment of the period in demanding poetry recognizably *Australian* in nature: "From a new country should come, in time, a new literature. Those images of a virgin nature, found in the sky and landscape, in the Fauna and Flora of Australia, must one day speak to the true poet and find an utterance in his song.... One day or other, we shall catch the brightness of an Australian sky on the page of an Australian bard."[48] Even as the shipboard poems show emigrant nostalgia to operate in both backward- and forward-looking registers, the question of indigeneity here reveals a similar duality in the ways British emigrants understood themselves after having arrived in the colonies. Second- and third-generation emigrants continued to eye Great Britain from afar and to question the degree to which they could ever belong in the lands where they were born.

As part of the effort to establish local culture, British colonies looked for local poets. These "colonial laureates," the subject of chapter 5, acted as arbiters of poetic taste and culture. Among the most significant was Richard Henry (later Hengist) Horne, a minor midcentury English poet who arrived in Melbourne in 1852 and produced two years later "the first Poetical Work ever published in this Gold-trading Colony."[49] Over the next two decades, he would go on to publish in Australia a handful of mildly well-received volumes, including an epic drama. Horne, now known primarily as a correspondent and sometime collaborator with Elizabeth Barrett Browning, was called "Melbourne's official literary spokesman" for this period, "the unofficial Laureate of Victoria."[50] Similar accolades accompanied the publications of Susanna Moodie and Charles Sangster in Canada. The work of these pioneers, these colonial laureates, was foundational to the culture of Anglo settler colonialism: the transportation and revision of cultural institutions from home to abroad.

This book concludes with the late-century turn to nationalism throughout British colonial spaces. Significantly, these emerging forms of nationalism were accompanied by an equally enthusiastic celebration of imperial federation: the notion that all of Britain's colonies—"Greater Britain," as it was often called—would remain part of a larger Anglo community, united by both loyalty to the queen and shared Anglo-Saxon blood. Race, then, emerged at the end of the century as an organizing principle for "nationalist" feeling. In poetry by the Bulletin School in Australia and the Confederation Poets in Canada, we see how racial identification complicated the turn from British loyalty to national sentiment. Believing themselves to be part of a global Anglo-Saxon community, poets at the turn of the twentieth century experimented with verse forms that were thought to reflect both that imagined racial origin *and* innovations unique to the specific colonial spaces in which they found themselves.

If we take seriously Isobel Armstrong's claim that "the effort to renegotiate a content to every relationship between self and the world is the Victorian poet's project," then a literal world of new possibilities opens itself to readers of poetry composed in nineteenth-century British colonies.[51] I first glimpsed some of these possibilities as a reader at the State Library of New South Wales, gingerly turning the pages of shipboard newspapers and trying to imagine the ocean-bound worlds their contributors might have inhabited. What emerged for me over the following years of archival searching was not just a trove of emigrant poetry but a reorientation toward poetry itself: alternate ways of reading and making sense of poems few scholars have thought worthy of attention. Our traditional, canon-based disciplinary practices have by and large excluded colonial poetry. In decentering the established geography of British poetry, I found I needed new strategies for making sense of literary objects that have fallen outside our established reading practices. This volume foregrounds these strategies: argumentative and methodological frameworks for understanding the cultural work of British poetry in the global nineteenth century.

CHAPTER 1

Floating Worlds
Poetry and the Voyage Out

Let us begin, like British emigration in the nineteenth century, with a long sea voyage. Stretching to upward of four months at midcentury, the journey out was an especially "defining moment" for those heading to Australia and New Zealand.[1] Anthony Trollope, who sailed with his wife to Australia in 1871, described the peculiarity of emigrant ship culture in his 1879 novel *John Caldigate*: "No work is required from anyone. The lawyer does not go to his court, nor the merchant to his desk. Pater-familias receives no bills; mater-familias orders no dinners. The daughter has no household linen to disturb her. The son is never recalled to his books. There is no parliament, no municipality, no vestry. There are neither rates nor taxes nor rents to be paid. The government is the softest despotism under which subjects were ever allowed to do almost just as they please."[2]

Trollope's perspective is distinctly middle class, suitable for lawyers and merchants, but the experience of extended leisure would have been shared by both steerage and upper-deck passengers. That in-between state of seeming inertia, monotonous days with little change of scenery, gave passengers ample time to consider the futures that awaited them in the antipodes. Catherine Helen Spence's novel *Clara Morison: A Tale of South Australia during the Gold Fever* (1854) opts not to dwell on "the monotonous life on board a passenger ship during so long a voyage," but in her autobiography Spence recalls "all the young men" onboard "reading a thick book [about sheep] brought out by the Society for Promoting Useful Knowledge" and then, in the evenings, passengers dancing "to the strains of Mr. Duncan's violin."[3]

Long weeks at sea were punctuated by the circulation of newspapers that were edited and printed onboard (see figures 2 and 3 for examples of ship newspaper mastheads). By the 1860s, passengers embarking for Australia or New Zealand would have expected a shipboard periodical. A writer for *Chambers's Journal* explains in 1867 that "in not a few of our large, long-voyaging clipper-ships, it is customary . . . to publish a weekly newspaper. Some person of talent among the passengers undertakes to edit it; its literary contributors are volunteers from all quarters of the ship—Saloon, Second Cabin, Intermediate, and Steerage; the captain generally favours it with quotations from his Log . . . and the medical officer promulgates in it his bulletins of health."[4] Imagine the delight of receiving a newspaper after weeks at sea, the comfort of a periodical's generic familiarity. In their shipboard formats, short works of serial fiction were not uncommon; in many cases, fully one-third of the newspaper content, and sometimes more, was poetry.[5] Emigrant ships from earlier in the century had circulated newspapers as handwritten manuscripts, sometimes accompanied by ornate watercolor illustrations.[6] As shipboard printing became more commonplace, subscriptions were taken out among passengers for bound editions, keepsakes for subscribers printed after ships had reached their destination.[7]

While still onboard, the journals were important in framing the first experiences of emigration. Insofar as passengers at sea had few ways of knowing what was happening outside their ship—"cut off for the time from communication with the great world," one contributor put it in 1870—the ship journals offered emigrants local news, documenting the goings on of their isolated community: this "small world in which we are now moving," wrote one journal in 1860; "our own floating world," wrote another, "which, for the time being, is all the world to us."[8] Drawing from the traditions of British periodical printing, including serialization, the mixing of genres, and the anonymity of contributors, the shipboard journals' foremost duty, attested to in editorials and letters printed in their pages, was to alleviate the monotony of ocean travel: the 1875 *Sobraon Occasional*, for example, "wishes to encourage the fine arts of sea-life—arts of killing time, of grumbling, of gossiping, of chaffing."[9]

In their negotiation of British literary traditions, however, emigrant ship compositions also contributed to the necessary work of locating passengers both physically and psychologically as they approached the colonial periphery. If passengers aboard emigrant ships were "[not] exactly British," as Elleke Boehmer writes of British settler colonialists more generally, then their literary productions were not quite British either.[10] Both the passengers and the periodicals reflect an in-between status: not exactly British,

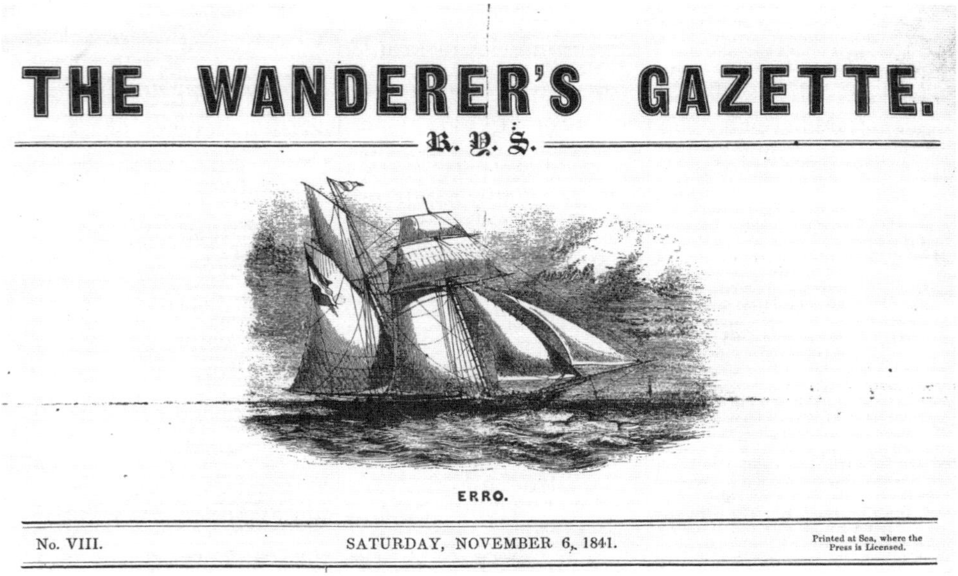

Figure 2. *The Wanderer's Gazette* (6 November 1841). "Printed at Sea, where the Press is Licensed." State Library of New South Wales, Sydney. Q84/156.

but not quite colonial. In neither subject position could passengers imagine themselves fully *at home*.

Shipboard publications point to this sense of homelessness by thematizing the ambivalences of geographic displacement and the anxieties of abandoning home for unknown futures abroad. Though necessarily implicated in greater networks of imperial power, the individuals whose poems I read in this chapter generally imagine themselves without authority, reflecting what the authors of *The Empire Writes Back* call "the backward-looking impotence of exile."[11] Victorian emigrants heading to Australia and New Zealand were themselves between continents and between cultures. The poetry they published en route to the colonies reflects their persistent engagement with both British poetic traditions and emerging diasporic, emigrant identities. Their work points as well to the ways poetry offered British emigrants vehicles for cultural mediation unavailable in prose writing: specifically, by echoing, revising, and parodying popular lyrics and songs recognizable to nearly all nineteenth-century British subjects. Through parodic revisions of canonical British poems, emigrants discovered strategies for mediating feelings of impotence, for exerting control over the in-between states of transition.

Communities in Transit

An impressive number of British citizens emigrated to Australia and New Zealand in the nineteenth century. In 1852 alone, according to *Blackwood's*, 568 ships sailed from Britain for Australia, carrying 87,881 adult passengers.[12] More recent estimates suggest roughly a half million persons emigrated to Australia and New Zealand in the 1850s, the height of the Australian gold rush and the point at which the stigma of the continent's convict history seems to have abated (transportation of convicts to New South Wales stopped by 1840; transportation to Van Diemen's Land, now Tasmania, came to an end in 1853 and continued to Western Australia up until 1868, at which point the entire system was brought to a close).[13] Life would have varied on board those hundreds of ships, sometimes significantly, but overall there would have been a mix of passengers from different classes. The *White Star Journal*, published on board a ship headed from Liverpool to Melbourne, writes that "if we have on board no members of the titled classes, there are scions of families so old and distinguished, that title would add little to their honors; and there are individuals and families representing the various grades of middle-class life, skillful artisans, and laboring men."[14] Passengers of all classes would likely have shared the desire for a better life ahead and experienced what one traveler in 1842 described as the "becoming and kindly spirit of intercourse which ought to prevail among fellow passengers who are bound together by a community of hopes and circumstances."[15]

We might imagine the emigrant ship as a community in transit, connected not only by a shared destination and the conditions of the journey but also, for the majority of passengers, by roughly common socioeconomic aspirations. Benedict Anderson's understanding of an imagined "national consciousness" coming into being "via print and paper" applies here in microcosm.[16] Ship newspapers linked individuals onboard by means of a shared, if imagined, *emigrant* consciousness, both reflecting and shaping the enthusiasms, hopes, dreams, and anxieties accompanying the move from home to abroad. "We have left our homes for a strange land," writes the editor of the *Maori Times* onboard a ship headed to Auckland in 1867, invoking with his "we" a shared experience among all his readers: "left friends, and all home-ties, to seek a fortune, and live a new life in another country."[17] The anonymity of most contributors deepened the newspapers' sense of shared purpose: the essays, stories, and poems published onboard reflected communal experiences more than individual viewpoints. In most circumstances, we cannot know whether their authors were male or female, privileged or poor. And while the newspapers depict some of the more grueling elements of long ocean voyages—deaths at sea, violent storms, sea-sickness, contagious diseases, close quarters—they more commonly offer a brighter, idealized version of emigration.[18] By and large, the ship newspapers project a *beau ideal* of life in transit, constructing versions of emigrant experience that might replace the otherwise alienating and painful realities of life at sea. When at their journeys' end passengers paid the subscription fee for a bound edition of the ship journal, they were getting not just a keepsake or a marker of their time at sea but an important alternative to displacement, physical pain, and emotional trauma.

Indeed, accounts from emigrant crossings suggest predominantly horrid conditions. An 1852 article in *Household Words* jokes that "taking a berth in a ship to Australia is like taking apartments with no exit for four months." Passengers consigned to rooms without windows or air pipes faced "the risk of being, if not quite stifled, half poisoned."[19] A decade later, *All the Year Round* describes the steerage compartment as "a long low narrow apartment, with a very narrow, immovable table and two benches running its entire length." On either side of this table were small, closet-like spaces "designed for sleeping-rooms." "For six persons to inhabit a closet of this size day and night without quarrelling," the author concludes, "must require a miracle of good sense and good temper."[20] John Davies Mereweather, a passenger onboard a ship bound for Adelaide in 1852, describes the "most lugubrious and dungeon-like aspect" of the steerage compartments. "The emigrants complain sadly of the skuttles leaking. Some of their mattresses are saturated with water; consequently they rise in the morning with severe colds." Mereweather finds fault with his fellow passengers as well: the rough, "heterogeneous mass," which includes some "wretchedly dirty peasantry with large families" among others who are "small tradesmen" and "respectable mechanics."[21]

Given the strain of the outbound journey, even for those fortunate enough to be in upper-class accommodations, passengers were no doubt grateful for the distraction offered by ship newspapers. Opening a ship journal from the 1850s or '60s, one might encounter a poem celebrating Florence Nightingale, a humorous lyric on seasickness, a gossipy work entitled "Sketches by Booze," or a "Lament of the Single Ladies," voicing the frustrations of women on board.[22] Predictably, one also finds passages from Samuel Taylor Coleridge's "Rhyme of the Ancient Mariner" and various other poems on sea travel,

Figure 3. *The Lightning Gazette* (3 November 1855). National Library of Australia, Canberra. Nq 994.03. LIG.

homesickness, and exploration.[23] One journal, the *Pioneer*, offers a log of the ship's journey in tetrameter couplets:

> The 16th of November at four o'clock
> We left the South West India Dock,
> The fog cleared off, and with the tide
> The Thames embraced his peerless bride.[24]

Though these poems may at first seem like entertaining filler, recent scholarship on poetry and Victorian periodicals offers a more compelling interpretive framework. Linda K. Hughes notes two important functions for poetry in the mainstream Victorian periodical press: first, poems "could enhance the cultural value and prestige of the periodical itself," and second, they "could mediate the miscellaneousness and ephemerality" of the newspaper's content.[25] Poetry, then, was vital to Victorian periodical culture in ways that modern reading practices have tended to obscure.

I propose three characteristics especially constitutive of Victorian shipboard poetry, and I examine each in turn in the sections that follow. First, poetry in ship newspapers regularly turned to a revisionary mode, rewriting well-known poems and poetic forms from the perspective of emigration and colonialism. Building on the rich British tradition of literary revision and parody, emigrant poets actively borrowed metrical forms and rewrote canonical lyrics, often in parodic registers. I follow Margaret A. Rose in taking a broad view of parody, a mode encompassing not only mockery but also loving imitation, sympathy with the original work.[26] Parody, Carolyn Williams argues, "is a rhetoric of temporality, projecting the difference between a 'before' and an 'after' as part of its structure."[27] For Victorian emigrants, *before* and *after* marked not only a temporal relationship between old and new, but differences between home and abroad, British and colonial, domestic and foreign. Poetic revision and parodic structure in the ship journals, that is, may be read as an index of shifting identifications, denoting the transition of those on board away from an easy or uncomplicated relationship to the place of their birth.

Second, emigrant shipboard poems often inhabit a structure of nostalgia (from the Greek, the longing to return home). Both "a sentiment of loss and displacement," as Svetlana Boym suggests, as well as "a romance with one's own fantasy," nostalgia often inspires the emigrant's turn to parody; parody, we might say, becomes a productive way for emigrants to negotiate nostalgia.[28] The emigrant nostalgic casts herself forward, spatially and temporally, toward the colony, all the while glancing back, with mixed feelings, at what she's left behind. Historians have described British emigrants alternately as having an "umbilical attachment" to their place of birth and, by the end of the nineteenth century, as developing various forms of "colonial nationalism[s]," resistance both to the British government and to imported British culture.[29] The nostalgic poems I read here constitute a midpoint between these two historical models, demonstrating both imagined belonging to an originary (British) homeland *and* departure from that culture. Ship poetry, I argue, provided ways for emigrants to imagine colonial identities as neither umbilical nor fully independent: strategies for becoming colonial subjects without abandoning nostalgic attachments to home.

Lastly, Victorian emigrant poems express concern for the place of culture, and poetry especially, in the colonies. The British press, quick through the 1850s to encourage emigration among those "willing and skilled to work at useful employments," also warned that "the colonies are still in a state in which the most robust in body make their way best."[30] When the English poet Richard Henry (later Hengist) Horne emigrated to Melbourne in 1852 to dig for gold, he publicly distanced himself from his identity as a poet, writing in a letter to the colony's primary newspaper, "I never thought of coming out to Australia as a man of letters, but as one possessing active energies and a very varied experience. I did not wish to exercise any abstract thinking, nor to write either poetry or prose, but to *do* something. . . . This Colony does not desire literature, or the fine arts at present, and I do not desire to contribute to them."[31] To emigrate in the mid-Victorian period, then, was to risk the loss of literary culture, and perhaps "culture" more broadly construed. Emigrant poems voice real concern about this possibility.

Parody at Sea: Tennyson, Hood, Longfellow

I'll begin with a mostly lighthearted parody, published in the *Rodney World* aboard the ship *Rodney* on her 1885 voyage from London to Melbourne.

> Come into the boat, my lads,
>   For the strong north wind has flown;
> Come into the boat, my lads,
>   I sit on the thwart alone,
> And soon on the sea, we'll be wafted abroad;
>   Tho' we pull, we shall never be blown.
>
> For the good ship scarcely moves,
>   And white sails flapping on high.
> The mate, he turns into the bunk he loves,
>   For scarce there's a cloud in the sky,
> He lays himself down in the bunk he loves,
>   To have forty winks, or he'd die.
>
> Come, lads of the *Rodney*, be not like girls.
>   Come hither, your luncheon is done.
> The ship in the distance, like glimmer of pearls,
>   Be our goal, and worthy a one.
> Come down, little Cohn, with your beautiful curls,
>   And row in the blazing sun.[32]

Stuck at sea without wind to carry their sails, the young lads of the *Rodney* decide to row a smaller boat over to a nearby vessel, "the ship in the distance." The likely goal is to break the monotony of the day. The ship in the distance glimmers, mirage-like: a worthy destination, if for no reason other than its proximity and the relief it offers from mind-numbing, sleep-inducing tedium. But the sailors find themselves in trouble halfway between the two ships when a trade wind finally picks up, setting the *Rodney* on its way. For a horrifying moment it seems their ship will leave them behind, until finally it stops to wait for their return:

> She is stopping, our ship, so sweet;
>   She is waiting for us a-head;
> We never will own we're beat,
>   Tho' we all will go early to bed.³³

What might be lost to the modern reader, but would have been heard loud and clear in the nineteenth century, is this poem's playful rewriting of Tennyson's "Come into the Garden, Maud," one of the most celebrated lyrics of the period. Tennyson was among the most parodied of Victorian poets; Walter Hamilton's 1884 collection of *Parodies of the Works of English and American Authors* opens with a section on the poet laureate, whose every work seems to have inspired a parodic rewriting.³⁴ The original "Come into the Garden, Maud," part of Tennyson's 1855 long poem *Maud*, would have been recognized by most passengers as the model for the ship parody:

> Come into the garden, Maud,
>   For the black bat, night, has flown,
> Come into the garden, Maud,
>   I am here at the gate alone;
> And the woodbine spices are wafted abroad,
>   And the musk of the rose is blown.³⁵

"Come into the Garden, Maud" was published regularly on its own as an isolated lyric. Within the larger context of *Maud*'s narrative, the poem serves as the pinnacle of the speaker's delusional, likely imagined romance with his object of desire, Maud. The tone is bittersweet, apprehensive even, anticipating violence to come (the speaker and Maud's brother duel immediately after, resulting in the brother's death) and the collapse of the speaker's romantic fantasy. The differences between the playful, jocular "Come into the boat, my lads" and Tennyson's longing and ultimately tragic lyric are severe.

Those differences, of course, are part of what make the latter poem both humorous and important. We might, for example, notice that the "woodbine spices . . . wafted abroad" in Tennyson's lyric become in the ship poem the sailors themselves, "wafted abroad." The two poems' sonic and structural resonances foreground the differences in their content: foreground, among other things, the differences between *Maud*'s domestic, quintessentially English garden and the unforgiving sea of the emigrant ship. Consider the following two stanzas (Tennyson first, followed by the ship poem), which align an imagined romantic idyll—the hero's wished-for tryst with Maud—with the labor of the sailors in their small boat:

> From the meadow your walks have left so sweet
>   That whenever a March-wind sighs
> He sets the jewel-print of your feet
>   In violets blue as your eyes,
> To the woody hollows in which we meet
>   And the valleys of Paradise.[36]

> In the sails of the ship there comes so sweet
>   The faintest of trade wind sighs;
> While, in the boat, all wetting our feet,
>   The water commences to rise—
> And bailing her out, in this tropical heat,
>   Is certainly not Paradise.[37]

Tennyson's lines imagine a sympathetic relationship between Maud and the English landscape so profound that violets the color of Maud's eyes spring from paths she wanders. The ship poem highlights instead the sailors' dislocation from the natural world, their misfortune at being separated from the *Rodney* at just the moment a trade wind picks up, stranded in a boat slowly filling with water.

"She is sailing, our ship!" cry the sailors, "'Tis clear / She'll leave us alone to our fate." I want to suggest that the *Rodney*, the departing ship—ship of state, mother ship—stands for a version of imagined abandonment against which the poem's form struggles. Not only will the ship wait for her sailors to return ("She is stopping, our ship, so sweet; / She is waiting for us a-head"), those sailors will carry along with them the cultural structures of their original home: aesthetic forms, like *Maud*'s meter and rhyme patterns, whose iterations will maintain connections to the domestic scenes they've left behind. "Come into the boat, my lads" frames with a knowing, humorous style the traumatic separation between home and abroad, British culture and an unknown colonial life.

Through parodic echo and emendation, the ship poem establishes a nostalgic relationship to Tennyson's original lyric and suggests strategies for overcoming feelings of abandonment and isolation. Parodies of Tennyson published back home, such as those in Hamilton's 1884 collection, would necessarily have functioned in different registers, given the absence of the specific context—the emigrant ship itself—to make sense of the parodic frame. That so many emigrants turned to parodic rewriting in the ship journals points both to the larger culture of Victorian parody, of which their poems were a part, and to the specific uses of parody within the context of emigration and colonization. The ship poems demonstrate that parody was a crucial mode of colonial reading and writing; the parodic double gesture—lovingly holding something at a distance—was constitutive of the colonial literary scene.

Take as another example the following play on Thomas Hood's 1843 "Song of the Shirt," among the most important political poems of the British mid-century. Published in the *Nemesis Times* in 1876, en route to Melbourne, "The Song of the Ship" transplants Hood's poem about working-class women's labor—"Stitch! stitch! stitch! / In poverty, hunger, and dirt"[38]—into a poem about the monotony of emigration:

> With features pallid and wan,
>   With colourless cheek and lip,
> A lady sat on the quarter-deck,
>   Watching the heaving ship.
>
> Pitch, pitch, pitch,
>   As her bow in the water dip,
> In a tremulous voice, with a nervous twitch,
>   She sang the Song of the Ship.[39]

"The Song of the Ship" exists in a moment predicated on the past; its representation of shipboard monotony comes into focus by way of the Victorian seamstress's monotony. Life aboard the emigrant ship, in this instance, depends on a backward-looking formal gesture (the ship poet's echoing of Hood's poem). As far as the unhappy lady moves from her native England, she remains at a structural level in much the same place. In some ways her stagnation resembles the early British cartographers described by Paul Carter in *The Road to Botany Bay*, those newcomers to the Australian landscape who saw it less in terms of *what was actually there* than of *what they expected to find*. "What was named" by white settlers in Australia, argues Carter, "was not something out there; rather it represented a mental orientation, an intention to travel. Naming words [for mountains, bays, and sundry geographical phenomena] were forms of spatial punctuation, transforming space into an object of knowledge, something that could be explored and read."[40] Like those early British explorers, who made use of what they already knew, the shipboard poets borrowed from a shared metrical vocabulary, using formal structure to make sense of the new worlds in which they found themselves. The map of established, familiar meter transformed the unfamiliar into recognizable, navigable space.

Of course there's more than meter in the backward gesture of "The Song of the Ship"; the poem wouldn't succeed if not for the specific verbal cues, the sonic echoes that recollect "Stitch, stitch, stitch" in the ship poet's "Pitch, pitch, pitch." But the converse argument is also true: the verbal cues wouldn't work if not for the metrical backbone to which they're bound. Arguments about class (the working-class seamstress who becomes an upper-class British *émigrée*) or gender (stultifying women's labor, a constrained spatial compass) will be incomplete without attention to the poem's formal tensions between metrical stasis (evoking structural historical fixedness) and the "pitching and tossing work" of the poem's content (drawing attention to the specific contingencies of its composition).[41] The metrical scaffolding helps make sense of the unfamiliar. One both knows and does not know "The Song of the Ship"; it is at once recognizable and foreign.

Metrical structure in the shipboard compositions offers a framework for feeling at home in a poem, whether one recognizes the specific referent—here Hood's poem, which itself echoes Tennyson's 1842 "Break, Break, Break"—or not. I understand meter, both in this example and more generally, to be historically located and culturally ordered, particular to specific times and places.[42] As such, the shipboard poet finds space for herself within Hood's metrics because she recognizes her experience of monotony to be similar to those of the seamstress. The point is not that Hood's meter is necessarily monotonous, but that "The Song of the Shirt" had, through its circulation and absorption within popular Victorian culture, become representative of monotony, allowing the shipboard poet to manipulate that sense of monotony for her own specific purposes.

Another style of parodic imitation appears in the *Fiery Star Gazette*, a journal printed in 1863 on a voyage from Cork (via London) to Brisbane. A play on Henry Wadsworth Longfellow's 1855 *Hiawatha*, the *Fiery Star* poem makes explicit its connection to Longfellow in its title: "Lines after the Style of Hiawatha."

From the shores of dear old England,
From the mighty town of London,
Sailed forth our godly vessel,
Sailed forth upon the ocean;
To contend with storms and tempests,
And in triumph bear us onwards
To the distant Port of Brisbane—
To the colony of Queensland.[43]

Though an American poem, *Hiawatha* circulated globally as one of the best-known English-language poems of the century. According to *Chambers's Journal* in 1856, Longfellow was "the most popular poet living" and *Hiawatha* "America's first written epic."[44] At least one British critic found Longfellow's meter especially suited to his theme—"In it, we hear, as it were, the swaying of trees, the whirr of wings, the pattering of leaves, the trickling of water"[45]—but more readers delighted in its parodic iterability. Not only in America and Britain, but in Australia, too, parodies of *Hiawatha* proliferated. The *South Australian Register*, for example, notes that the poem "has created quite a furor amongst the satirical parodists." The journal then reprints a San Francisco paper's metrical report on court proceedings:

In the Mayor's Court this morning,
Monday morning, blue and blear-eyed,
Blear-eyed soakers from the lock-up,
Came like Falstaff's ragged army.[46]

Unlike this particular parody, however, which attaches Longfellow's trochaic tetrameter to material entirely dissociated from the original poem, the ship parody—"Lines after the Style of Hiawatha"—edges close enough to *Hiawatha* itself to raise the interpretive and political stakes of its publication.

The original *Hiawatha* concludes dramatically with the Native American chief retreating from earth by canoe as the white man, bearing Christianity, comes to usurp his power.[47] Longfellow strains to present the Europeans' arrival in North America as benign and even beneficent, to celebrate a moment that from other vantages reads as tragedy:

And the evening sun descending
Set the clouds on fire with redness,

Burned the broad sky, like a prairie,
Left upon the level water
One long track and trail of splendor,
Down whose stream, as down a river,
Westward, westward Hiawatha
Sailed into the fiery sunset,
Sailed into the purple vapors,
Sailed into the dusk of evening.

    And the people from the margin
Watched him floating, rising, sinking,
Till the birch canoe seemed lifted
High into that sea of splendor,
Till it sank into the vapors
Like the new moon slowly, slowly
Sinking in the purple distance.[48]

Hiawatha sails toward the descending sun, conscious of his people's eminent decline. His death participates in a larger Victorian narrative trope of dying Indians that, according to Kate Flint, "found resonances in a British readership well prepared to celebrate its capacity for compassion at the loss both of a specific people and of an unrecapturable version of preurban society."[49]

I will have more to say about the trope of the dying Indian and its specific manifestations in Australia, New Zealand, and Canada, in chapter 4. For now, I want to point out that in borrowing both the *Hiawatha* form and the specific language of sailing toward a distant horizon (echoing even Longfellow's anaphoric "Sailed into" with his own "Sailed forth"), the poet on board the *Fiery Star* implicitly places his fellow passengers within a colonizing narrative, projecting their personal experiences of shipboard travel onto the map of European expansion:

Then arose the mighty east wind,
Rushing, roaring, from the eastward,
Raised on high, the surging billows,
Blew the spray into our faces.
Stowed, or reefed, was all our canvas,
Close reefed was the mizzen-topsail,
Still the ship was struggling onward—
Onward to her destination.[50]

Like "Come into the boat, my lads," the *Hiawatha* parody points back to a familiar, popular poem and entertains both affinities to and distinctions from that original work. The gesture back to home would have been doubly complex on board the *Fiery Star*, as the ship had been chartered by a priest, Father Patrick Dunne, to transport poor Irish families to Queensland in the aftermath of the great famine: "for the benefit of his poor, sorely-tried countrymen and countrywomen, many of whom were saved by his splendid exertions from the fearful effects of famine or the dreaded degradation of the poor-house."[51]

Other poems in the journal reflect an explicit Irish nationalism:

When Ireland's released from the yoke of Saxon,
Och! then will our hearts beat with glee;
. . . .
   Och! Erin Machree,
   It's dear ye're to me,
   Thou small little isle of the sea.[52]

More accommodating to the British, an essay titled "Our Adopted Land" suggests that "one of the brightest features of the present emigration is the combination of the Celtic and the Anglo-Saxon races." Irish emigrants, the essay goes on to say, will now work alongside the British to build the Queensland colony together: "There will the dauntless spirit of the Celt find ample scope to vie in honest rivalry with the boundless enterprise of the Anglo-Saxon. Through their united energy will be ensured the prosperity of their adopted country."[53]

The Irish at home, long accustomed to thinking themselves under the thumb of British imperialism, may well have identified in some respects with the colonized Hiawatha rather than the colonizing white man. A scathing 1856 *Irish Quarterly Review* essay, for example, described Longfellow's arriving colonists as "Iagoos" [sic] to Hiawatha's Othello.[54] But en route to Australia, now colonists themselves, the Irish aboard the *Fiery Star* seem more easily to occupy the aggressor's role. The *Fiery Star* publications reflect what Katie Trumpener identifies as the "reconciliation" of local tensions in colonial spaces: "The empire is not a site of struggle and conquest [among the English, Scottish, and Irish] but a place in which Britain is successfully reconstituted, in miniaturized form."[55] Hiawatha's death sail thus becomes, via revision and parody, the triumphant struggling of a people bound for a greater destiny. According to the *Fiery Star Gazette*, the emigrating Irish will now join the British in "defend[ing] the ruined hut against the aborigines of Australia."⁵⁶

"Come into the boat, my lads," "The Song of the Ship," and "Lines after the Style of Hiawatha," then, all work playfully to situate emigrant experiences both within a larger literary tradition and in relation to homelands left behind. That these poems would also have resonated politically among their shipboard readers—both explicitly, through their content, and implicitly, through their formal echoing and revision—should, I hope, be clear. The ship poems work in one register to confront the monotony and dislocation induced by ship travel, but they also suggest a greater communal purpose, providing a venue for reflecting on passengers' shared experiences of emigration. "Here are a number of people, all of them perforce separated for a time from their ordinary circumstances," writes one contributor to the *Caldera Clippings*, published in 1877 on a trip from England to Cape Town. It will be beneficial, the essay continues, to "disconnect one's-self temporarily from one's natural prejudices and tastes, and to be ready to accept the general conditions of the moment . . . to forget one's-self, in short, and to think first of the general comfort of the little community."⁵⁷

Many of the journals address head-on their political aspirations. A good number proclaim absolute removal from partisan viewpoints: for example, the *Sobraon Occasional*, sailing to Melbourne in 1875, "recognizes no law but that of its own spasmodic existence, which is that it should appear in public whenever it feels so disposed. It has no great cause at heart. It does not care what Party is in. It deals impartially with Tory, Liberal, and Radical."⁵⁸ On the other hand, the *Aconcagua Times*—sailing from Adelaide on a return trip to Plymouth in 1879—pointedly insists that on "our floating commonwealth," the journal's "principles will be strictly Conservative. It will support by its influence the government, the discipline, the good order of the organised society in which for six weeks we are here to live."⁵⁹ The journal of the *Argo*, a naval ship sailing from Portsmouth to Madras in late 1857—carrying the Left Wing 68th Light Infantry to support British forces in India after the rebellion earlier that year—declares that its "political opinions . . . are liberal—very liberal, and it will on all occasions, to the best of its ability, do all that lays in its power to forward the liberal interests of the country."⁶⁰

My point here has less to do with the specific politics of any one ship and more with the fundamental idea that the ship journals would have been understood by their contributors and readers to be political ventures, to have political value: more often than not, they were explicitly framed as such from the outset. Within this context, the shipboard revisions and parodies open themselves to a variety of political uses. Parody itself, as Williams argues, "can be—and often simultaneously is—both conservative and progressive, since it preserves the memory of past forms while turning away from them into its own, more highly valued, present."[61] When poems like "Come into the boat, my lads," "The Song of the Ship," and "Lines after the Style of Hiawatha" look both behind and ahead, they acknowledge their literary and cultural origins while writing their own present and future. Emigrant ship poets began the process, continued on arrival in the colonies, of constructing new settler identities without fully abandoning the old. The circulation of these poems on board established these identities in necessary relation to broader emigrant communities.

Forms of Remembering

Like parody, nostalgia also works in divided temporal and spatial registers. Nicholas Dames suggests that "a nostalgic looking-backward is . . . necessarily a looking-forward—a dilution and disconnection of the past in the service of an encroaching future."[62] One contributor to the 1870 *Commissary Review* captures this nostalgic double gesture, noting that "we, on board this vessel, going out to seek a new home, in a country to most of us unknown—going, some to seek a livelihood, others for the conservation of that boon good health—although our faces are turned toward the South, yet cherish the fond remembrance of our dear old English home."[63] An 1866 lyric from an emigrant ship headed to Cape Town elegantly echoes those thoughts and feelings:

> Far from that best of harbours, home,
> From all that's dear to me;
> Where'er I stray, where'er I roam,
> My thoughts are still of thee.[64]

The sentiments of this poem—no matter how far I go, my love, I think of you—appear consistently throughout the shipboard publications, their significance regularly augmented by way of metrical structure. The poet who thinks of his love "where'er [he] roam[s]" does so by way of common meter: alternating lines of iambic tetrameter and trimeter, a structure standard in both English hymnody and ballad poetry.[65] His loving thoughts, then, are mediated by a metrical form that itself enacts a nostalgic looking-backward, to the songs of childhood, the sounds of home.

As poetic structures that would have been familiar to anyone growing up in nineteenth-century Britain, ballad meters especially communicated the sense of home and the new pain of distance from that home.[66] The following ballad-like poem, which imagines a fantastical "fairy land" only to be brought back harshly to the cold present of an emigrant ship, was published on an 1872 journey from Liverpool to Melbourne.

> I stood in a land, a fairy land,
>   Of fruit, and flower, and tree,
> Of sunny mount and sparkling fount,
>   The flower of my heart with me.
>
> I clasped her hand—a fair, soft hand,
>   And gazed into eyes of blue,
> More deep and clear than the azure sphere,
>   Than the light of heaven more true.
>
> As I clasped the hand—a fair, soft hand,
>   Of her I treasured most,
> I awoke, half mad, for I only had
>   Fast hold of my cold bed-post.[67]

Unlike most ship poems, this lyric is signed by its author, Xaverius Thomas McNiven; the following month's issue posts an obituary notice for McNiven, who "suffered from what is supposed to have been bronchial decline.... The damp climate of Ireland proving too much for him, he [had] determined, if the climate suited him, to reside permanently in Australia."[68] The dying McNiven's lyric reads as doubly desperate, straining toward a fantastical future with his beloved while at the same time nostalgic for a past, perhaps equally fantastical, when they were once together. The poem's ballad meter contributes to its pathos, gesturing toward the lost comforts of familiarity and home.

Among a subset of educated emigrants, complex metrical structures offered further layers of historical and cultural resonance. For example, an 1875 lyric published on board the *Sobraon* during a voyage from Plymouth to Melbourne frames nostalgia by way of elegiac couplets, the metrical form Ovid used in composing his poem of exile, the *Tristia*. Unlike the parodic poems discussed in the previous section, "A Dream" maintains a sincere, devotional relationship to Ovid's original work, offering an elegant and moving meditation on the author's beloved, left behind in England while he ventures out to Australia:

Was it a voice, or a dream, or a sigh of the wind through the gloaming
    Came to my soul in its pain, soothing the sorrow to sleep?
Or was it thy spirit, my darling, over the blue waters roaming,
    Sought me, and found from afar, murmuring—"Love, do not weep"?

Why did you come to me, O my love; were you sleeping or waking?
    How did you find me so far over the sorrowful seas?
Did your heart, in its loneliness, feel that my heart in its anguish, was breaking?
    Did the wings of some pitying dream waft you safe to me here on the breeze?[69]

Elegiac couplets—alternating lines of dactylic hexameter and pentameter—were written before Ovid, but primarily as epigrammatic witticisms; it was the Roman poet who opened up their expressive potential.[70] Exiled from Rome in the year 8 CE, he was sent to Tomis, an outpost colony on the peripheries of the Roman empire, where he spent his remaining years dwelling among those he called "barely civilized."[71] Peter Green argues that Ovid's exile in Tomis "cut him off, not only from Rome, but virtually from all current civilized Graeco-Roman culture" and "rubbed the poet's nose in the rough and philistine facts of frontier life."[72] Ovid composed the first part of his *Tristia* while voyaging from Rome to Tomis. "Every word," he informs his readers at the end of the poem's first part, "was written during the anxious days / of my journey."[73]

One begins to see why an educated British emigrant, feeling dislocated from his love, traveling by ship to the far reaches of empire, might settle on the elegiac couplet as an appropriate vehicle for expressing himself. Both Tomis and Australia represent, for ancient Rome and Victorian Britain, respectively, the outermost limits of empire; both colonies impose a near-total isolation from home. More particularly, both Ovid and the ship poet are compelled to leave behind their loved ones and find themselves cast off, alone, adrift. Though not British in origin, Ovid's elegiac couplets represent for a European emigrant the larger compass of Western civilization: a cultural frame one might fear losing while voyaging to the antipodes. Much as Anderson understands ideas of both home and nationality as "less experienced" by exiles "than imagined, and imagined through a complex of mediations and representations," poetic form becomes in the ship publications a mediator of cultural identification, a nostalgic structure through which *home* might be imagined.[74] As in the parodic structures of "Come into the boat, my lads" and "Lines after the Style of Hiawatha," this sort of formal echoing operates on both conservative and progressive registers, looking behind to the poet's native England while also looking ahead, tentatively, to a new life beyond. The author of "A Dream" remains haunted by his past, the voice that follows him out to sea; he tries by way of the poem to understand his relationship to the past, the present, and the future. The poem thus becomes a tool for mitigating nostalgic pain.[75]

The third and fourth stanzas of "A Dream" further clarify the poet's nostalgic relationship to formal imitation, suggesting the ways metrical repetition might have been understood as a coping mechanism for traumatic loss and profound change:

> I saw you not, dear, though I felt your presence around and about me,
>   Like a girdle of infinite calm, and your voice for a moment I heard,
> Like the wail of a harp by the wind softly touched, thro' the spell that enwound me,
>   In a language that souls understand, or the sweet weary song of a bird.
>
> And over my soul there swept a measureless, infinite longing
>   To clasp you again to my heart, in spite of the years and of fate,
> And I turned from the blaze of the sun, and saw where the shadows were
>   thronging,
> But you were not there—you were gone, and I wept, for I knew I must wait.[76]

Invoking the Romantic figure of an Aeolian harp, the poet feels an absent presence: fleeting, ephemeral, and yet unmistakable, like the bounds of Englishness that girdle round the Australian emigrant. The voice that follows him from shore, felt bodily and emotionally with "infinite longing," structures his outbound journey, his venture into the unknown. Through its iteration and the gradual changes in its echoing form, the emigrant poet inhabits a nostalgic structure so as to understand his own experience of difference and distance. Ovid's elegiac couplets allow the *Sobraon* poet to recognize what it means to be displaced and yet still attached, an emigrant cast off and yet still a European deeply rooted in Western culture and tradition.

Anticipating Colonial Culture

But what was to be the place of culture and tradition at the far reaches of British colonization? How would emigrants replace the homelands they'd left behind? The five chapters that follow explore in different ways the complexities of these questions. Onboard emigrant ships, the answers tended to be exhortative: "Be men, be gentlemen," proclaims one ship journal in 1870, "and let each one feel that the heritage of our England is a noble patrimony and one we will seek to hand down as the richest dowry untarnished to our children."[77] "Emigrant!" writes another ship journal in 1862, "cultivate polite literature in order to be worthy of your future learned fraternity!"[78]

According to the British press, however, that literary heritage was not manifesting in a culture of colonial poetry. Francis Adams, writing in the *Fortnightly Review* in 1892, criticizes "Australia's neglect of her 'men of letters,' and especially of her poets": "the average Australian cares nothing for, and indeed knows nothing of" the foremost Australian poets of the day, "[Henry] Kendall, and [Charles] Harpur and [James Brunton] Stephens.... The case for the hopeless illiterateness of the average Australian seems made out."[79] Not only were colonial Australians, so it was said, uninterested in poetry, but poets themselves found their labors at odds with the requirements of colonial life. An 1884 *Temple Bar* essay on Adam Lindsay Gordon, the best-known midcentury Australian poet, suggests that Gordon may not have committed suicide at the age of only thirty-six if not for his commitment to poetry: "It may be maintained that Gordon's troubles sprang from his cultivation of the Muses; and here the average emigrant is not likely to follow his example."[80] Poetry in fact was thriving in Australia by the later Victorian period, as the final chapter of this study shows. But for British citizens embarking on emigration, the perception of colonial culture, mediated by the British periodical press, was more important than the reality.

Fin-de-siècle British critics mostly agreed on the derivative nature of Australian colonial poetry. But the *Westminster Review* points out with a mix of encouragement and patronization that, "during the earlier stages of 'nation-making,' intellectual progress and development naturally remain in abeyance"; poetry, then, will come to Australia once it establishes itself on firmer political ground:

> The fact that the Muse of the Antipodes has not yet wholly cut her leading-strings and abandoned an almost slavish imitation of English and American models, results from the circumstance that hitherto the mass of the inhabitants has been too busily engaged in "nation-making" to permit primarily of the enjoyment of those years of widely diffused liberal education indispensable to the creation of the literary taste and "atmosphere" of culture; and, secondarily, of that patient, studious development of the imaginative faculty, and of the cultivation of its "voice" in metrical expression which learned leisure and the existence of a literary class *in se* tends to foster.[81]

According to the *Westminster*, the Australian poetic impulse is, for the time being, doomed either to silence or to "slavish imitation," not only because of unsettling geographic and cultural displacement, but also because of the absolute commitment—and subsequent loss of leisure time—required by the colonial enterprise. The poet Richard Hengist Horne, who spent nearly two decades in and around Melbourne, reflects on these views in an unpublished epic from 1866, *John Ferncliff: An Australian Narrative Poem*: "Here was reality, and no romance:/ No words his practiced [hand?] could enhance."[82] Especially in the middle decades of the nineteenth century, Australia was characterized as a place of gritty realism ("no romance"), a place unconducive to the imaginative work of poetic composition.

The sixth issue of the *Superb Gazette*, published in 1882 during a journey from England to Melbourne, offers what might be read as a poetic meditation on this theme. "Lines: Composed on the death of a chaffinch, which flew on board while going down Channel, and died in lat. 42° S., long. 82° E.," was written by one H. Alderton, and it mourns the death of a bird whose ill fate landed it onboard the ship as it sailed from the English shore.[83]

> Poor little bird, how sad a fate,
> How sorrowful, how desolate;
> Far from green fields and pleasant lane,
> To perish on the mighty main;
> No loving mate or kindred near,
> But all so bleak, so cold, and drear.[84]

Though far from achieving the gravitas of Percy Shelley's skylark ("Hail to thee, blithe spirit!"), Alderton's chaffinch nonetheless takes on attributes of a Romantic songster.[85] Notice in the lines that follow how the diminutive bird's song comes to signal, first, national belonging, and then the experience of captivity and exile:

> Poor little bird, two months before,
> Sweetly thou sang on England's shore,
> And hopping gaily all the day,
> How happy passed the time away,
> With sweet young mate to cheer the hours,
> In hawthorn hedge or shady bowers.
> But venturing upon the sea,
> You fell into captivity;

And on a ship far outward bound,
This luckless little bird was found;
And torn from every earthly tie,
Was caged to pine away and die.
Week after week thy fragile form
Endured the tempest and the storm;
Week after week! oh, what an age,
Within a narrow prison cage,
With nought but bitterness and pain,
An aching heart and throbbing brain.
But Death at last, poor suffering bird,
Thy sorrowful lamenting heard,
And touched thee with his magic hand;
When nearer drew the distant land,
When hope beat high in every breast,
Thy weary spirit sank to rest.[86]

Alderton points to the English landscape—"green fields," "pleasant lane," "hawthorn hedge," and "shady bowers"—with a nostalgia characteristic of emigrant writing. Within this space, its rightful home, the chaffinch sings with full-throated ease. Caught unwittingly aboard an emigrant ship, the poor bird suffers, pines away, and finally dies. Its "fragile form" cannot endure the loss of English landscape, the change of climate, and the experience of captivity aboard the ship.

Birds such as the chaffinch were regular freeloaders on emigrant vessels: "Sometimes," notes an 1858 *Chambers's Journal* essay, "birds seem to be induced by mere curiosity or love of mankind to put out from their native shore, and alight on ships at sea."[87] I read in the death of this particular chaffinch a degree of skepticism about the culture of Australian colonialism and the possibility for genuine belonging available to British emigrants. Though the passengers aboard express enthusiasm as they approach their new home—"hope beat high in every breast"—the chaffinch cannot bear the final mark of separation from its original home, the arrival in the colony. Perhaps the bird's "aching heart" and "throbbing brain" reflect the experiences of any British citizen transplanted so far from home, "torn from every earthly tie." More specifically, birdsong was understood throughout the nineteenth century as a figure for lyric poetry; the chaffinch poem suggests that lyric song, or even poetry more generally, will not readily thrive on foreign soil.[88]

Both the anxieties implicit in Alderton's 1882 poem and the critiques of colonial "slavish imitation" from the *Westminster* remind us of how poetic revision and parody shaped works such as "Come into the boat, my lads," "The Song of the Ship," and "Lines after the Style of Hiawatha": poems that both foreground imitation and insist, with a wink and a smile, on difference. Emigrant ship poets embraced imitation strategically, to negotiate the emotional trials inherent to geographical and cultural change. The elegiac couplets of "A Dream" may similarly be called *imitative*, and yet their recontextualizing of classical poetic tradition should instead be seen as a self-conscious, stylized work of replication, one with clear emotional value.

Poems such as these challenge commonplace assumptions about colonial derivativeness such as those voiced by the British press at home. British emigrant poetry intentionally maintained the structure of a greater cultural replication (from core to periphery, home to abroad); to critique it on account of its derivativeness misses the point of its composition. The chapter that follows turns to the colonies themselves and to the circulation of imitative poetry within emigrant communities. What we see there expands the ship journal paradigm and points to the foundational place of imitation in British colonial poetics.

CHAPTER 2

Colonial Authenticity
Circulation, Sentiment, Adaptation

Plagiarizing Culture

We have seen that nineteenth-century colonial poetry, according to Victorian critics, was essentially derivative and drawn primarily from British sources. The accusation of plagiarism—direct and intentional copying—naturally weighed heavily on colonial writers. For Oscar Wilde, the connection between Australia and fraud was axiomatic, originating in Australia's foundations as a penal colony. His 1889 essay "Pen, Pencil and Poison" showcases the common nineteenth-century association between forgery and penal transportation by way of the poet, painter, and poisoner Thomas Griffiths Wainewright (1794–1847). A minor literary figure in the 1820s, Wainewright in 1837 was found guilty of forgery, sentenced to transportation for life, and sent to the British colony at Hobart (charges that he had murdered several family members by poisoning were never proved).[1] Wilde writes of Wainewright as "an art-critic, an antiquarian, and a writer of prose, an amateur of beautiful things and a dilettante of things delightful, but also a forger of no mean or ordinary capabilities, and . . . a subtle and secret poisoner almost without rival in this or any age."[2] Wainewright's crimes, in Wilde's view, "seem to have had an important effect upon his art," bringing a "strong personality to his style" that had been lacking before his turn to sin.[3]

As a forger in what was to become Australia, Wainewright would have been in good company. Sydney's most important colonial architect, Francis Greenway (1777–1837), had been transported in 1814 for forgery.[4] One of Australia's noted early landscape artists, Joseph Lycett (c.1774–c.1825), was also transported to Sydney in 1814 on conviction of forgery.[5] Both thrived in the antipodes. In general, Britain tended to transport not violent criminals but instead those convicted of "minor theft," robbery, larceny, swindling, and forgery: all "crimes against property," as Robert Hughes has shown.[6] One writer in the 1830 *Sydney Gazette* argued for leniency toward those convicted of forgery, which in both Britain and Australia was still a capital offense: "We are of opinion, notwithstanding its injurious consequences to society, that it ought not, except in cases of singular enormity, to be punished with death."[7] With so many rehabilitated forgers contributing to Sydney's early development, such a position made good sense.

Establishing literary culture in a new colony always raises questions of authenticity, and this would have been especially true on the Australian continent, a space already associated in the British mind with crimes of unauthorized replication. Even in nineteenth-century America, as Lara Langer Cohen has shown, *fraudulence* and *literature* were intertwined terms, a result of "the hopelessness of distinguishing impostures, forgeries, plagiarisms, and hoaxes from literature proper."[8] In imagining new homelands on the Australian continent, colonial poets regularly demonstrated what Susan Stewart in a different context identifies as "cris[e]s in authenticity."[9] Nonetheless, this chapter takes Wilde's lead in finding positive aesthetic consequences to Australia's criminal origins. Like Wilde, who sees Wainewright's acts of forgery as foundational to his artistry, I reframe unauthorized literary replication as constitutive of emerging British colonial cultures, both in Australia and elsewhere.

Let's start by considering cultural replication from a different perspective. When Oliphant Smeaton wrote in the 1895 *Westminster Review* of the "slavish imitation" practiced by nineteenth-century Australian poets, he was casting in a negative light what James Belich calls the "cloning system" of nineteenth-century Anglophone settlerism.[10] The accusation of "slavish imitation" registers differently when read against the history of Australia's great forgers; *derivativeness*, along with *copying* and *forgery*, should be understood as dismissive terms for what in other contexts is called "cultural replication." Such dismissiveness tends to be yoked primarily to literature and the arts, and not to other cultural institutions. For example, when in 1835 the *Eclectic Review* wrote about the just-approved colony of Adelaide, replication and derivativeness appeared as entirely positive outcomes for South Australia: "If the present experiment should . . . be attended with success, a foundation will be laid for the existence, in the southern hemisphere, of a nation, in which the laws, the language, the religion, and the institutions of England may be perpetuated; and in which they may form the character, and ensure the happiness of unborn millions."[11] We see here and throughout the nineteenth century a profound double standard between replicating cultural institutions (laws, language, and religion), understood as a moral good, and replicating works of art, which critics deride without mercy.

Often lost among high-minded readers of nineteenth-century colonial literature is the comfort such derivativeness offered migrants arriving on the shores of Adelaide, Halifax, and Cape Town, among many other places. Weary from their long journeys, British emigrants found relief and pleasure in just the sort of derivativeness that Smeaton treats with contempt. Richard Henry Horne writes in 1853 that on "reach[ing] Melbourne, we were landed on a wharf which was overwhelmed with a confusion of men and things and carts and horses." Horne and his compatriots are "exhausted" and prone to "despair" as they attempt to secure lodgings on their first night in the colonial city.[12] An 1842 arrival to Wellington writes in a similar vein that "great numbers of our fellow-passengers are half-starved through want of employment.... A poor man can hardly be in a worse place than this. It is a most miserable country in the winter; such continual storms and tempests of rain and wind prevail as you in England have no notion of."[13] Emigrants in such circumstances valued the comforts of familiarity. Catherine Helen Spence recalls in her autobiography that, on arriving in the new colony of Adelaide in 1839, she "read over and over again" John Aikin's *Select Works of the British Poets* (1820), along with "[Oliver] Goldsmith's complete works," both of which she "thoroughly mastered."[14] According to Geoffrey Serle, emigrants in the colony of Victoria through the 1850s "took immense pride in their creation of 'another England', and assumed that it was the virtue of British institutions which had made such success possible."[15] Here again the focus remains on "institutions" such as religion and the law, but for immigrants like Spence the aesthetic sphere would have been equally significant.

Given the weight nineteenth-century emigrants attached to cultural replication, we need a new set of strategies for considering early colonial literary derivativeness and reprinting, strategies that move beyond the simply dismissive. Rather than noting condescendingly that "the spirits of Felicia Hemans and Martin Tupper haunted the antipodean air"—this from the *Oxford History of New Zealand Literature in English*—we should instead reflect on the important and even necessary work of colonial derivativeness and the ways poems by Hemans and Tupper actually circulated in those spaces.[16] Like the nostalgic structures of the shipboard poems discussed in chapter 1, early colonial poetry looked both ahead and behind in temporal and geographic registers, often inhabiting simultaneously both past and present, British and colonial. If the spirit of Felicia Hemans "haunted" the air of colonial Melbourne or Auckland, that was no doubt because Hemans was among the most popular English poets of the early nineteenth century. In recreating British culture in the antipodes, it would have been odd if emigrants in the new Victorian colony had *not* turned to Hemans—or to Martin Tupper for that matter, "the Royal Family's favorite poet, one of the best-selling Victorian bards, who was a household name on both sides of the Atlantic until tastes changed in the 1860s."[17]

We should also remember the larger context of nineteenth-century literary copying and reprinting, which allows us to see British colonial "derivativeness" as part of a global culture of replication and circulation. Writing of the nineteenth-century "culture of reprinting" in the antebellum United States, Meredith McGill argues that "the mass-market for literature in America [was] built and sustained by the publication of cheap reprints of foreign books and periodicals" and that "the primary vehicles for the circulation of literature were uncopyrighted newspapers and magazines."[18] A similar story plays out in Britain's colonial spaces. In early nineteenth-century colonial cities around the world, first newspapers and then magazines were largely responsible for establishing and maintaining a sense of literary culture. Booksellers such as "Connell & Ridings," featured in Auckland's *Daily Southern Cross* (1 Sept. 1857), advertised in colonial newspapers the volumes they had for sale (figure 4), and those same newspapers published poems and prose excerpts—almost certainly unauthorized—that would have helped establish the sense of a canon (works by Boswell, Young, Dryden, and Milton) while also maintaining enthusiasm for more recent authors (Dickens, Scott, and Hemans). None of the authors advertised in the *Daily Southern Cross* were of the New Zealand colony itself.

This chapter focuses on three scenes of colonial publication. With each, I show unauthorized poetic reproduction to be foundational to colonial culture. More specifically, these three scenes demonstrate the centrality of genre—and genre's eminent reproducibility—to the work of colonial reproduction. From the 1828 printing of South Africa's first anthology of English-language poetry, to the circulation of Felicia Hemans's poetry in 1830s Can-

Figure 4. (FACING PAGE) "Valuable Books and Engravings," advertised in the *Daily Southern Cross* (Auckland, 1 September 1857). National Library of New Zealand, Wellington.

Valuable Books & Engravings

CONNELL & RIDINGS

Will sell by Auction, at their Mart, Queen-street, TO-MORROW, (Wednesday) 2nd September, at 1 o'clock,

A LOT of Valuable BOOKS and ENGRAVINGS

Amongst the Books will be found—

Rev. Lionel T. Berguer's British Essayists, 44 vols., elegantly bound
Boswell's Johnson, 4 vol.
Benjamin Franklin's Works, 2 vols.
Al Koran, fourth edition
Marcet's Conversations on Chemistry, 2 vols.
Grant's Superstitions of the Highlands
Young's Works, complete, 5 vols.
Fine old Bible, 1626
Dicken's Master Humphrey's Clock, complete
Maynard's, Josephus, folio, with plates
Dryden's Fables, by Dr. Aikens, with plates
French and English Dictionary
Directions for English Traveller
Curious old Work, 1643
Collens' Anatomy, 2 vols folio, with fine plates
Doddridge's Family Expositor, (handsomely bound)
Burkitt's Notes on the New Testament, large quarto
Gifford's English Lawyer
Milton's Works
Buffon's Natural History, 15 vols., plates,
Village Farrier
Munroe's Anatomy, 4 vols 1 vol. plates
Memoirs of Mrs. Hemans, 2 vols.
Scott's Rokeby and Lady of the Lake
Wilson's Ornithology, 4 vols.
A Mirror for Saints and Sinners, very curious 1671
Lord Bacon's Sylva Sylvarum 1631, original edition, very curious
With numerous Standard Works, and
Several Account Books

ENGRAVINGS.

Jones' Views of the seats of Noblemen and Gentlemen
National Gallery
Heath's Gallery of Engravings
Views in Switzerland
Book of the Illustrations

Also,
A superior Microscope.

ada and Australia, colonial poetic cultures emerged in relation to the genres of Anglo-American poetics.

Generic Adaptations: William Cullen Bryant in Colonial South Africa

In 1828, R. J. Stapleton published the first anthology of English-language poetry in South Africa, *Poetry of the Cape of Good Hope*, an effort "to rescue . . . from oblivion" poems printed originally in Cape Town newspapers.[19] Likely unbeknownst to Stapleton, the opening poem of his volume was written not by an English-speaking emigrant to Britain's Cape Colony but by the American poet William Cullen Bryant, who, in the late 1820s, was emerging as one of the United States' most respected literary figures. In its original American contexts, Bryant's "To a Water Fowl" was first printed in the 1818 *North American Review* and then reprinted in the poet's 1821 volume *Poems*. The poem subsequently appeared in a Cape Town newspaper, the *South African Chronicle, and Mercantile Advertiser*, in November 1824, noted there as having been "extracted from a sailor's album, on Dyer's Island," a small island off the South African coast near Cape Town.[20] Four years later, Stapleton lifted the poem from the *South African Chronicle* and gave it pride of place as the introductory poem of his volume, thereby establishing Bryant, anonymously, as the first anthologized writer of English poetry in the South African colony (figure 5).

That Bryant's poem was mistaken as an original of the Cape Colony was perhaps not entirely coincidental. Though Bryant was central to an emerging American literary culture, reviews of his poetry in the 1820s in both the United States and Britain characterized the poet as a *colonial* writer. For example, the inaugural issue of the *United States Literary Gazette* in 1824 highlighted not Bryant's essential Americanness but instead his indebtedness to English poets: "['To a Waterfowl'] is a beautiful and harmonious blending of various beauties into one. We have been awed with the boldness and sublimity of the metaphoric language of Wordsworth, have been soothed by the deep and quiet tone of moral sentiment, which pervades many of the works of Southey, and delighted with the skillful adaptation of epithets in the odes of Collins; but we do not remember any poem, in which these high excellencies are more happily united, than in the short ode mentioned above."[21] The *New York Mirror* in 1825 reprinted an article from the London *Monthly Magazine* that addressed Bryant's poetry, and specifically "To a Water Fowl," after noting that, "in point of literary dependence, America

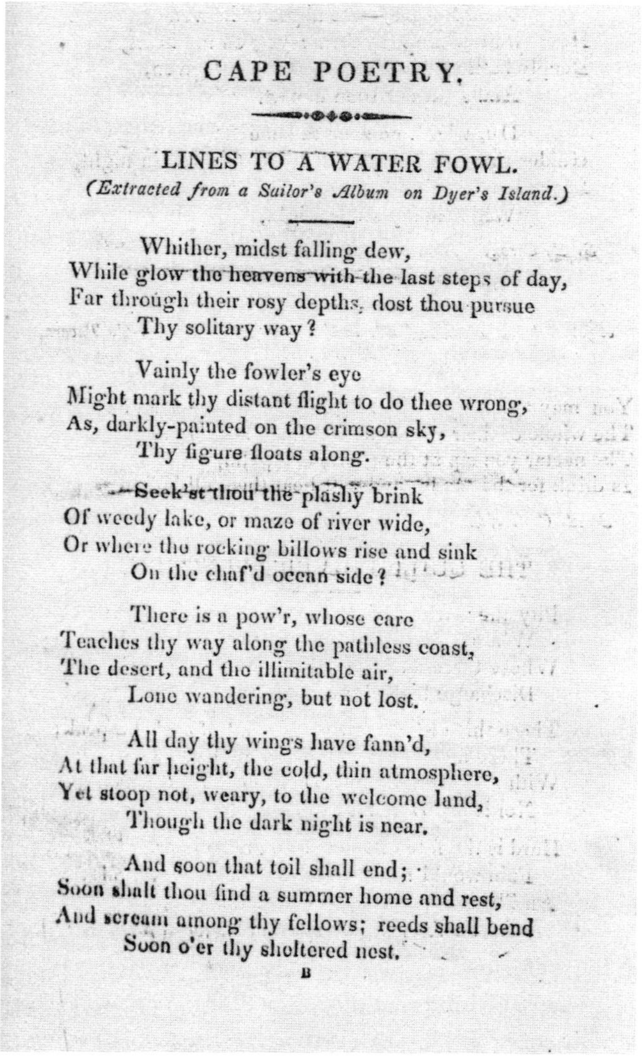

> ## CAPE POETRY.
>
> ### LINES TO A WATER FOWL.
> *(Extracted from a Sailor's Album on Dyer's Island.)*
>
> Whither, midst falling dew,
> While glow the heavens with the last steps of day,
> Far through their rosy depths, dost thou pursue
>   Thy solitary way?
>
> Vainly the fowler's eye
> Might mark thy distant flight to do thee wrong,
> As, darkly-painted on the crimson sky,
>   Thy figure floats along.
>
> Seek'st thou the plashy brink
> Of weedy lake, or maze of river wide,
> Or where the rocking billows rise and sink
>   On the chaf'd ocean side?
>
> There is a pow'r, whose care
> Teaches thy way along the pathless coast,
> The desert, and the illimitable air,
>   Lone wandering, but not lost.
>
> All day thy wings have fann'd,
> At that far height, the cold, thin atmosphere,
> Yet stoop not, weary, to the welcome land,
>   Though the dark night is near.
>
> And soon that toil shall end;
> Soon shalt thou find a summer home and rest,
> And scream among thy fellows; reeds shall bend
>   Soon o'er thy sheltered nest.
>
> B

Figure 5. *Poetry of the Cape of Good Hope*, ed. R. J. Stapleton (Cape Town: G. Greig, 1828). National Library of South Africa, Cape Town. Grey Collection. G.13.b.45(1.1).

seems to be still a British colony, and to draw her supplies, in a great degree, from the mother country."[22] Bryant reads as a *colonial* poet because his poems are generic congeries: they "blend . . . into one" elements borrowed from Wordsworth, Southey, and Collins.

"To a Water Fowl" succeeds as a South African poem precisely because of its generic nature. Like the bird in "Lines: Composed on the death of a chaffinch," the *Superb Gazette* poem discussed in chapter 1, the water fowl of Bryant's poem signals that we have entered a particular version of lyric space: internalized, reflective, and universal. "To a Water Fowl" is meant to reflect human interiority abstracted from the particulars of time and place, so readers might imagine themselves anywhere historically or geographically. "Water fowl" should additionally be understood as categorical rather than specific, referring to varieties of "ducks, geese, and swans considered as a class."[23] Whereas a poem such as Barron Field's "The Kangaroo" (1819) uses wildlife to mark the specific place of its origin (the poem could only describe Australia), Bryant's poem instead addresses a bird that could be from nearly any temperate climate the world over.

Like the bird he describes, Bryant's landscape is also generic and indistinct:

>   Whither, 'midst falling dew,
> While glow the heavens with the last steps of day,
> Far through their rosy depths, dost thou pursue
>   Thy solitary way?
>
>   Vainly the fowler's eye
> Might mark thy distant flight to do thee wrong,
> As, darkly-painted on the crimson sky,
>   Thy figure floats along.[24]

For Bryant, the waterfowl is a sign that all life on earth has purpose and is guided by a greater spiritual truth. As a meditation on anxiety, feeling lost and without direction, and finally overcoming those feelings, the poem unintentionally articulates one of the fundamental experiences of emigration. More than just a poem resonant with emigrant experience, "To a Water Fowl" locates a horizon on which present anxieties fade into the comforts of domesticity, family, and rest:

>   And soon that toil shall end;
> Soon shalt thou find a summer home and rest,
> And scream among thy fellows; reeds shall bend
>   Soon o'er thy sheltered nest.

Through its generic framing, the poem suggests a collective experience of existential anxiety and then comfort, a shared process of acclimating that would have been as resonant in the American nineteenth century as it was in British Australia, New Zealand, South Africa, and Canada. It's no surprise that "To a Water Fowl" circulated in Australia as well, reprinted in the *Sydney Herald* on 17 September 1832, this time with the author's name attached to his poem.[25]

Bryant's isn't the only unattributed poem in *Poetry of the Cape of Good Hope*. Stapleton notes that he found "The Emigrant's Song of Memory" in the *South African Chronicle*, but he leaves unsaid, and was likely unaware, that the poem was written by Margaret Holford (1778–1852), an English poet who never set foot in South Africa. Holford's poem "On Memory. Written at Aix-la-Chapelle," the source of "The Emigrant's Song of Memory," was originally published in London in 1823, in a collection edited by Joanna Baillie. When the *South African Chronicle* published the poem the following year (anonymously, so its place of origin was unclear, and with an entirely different title), the editor removed a stanza specifically detailing Charlemagne and troubadours, presumably to make the poem seem of South African origin.[26]

Unlike Bryant's poem, which works in its original form as a generic reflection on the natural world and human feeling, Holford's lines must be revised—abridged, adapted—into more general terms before it can fit into the South African locale: the poem must be made more generic. The specific context, Aix-la-Chapelle, must be excised, and the title changed entirely, transforming Holford's poem about one particular site of reflection into a general meditation on dislocation from an adopted homeland. Holford's poem on memory thus becomes, in its South African context, a poem whose publication history requires forgetting.

I print here the poem's first two stanzas, italicizing the stanza deleted from the *South African Chronicle* version:

> No! this is not the land of Memory,
>   It is not the home where she dwells:
>   Though her wandering, wayward votary
>   Is ever the thrall of her spells;
> Far off were the fetters woven, which bind
> Still closer and closer the exile's mind.
>
>   *Yet this land was the boast of minstrelsy,*
>   *Of the song of the Troubadour,*

> *Whence Charlemagne led his chivalry*
> *To the fields which were fought of yore;*
> *Still the eye of Fancy may see them glance,*
> *Gilded banner, and quivering lance!*²⁷

The poem's opening emphasizes a sense of dislocation; "the exile" of the first stanza lacks a sense of personal attachment to the place of the poem's genesis ("this is not the land of memory"). Since the original title indicates the poem was "Written at Aix-la-Chapelle," a reader of the poem as it appeared in Baillie's collection would have understood the deictic "this" as Aix-la-Chapelle, a placeholder then supported by the second stanza's references to troubadours and Charlemagne. Holford's readers are meant to reflect on the richness of storytelling and shared memory in Aix-la-Chapelle, or Aachen, now in western Germany, and to consider by contrast the absence of associated memory for the newcomer, "the exile." The original poem says in effect, "when I stand here in Aix-la-Chapelle, I have no personal history associated with the place, but I recognize the city to be one of great historical significance." The abridged version of the poem printed in South Africa says more generically, "as an emigrant I lack any connection to this land around me."

Far from being an isolated act of literary appropriation, the *South African Chronicle*'s removal from Holford's lyric of both author and context makes sense within a greater nineteenth-century culture of enthusiastic, unauthorized reprinting. Given that broader culture, there is nothing especially surprising about this particular example of unattributed reproduction. McGill's important work on the nineteenth-century American culture of reprinting helps frame Anglo-colonial print culture for us, especially with respect to periodical culture and the circulation of unauthorized reprints. We should consider, she writes, "what kinds of literature were demanded by a democratic public, what counted as literature in this culture, and how high art might be reconfigured for middle-class and working-class audiences."²⁸ A slightly emended set of considerations should be turned toward Stapleton's anthology, a work that seems keen to establish an English-language literary culture in the Cape colony.

What kind of literature might have been demanded by the Cape colony of 1828? Leah Price notes that an anthologist always "claims to stand within—and for—the same audience that he addresses."²⁹ Stapleton's anthology arrived in Cape Town at a moment of political and cultural transition. The authoritarian governor of the Cape colony, Lord Charles Somerset, had recently departed after fourteen years of firm control, which had included "unlimited powers of search, detention and banishment."[30] Somerset's regime had been criticized for its policies both within Cape Town (the governor famously refused freedom of the press) and on the colonial frontier (in particular his brutal treatment of the Xhosa).[31] With Somerset's removal, the Cape colony began to move toward more humanitarian policies, reflecting what Alan Lester describes as "a new bourgeois subjectivity" originating in "middle-class opposition" to old-fashioned aristocratic practices.[32] This included Ordinance 50, which "made 'Hottentots and other free people of colour' equal before the law with Whites,"[33] and Ordinance 60, which allowed the Cape press to "print whatever it liked short of the common law of libel."[34]

Stapleton thus published his *Poetry of the Cape of Good Hope* at just the moment British colonialists in the Cape elevated liberal progressivism as a goal for South Africa. The 1820s marked more generally, throughout Britain's colonial states, the beginning of a period of profoundly miscalculated confidence in the benefits European colonialists might bring to non-European spaces. In the middle decades of the nineteenth century, as Jennifer Pitts argues, political theorists across the ideological spectrum more or less followed John Stuart Mill in believing that "a British despotism was the best government to which . . . societies [perceived as undeveloped] could aspire, and also that such a despotism could be exercised knowledgeably and benignly to induce progress in such societies."[35] In Richard Price's words, imperialism through the period "morphed from [being perceived as] a problematic construct to [being perceived as] a benign concept."[36] Key to this developing sense of liberal progressivism within the colonies were the ideals promoted by literature, which explains at least in part what was at stake in Thomas Babington Macaulay's infamous 1835 insistence that "a single shelf of a good European library was worth the whole native literature of India and Arabia."[37]

Mill himself, model of a liberal progressive, believed poetry might represent the "sympathetic and imaginative pleasure, which could be shared in by all human beings."[38] Stapleton foregrounds this brand of idealized Romantic interiority in the poems of his anthology. Just five years after Stapleton's volume appeared, Mill would write that the "object of poetry is confessedly to act upon the emotions" of its readers.[39] Though not yet articulated in 1828, Mill's formulation resonates throughout *Poetry of the Cape of Good*

Hope. In taking poems "from the columns of the *South African Commercial Advertiser, South African Journal, South African Chronicle*, the *Verzamelaar*, and the *Cape Gazette*," Stapleton established space for shared affective experience, creating a version of universal humanism among English-language readers that was in keeping with the Cape colony's new progressive political ambitions.[40]

Stapleton's volume thus reflects the affective interiority that English-speaking settlers hoped to transport with them from Britain to their colonies. The status of those poems as copies is important—necessary, even—for a larger project of transportation and replication; their reproduction in *Poetry of the Cape of Good Hope*, following their reproduction in the pages of Cape Town's periodical press, is part of a broader, intentionally derivative colonial culture. Dipesh Chakrabarty describes this structure of colonial development—"first in Europe, then elsewhere"—as foundational to "what made modernity or capitalism . . . [become] global *over time*, by originating in one place (Europe) and then spreading outside it."[41] That we find the American Bryant and the English Holford as representative South African poets should thus be seen as neither a failure of the colonial literary scene nor as its success, but rather as a *feature* of the period and of colonialism itself. Indeed, a significant portion of Stapleton's volume is not of South African origin. In addition to other unattributed poets, the Scottish poets Henry Scott Riddell (1798–1870) and James Montgomery (1771–1854) each make an anonymous appearance, along with an unsigned "Ode to Enterprise" by English clergyman and mineralogist Edward Daniel Clarke (1769–1822).[42] These poems' shared affective interiority indicates the degree to which genre—here the Romantic lyric—mediated the transportation of culture from home to abroad.

Affective interiority similarly marks the poems in Stapleton's volume of South African origin, including Thomas Pringle's now canonical "Afar in the Desert," originally published in the *South African Journal* in 1824. Unlike the poems by Bryant and Holford, Pringle's landscape is distinctly South African, starting with the poem's opening lines: "Afar in the desert I love to ride, / With the silent Bush-boy alone by my side."[43] Stapleton also prints detailed footnotes explaining Pringle's more specialized South African terms: *Gnoo, Hartebeest, Gemsbok, Eland*.[44] But Pringle's metaphysical concerns—his feeling of dislocation and hopelessness followed by a reprieve—are without question of a piece with Bryant's "Waterfowl," signaling the poem's generic affinities with the volume's imported works.

In brief, the poem's speaker rides out into South Africa's vast and apparently uninhabited expanses; he discovers there "freedom, and joy," but also, as he moves farther from the British colony, "a region of emptiness, howling and drear.... A region of drought ... void of living sight or sound." Scholars have criticized Pringle for silencing his "Bush-boy" companion; they have also read the poem as a diagnosis of the South African colony, doomed, in Pringle's view, to failure.[45] The emptiness of Pringle's landscape might be located near the start of an English-language tradition in South Africa, described by J. M. Coetzee as "a failure to imagine a peopled landscape, an inability to conceive a society in South Africa in which there is a place for the self."[46] In the poem's final verse paragraph, the absolute visual and aural blankness is at last relieved by a "still small voice," which comes at a moment of absolute despair, offering the possibility of optimism:

> And here—while the night winds round me sigh,
> And the stars burn bright in the midnight sky,
> As I sit apart by the Desert Stone,
> Like Elijah at Sinai's cave alone,
> And feel as a moth in the Mighty Hand
> That spread the heavens and heaved the land,—
> A "still small voice" comes through the wild,
> (Like a Father consoling his fretful Child),
> Which banishes bitterness, wrath, and fear—
> Saying "Man is distant but God is near."[47]

Pringle's referent is the Old Testament, the "still small voice" that comes to Elijah in the wilderness, suggesting the presence of a higher power even in the remotest of spaces. Like the missionary John Campbell, who discovers in the South African landscape both poetry and "the living word" (discussed in my introduction to this book), Pringle intentionally conflates religious epiphany with the overhearing of a Romantic breeze, a voice that comes to him, inspired, on the wind.

In the context of *Poetry of the Cape of Good Hope*, we might imagine Pringle's poem overhearing not just the sound of the Old Testament's deity or the inspiration of a Romantic breeze but, more particularly, an internalized voice of Anglo culture and tradition. Cape Town's polyglot community was not welcoming to English speakers in the way of Australia, New Zealand, and Canada. In 1877, a half-century after Stapleton's anthology, Anthony Trollope visited Cape Town and noted that it was predominantly "not ... an English-speaking population."[48] Pringle absents himself from this cacophony of non-English speakers, riding out into the mostly unpopulated—and therefore *quiet*—landscape, looking to hear again an internalized and familiar voice. Coetzee finds fault in this, suggesting that Pringle was guilty of "uninventively assimilat[ing] his data under the categories provided for him by the dominant poetic models of his time and place," leaving him unable to perceive "the specificity of Africa."[49] This assessment is as true as it is unsurprising. Like the editors of the Cape Town newspapers, which sought to assimilate English-language poetry to South Africa, and like Stapleton, who reproduced without scrutiny their already derivative poems, Thomas Pringle seemingly wished to find a place for British culture in a space unwelcoming to it. Like most of his fellow colonialists in the early nineteenth century, Pringle's aspiration was not to reinvent culture for the South African colony but to find a place for British culture within it.

Circulating Sentiments: Felicia Hemans in Canada and Australia

When Isabella L. Bird (1831–1904), an "Englishwoman in America," took her "first view of Niagara," her mind turned to Felicia Hemans to make sense of what was before her: "I forgot my friends ... I forgot everything—for I was looking at the Falls of Niagara."[50] In the midst of so much forgetting, Bird remembers Hemans's 1826 poem "The Traveller at the Source of the Nile," two stanzas of which—slightly altered from the original—she prints:

> No more than this!—what seem'd it now
>   By that far flood to stand?
> A thousand streams of lovelier flow
>   Bathe my own mountain land,
> And thence o'er waste and ocean track
> Their wild sweet voices call'd me back.
>
> They call'd me back to many a glade,
>   My childhood's haunt of play,
> Where brightly 'mid the birchen shade
>   Their waters glanced away:
> They call'd me with their thousand waves
> Back to my fathers' hills and graves.[51]

These stanzas seem at first an odd choice for Bird, given their suggestion that a traveler's present will always be mediated by her past. Whereas Bird claims to have forgotten everything once in sight of Niagara, Hemans's lines show James Bruce, the Scottish author of *Travels to Discover the Source of the Nile* (1790), recalling the landscape of his childhood at just the moment he comes upon "the marsh and the fountains of the Nile." Bruce's experience of the Nile seems the opposite of what Bird says of the Niagara: "Upon comparison with the rise of many [Scottish] rivers," writes Bruce, "[the Nile] became now a trifling object in my sight. I remembered that magnificent scene in my own native country, where the Tweed, Clyde, and Annan, rise in one hill."[52]

What connects Bird to Bruce, via Hemans, is disappointment. Bird is first overwhelmed by the sight of Niagara, then disappointed by the "collection of mills" that "disfigures this romantic spot." The tourists, too, challenge Bird's romantic inclinations: "Not far from where I stood, the members of a picnic party were flirting and laughing hilariously, throwing chicken-bones and peach-stones over the cliff."[53] Here the sublime wrestles with the mundane: the immensity of Niagara versus the offensive minutia of chicken bones. Though she turns from Niagara for reasons quite different from those that turned Bruce from the Nile, Hemans's poem nonetheless offers Bird an affective register for making sense of the jarring North American scene. Bird adapts Hemans's lines to her own particular situation, both thematically and literally, shifting Hemans's third-person perspective on Bruce—"They called him, with their sounding waves,/Back to his fathers' hills and graves"—to Bird's own first-person: "They call'd *me* with their thousand waves/Back to *my* fathers' hills and graves."[54]

Hemans would have been among the more readily available poets for such appropriation and adaptation. A midcentury British or American reader like Bird could have encountered Hemans's poem in any number of places, including Fanny Bury Palliser's *The Modern Poetical Speaker, or a Collection of Pieces Adapted for Recitation . . . from the Poets of the Nineteenth Century* (1845) and Frederic Rowton's *The Female Poets of Great Britain* (1848), two anthologies that were part of an emerging transatlantic culture of lyric circulation and recitation. Palliser's volume, which also contains Pringle's "Afar in the Desert" and Bryant's "To a Waterfowl," appeared at just the moment, according to Catherine Robson, that poetry began to "appear in British elementary classrooms in . . . significant quantities."[55] Bird would have been fourteen at the time Palliser's volume was published, seventeen at the time of Rowton's, and she was living at a moment that saw memorization and recitation as necessary components of education.

More than that, it was a time, in Virginia Jackson's words, when lyric poetry "emerged" as a genre "independent of social contingency": a period when poetry was more readily severed from its historical and cultural contexts and put to a reader's personal uses.[56] This helps to explain why Hemans's lyric about Bruce's experience at the Nile was so readily decoupled from its original context, signaling not the specific story of an eighteenth-century Scots explorer but the universal experience of disappointment. "The Traveller at the Source of the Nile" thereby transforms into a vehicle for personal use, a way for Bird—or anyone else—to make sense of the present in relation to the past: "The feelings which Mrs. Hemans had attributed to Bruce at the source of the Nile," she writes, "*were mine* as I took my first view of Niagara."[57]

That feelings circulated via poetry through nineteenth-century Anglo-American reading publics has long been understood.[58] Hemans's lyrics were among the most successful in this regard, offering frameworks for readers to experience feeling in manageable doses. A review in the *Edinburgh Monthly Review* offers a representative perspective: "The verses of Mrs. Hemans appear the spontaneous offspring of intense and noble feeling, governed by a clear understanding, and fashioned into elegance by an exquisite delicacy and precision of taste."[59] Bird's use of Hemans suggests an understanding of lyric poetry in keeping with Lauren Berlant's reading of sentimentality, in which she provocatively describes genre as "an aesthetic structure of affective expectation, an institution or formation that absorbs all kinds of small variations or modifications while promising that the persons transacting with it will experience the pleasure of encountering what they expected, with details varying the theme."[60] Hemans's poem "absorbs" the "variations" of Bird's particular narrative, offering an aesthetic "structure of affective expectation" through which readers might recognize and imaginatively share in Bird's own experiences.

Such uses of Hemans might be found throughout the nineteenth-century Anglo world, making it literally true that "the spirit . . . of Felicia Hemans . . . haunted the antipodean air," just as it haunted British North America. To be clear: I employ the word *haunted* here in a positive sense, rather than the pejorative of its original use in *The Oxford History of New Zealand Literature in English*. The spirit of Hemans haunted colonial Australia, New Zealand, and Canada not only because of the global culture of reprinting but also because Hemans's affective style resonated among readers in those spaces, just as it did among readers in Britain. For colonial readers, Hemans's poetry was representative of the affective lyric genre.

For example, Hemans's poetry featured prominently in Sydney's periodical culture of the 1830s. In 1829 and 1830 alone, the *Sydney Gazette and New South Wales Advertiser* reprinted "The Image of the Dead," "The Dreaming Child," "The Nightingale's Death Song," "The Treasures of the Deep," "The Minster," "The Magic Glass," "The Requiem of Genius," "Triumphant Music," and "Music in a Room of Sickness."[61] The *Australian* reprinted "The Heart of Bruce, in Melrose Abbey" and "The Exile's Dirge."[62] Elizabeth Webby has shown that Hemans's poetry was increasingly popular in colonial Sydney. Hemans's volumes appeared in eight Australian book auctions in the 1830s and sixty-four in the 1840s. These are impressive numbers when compared to those for authors we now tend to consider more canonical: volumes of Tennyson and Robert Browning each appeared just once in 1840s auctions.[63] In 1838 the bookseller and printmaker William Moffitt advertised no fewer than five Hemans volumes for sale at his Sydney bookshop.[64] Across the Tasman Sea in New Plymouth, New Zealand, the Taranaki Institute's "Monthly Soirée" of August 1858 featured "a recitation from Felicia Hemans" in addition to "a reading from the Pickwick papers."[65]

As I suggested in the introduction to this study, Hemans's "The Homes of England" was an especially resonant poem for colonial readers, though its conservative politics inspired some important revisions. The poem circulated in its original form through a variety of Australian periodicals, appearing in three different journals in the 1840s alone.[66] In imagining an England unified across class lines, "The Homes of England" stands out as one of Hemans's more politically suspect works. Tricia Lootens points to the poem's linking of "'stately,' 'merry,' and 'cottage' dwellings within a harmonious national hierarchy" and rightly finds the lyric "sentimental, reactionary pastoral fantasy at its crudest":[67]

> The Cottage-Homes of England!
>   By thousands, on her plains,
> They are smiling o'er the silvery brooks,
>   And round the hamlet-fanes.
> Through glowing orchards forth they peep,
>   Each from its nook of leaves,
> And fearless there they lowly sleep,
>   As the bird beneath their eaves.[68]

Hemans's idyllic framing of English poverty would have been especially suspicious to those emigrants who had left Britain in search of greener pastures. In 1845, Adelaide's *South Australian* reprinted a Chartist revision of Hemans's lyric that makes explicit the original poem's conservative, obfuscating bent:

> The happy homes of England, alas! where have they gone?
> Like leaves in wintry weather, they have fallen, one by one;
> And where are now the rural sports that made the village gay?
> Some blight is, sure, upon the land, where all have pass'd away.
>
> The mansions of the great, 'tis true, still rise in pomp and pride,
> And round them rich demesnes are seen, extending far and wide,
> Where forest trees are waving green, and deer are bounding on;
> But the happy homes of England, O! where are they gone?[69]

Readers of the *South Australian* likely would have distanced themselves from the blighted and iniquitous scene painted here, as Adelaide in 1845 was enjoying an economic boom fueled by the mining of mineral deposits and a twenty-five-fold increase in the city's grain exports.[70] Adelaide's homes may have seemed happy indeed in relation to its residents' memories of England.

In Saint John, New Brunswick, an 1868 revision of "The Homes of England" serves first to reflect nostalgically on England and then to establish a new Canadian sentiment, distinct though tied to Great Britain (I print the poem in full to make this turn apparent). The author is Letitia F. Simson, who revised Hemans's poem after hearing it recited in a local church just one year after Canadian Confederation:

> The pleasant homes of England!
>   Oh how we love to praise,
> The dear Old Country of our birth,
>   The scenes of early days.
>
> The daisied fields and heath-brown hills,
>   O'er which we used to roam,
> E'er yet ambition stirred our hearts,
>   To seek our distant home.
>
> The cottage homes of England!
>   We never can forget:
> The calm, and sweet content, and peace,
>   Is lingering with us yet.

The palace homes of England!
    So ancient and so grand;
Are treasures of our memory still,
    In our adopted land.

Here, where a few short years ago,
    The Red Man's whoop was heard,
Nor sound of other human voice,
    Awoke the forest bird:

Here, where wild Nature reigned supreme,
    In deep, expressive praise;
And Art is hastening to unfold,
    Long hidden mysteries:

To cleave a highway for the feet,
    Of nations yet unborn—
Where fields and barren mountains top
    Shall wave with golden Corn.

From East to great Pacific's shore,
    The Iron Horse shall land,
Stores of great riches gathered up
    By many a toil-worn hand.

O England! Mother England!
    We render thanks to thee;
For all they guardianship to us,
    In helpless infancy.

And now we've grown to manhood's strength,
    We would go hand in hand,
To honour and to love thee still—
    Our dear old native land.
St. John, April 17th, 1868[71]

Simson finds in the newly formed Canadian Confederation Hemans's sense of domestic and national harmony. She finds as well a belief in upward mobility, enabled in part by westward expansion. Politically, then, the move to North America enables significant change, but in terms of sentiment—the affective ties imagined in Hemans's original lyric—the homes of England

and Canada remain nearly the same. Simson thereby imports the poem's genre and affective register, even as she alters its original content.

Hemans's haunting of both Canada and Australia might be traced not only in the reprintings and revisions of her own poems but also in poems that are clearly indebted to her in affective and thematic registers. Felicia Hemans proliferated through the works of colonial poets in the middle decades of the nineteenth century, contributing to the global culture of Anglo sentimentality. Among the more notable examples of this phenomenon were the poems of Eliza Hamilton Dunlop (1796–1880). Born in Ireland, Dunlop was newly arrived in New South Wales in 1838, the year she earned notoriety for publishing a poem on the real-life massacre of twenty-eight Indigenous Australians at Myall Creek. Scholars have rightfully positioned Dunlop's poem, "The Aboriginal Mother," in relation to other "crying mother" poems of the 1820s and '30s, including Hemans's "Indian Woman's Death Song" (1828) and Lydia Sigourney's "The Cherokee Mother" (1831).[72] More broadly, Dunlop's poem is distinctly that of a *political poetess*, a term Tricia Lootens has shown to be a lynchpin for thinking about race and sentimentality in the global nineteenth century.[73]

Dunlop's "Aboriginal Mother" invites sympathy from readers through the pathos of her speech, in much the same manner of Hemans's and Sigourney's Native American women:

> Oh! hush thee—hush my baby,
>   I may not tend thee yet.
> Our forest-home is distant far,
>   And midnight's star is set.
> Now, hush thee—or the pale-faced men
>   Will hear thy piercing wail,
> And what would then thy mother's tears
>   Or feeble strength avail![74]

Dunlop had been in Australia only a few months when the massacre took place. Widely reported and debated in local newspapers, the horrific event included the murder of a three-year-old boy and the decapitation of several Indigenous children.[75] The eleven stockmen accused of the crime were first acquitted by Sydney's Supreme Court, but in a second trial seven were found guilty and, on 5 December, sentenced to death.[76] Dunlop published her poem in the 13 December issue of the *Australian*, in between the contentious second trial and the execution of the murderers, which took place on 18 December.

The political register of "The Aboriginal Mother" stands out as distinct from Dunlop's earlier publications.[77] But stylistically Dunlop was using techniques on display throughout her writing, all of which fall within the broader work of sentimental lyric that Hemans epitomized. Dunlop's "Songs of an Exile" series, published in the *Australian* and including "The Aboriginal Mother" (the fourth in the series), demonstrates this stylistic consistency. For example, the third poem, from 29 November, considers the death of two Irish brothers who had emigrated to Vicksburg, Mississippi. A footnote indicates the poem's subject was lifted from a Dublin newspaper:

> He knelt beside a brother's bed—
>   Far in the stranger's land:
> And gently raised the dying head;
>   And clasped the lifeless hand.[78]

Dunlop's common meter and stock sentimental tableau are mostly cliché, but the same cannot be said of the poem's global purview. Dunlop casts a wide imaginative net in suggesting the affective resonances between an Irish emigrant's experiences in Mississippi and those of her readers in Australia. Like Bird's appropriation of Hemans's lyric, Dunlop's poem adapts the particular narrative she read in the Dublin newspaper, offering an aesthetic framework—what Berlant calls a "structure of affective expectation"—through which readers might recognize and make sense of their own experiences.

Dunlop's poem is both structurally and thematically generic, qualities that would have allowed colonial readers easy access to its affective register. In ways similar to Bryant's "To a Water Fowl," the emotions of the Mississippi deathbed scene would have resonated anywhere Dunlop's poem was published. Michael Richards, author of a historical catalogue of Australian books for the National Library of Australia, has shown that early Australian colonists "preferred imported literature to that written in New South Wales." Not only were such publications "cheaper," they also "reminded [colonists] of familiar scenes and themes."[79] Newspaper poetry falls into a different category from published books, but Dunlop's generic style is consistent with Richards's assessment; a colonial reader looking to buy one of Hemans's volumes for sale at William Moffitt's bookshop in Sydney would likely have appreciated the sentiment of the "Songs of an Exile" series. With the "Aboriginal Mother," we see Dunlop adapting the familiar, generic style of her earlier poems to the specific context of the Australian colony. What starts as an act of colonial replication—the "slavish imitation" described by the *Westminster Review*—transforms into a more distinct product of the Australian continent, borrowing an affective framework familiar to a global Anglo-American readership.

The sheer abundance of sentimental poetry in Sydney's newspapers pushes against the notion of a "crisis of authenticity" with respect to colonial poetry. Rather than critical self-consciousness, the proliferation of both sentimental reprints and derivative originals suggests an embracing of the global sentimental phenomenon. William Cullen Bryant's poetry again offers a fine example of how poetic feeling migrated in the early nineteenth century, moving with ease through multiple colonial spaces. In 1832, Washington Irving published a collection of Bryant's poems, writing in the dedication that his poems are "essentially American": "They transport us into the depths of the solemn primeval forest—to the shores of the lonely lake—the banks of the wild nameless stream, or the brow of the rocky upland rising like a promontory from amidst a wide ocean of foliage.... His close observation of the phenomena of nature, and the graphic felicity of his details, prevent his descriptions from ever becoming general and common-place."[80] The literary world outside the United States patently disagreed, finding his poems generic enough to designate spaces far from North America. We've seen already the extent to which "To a Water Fowl" circulated in South Africa and Australia. Bryant's "Indian Girl's Lament," a poem in keeping with the sentiment of Dunlop's "Aboriginal Mother," made its own global rounds, printed in the *Sydney Herald* (27 Sept. 1832) and Nova Scotia's *Bee* (17 June 1835). John Wilson, writing for *Blackwood's*, argues exactly my point in an 1832 review of Irving's volume, noting that, far from being a poem particular to American readers, "the 'Indian Girl's Lament' will inspire ... universal sympathy. Into her lips [Bryant] puts language at once simple and eloquent, such as the true poet fears not to breathe from his own heart, when in mournful imagination personating a sufferer, knowing that no words expressive of tenderest, and purest, and saddest emotions, can ever be otherwise than true to nature, when passionate in the fidelity of its innocence, nor yet unconsoled in its bereavement by a belief that pictures a life of love beyond the grave."[81]

What makes both Bryant's and Hemans's poems adaptable is their generic nature: their adherence to formal structures and emotional effects that would have been familiar to English-speaking readers around the world. This generic framing of sentiment makes sense of Wilson's claim—as a Scottish reader—to identify with the "Indian Girl's Lament" as much as a

North American might, or a colonist in Australia. Dunlop's "Aboriginal Mother" shows that she too understood the ways sentiment resonates generically. But her poem accomplishes something importantly distinct from the South African reprinting of Bryant's "To a Water Fowl." Whereas Bryant's poem suggests the replication of liberal progressivism in colonial spaces (his poem might be published as is around the world, with a similar effect in each locale), Dunlop's is instead an adaptation of liberal progressive beliefs to a specifically Australian context, not an exact duplicate or copy.

Other versions of Hemans abounded in colonial Australia. Caroline Leakey (1827–81) used sentimental adaptation to reflect on the challenges women faced both at home and abroad. After her 1847 arrival in Tasmania, the English-born Leakey spent most of her time there in a state of decline. She returned to England in 1853 and the following year published *Lyra Australia: or, Attempts to Sing in a Strange Land*. Striking in Leakey's volume is her logic of association, by which she uses her knowledge of England to make sense of what she discovered in Tasmania.[82] In the case of "Pale Oleander of the South," a Tasmanian oleander is the starting point for remembering scenes from an English childhood: "now I look on thee, / And know I've seen thee once before."[83] In Leakey's account, the oleander comes to represent first the tenuous position of women and then the specific death of a female childhood friend. The flower, she says, "didst unconscious lead me back / To that fair girl, in her once home of flowers, / Where tears alone now leave their track."[84] Much as Dunlop's "Aboriginal Mother" makes sense of the Australian present by way of Hemans's account of Native Americans, Leakey understands her experience of Tasmania by way of her past in England. She adapts her knowledge of the oleander and her particular experiences of the flower, to the specific context of the Tasmanian colony, finding solace even in painful connections between home and abroad.

Yet another colonial Hemans, Fidelia Hill (1794–1854), arrived in the fledgling town of Adelaide, South Australia, in late 1836 on board the HMS *Buffalo*. Hill was both the first European woman to set foot in the South Australian colony *and*, four years later, the first woman to publish a volume of poetry on the Australian continent. I will have more to say about Hill in chapter 5, but I note here that her poetry follows that of Dunlop and Leakey in suggesting the degree to which, in nineteenth-century Australia, *reproducing Britain* meant *reproducing sentiment*. "Here may I dwell," writes Hill while reflecting on her early arrival in the colony, "and by experience prove, / That tents with love, yield more substantial bliss / Than Palaces without it, can bestow."[85] Hill informs her readers that her poems were "written during seasons unfavorable to composition, of severe domestic calamity, and bodily suffering"; her poems suggest that these trials were mediated—and made endurable—by the domestic affections Hemans's poetry so consistently foregrounded.[86]

Plagiarizing Browning: The Case of Adam Lindsay Gordon

Adam Lindsay Gordon shot and killed himself outside Melbourne on 24 June 1870, a day after the publication of *Bush Ballads and Galloping Rhymes*, the book that would eventually make his reputation as Australia's most beloved midcentury poet. Born in the Azores into a Scottish military family and educated in England, he was sent by his father to Australia in 1853 at the age of twenty. Gordon planned to spend only a year or two in the colony before returning to England.[87] Instead, he remained as an officer in the South Australian mounted police, riding among settlements with only Macaulay's *Lays of Ancient Rome* for entertainment; according to his biographer, "he knew [the poems] by heart from end to end."[88] By 1857 Gordon had left behind the mounted police and was instead training horses and riding in steeplechases and hurdle races. An acquaintance from this time recalled riding with Gordon across the outback, amazed as the young man "recit[ed] quotations at length from Virgil, Homer, and Ovid," as well as "long passages from Racine's *Athalie*, and Corneille's *Cid*. . . . It was a puzzle to me how he managed to get books and carry them about and get time to read them."[89]

Gordon witnessed and participated in the rise of Melbourne as a major colonial city with genuine literary aspirations. In the early 1850s, when gold was discovered in Victoria, Melbourne was not yet two decades old. By 1873, three years after Gordon's death, Trollope would call Melbourne "the undoubted capital, not only of Victoria but of all Australia," and marvel at its quick ascent: "I believe that no city has ever attained so great a size with such rapidity."[90] As the colony of Victoria grew from a population of 76,000 in 1850 to 537,000 in 1860, the London press followed its progress with interest.[91] According to the 1856 *Tait's Edinburgh Magazine*, Melbourne had been "simply a provincial city" until the discovery of gold "agitated the whole civilised world," transforming the city "as if by the wand of a magician, into one of the most bustling emporiums in the world."[92] An 1858 contributor to the *Dublin University Magazine* concurs, writing of how the "gold-fever led to the growth of Melbourne so marvellously that in two years it sprang from the rank of a third-class English town to that of a first-rate English city."⁹³ Artist Henry Burn captured this moment of enthusiasm— "new opportunities, sudden wealth, and a hearty egalitarianism," in the words of historian John Hirst—in his iconic 1861 painting "Swanston Street from the Bridge" (figure 6).⁹⁴ By 1890, according to James Belich, "Marvellous Melbourne ruled Victoria, a colony as populous and rich . . . as the American state of California."⁹⁵

Both in Melbourne and back in Great Britain, critics voiced concern for the place of culture within the rapidly expanding city. "To bring about the future greatness which we have predicted for the colony, as the centre of a wealthy and powerful Anglo-Saxon empire in the Pacific, whose population are governed by British laws, and are in the enjoyment of British institutions," wrote *Blackwood's* in 1854, "it is most important that the British element should be as largely as possible infused amongst them. Society in Australia calls especially for the presence of an educated middle class, capable of ameliorating, by its example, the rudeness of character and manners which may be expected from amongst her successful gold-diggers, bush-farmers, and traders."⁹⁶

Ground was broken in July 1854 for a university and a public library, an ambitious project that would become the University of Melbourne and the State Library of Victoria. Sir Charles Hotham, governor of the colony, proclaimed at the groundbreaking ceremony that "he could conceive no institution more necessary, constituted as society was here, and taken in connection with the University, than the Library they were about to establish. . . . There was nothing more calculated to promote morality than sound knowledge and knowledge could not be better acquired than in a public library."⁹⁷ In 1856, after the opening of the library, a writer for the *Argus* wondered that "any well-conducted person has now nothing to do but to walk up stairs and take down the books he wants, conditionally only on his replacing them unharmed when he has done with them. No place that we have ever visited in Melbourne has so impressed us with a sense of the advance of civilisation in Victoria as the Public Library."⁹⁸

Adam Lindsay Gordon arrived on this enthusiastic colonial scene, a city that maintained higher literacy rates than those found in any other British colony or in London itself: 89 percent of the European men living in the colony of Victoria and 78 percent of women were to some extent literate in 1861.⁹⁹ These are especially impressive numbers when one considers Victoria's population explosion: the colony more than doubled, from 95,000 to 200,000

Figure 6. Henry Burn, *Swanston Street from the Bridge* (1861). St. James Cathedral, seen here, was moved in 1913–14 and replaced by St. Paul's Cathedral. The field on the canvas's left now features the Flinders Street Railway Station, and on the right now stands Federation Square and the National Gallery of Victoria, where this painting hangs. National Gallery of Victoria, Melbourne, Gift of John H. Connell, 1914.

between December 1851 and December 1852.[100] David Malouf describes Melbourne in the 1860s as

> related to London and all it stood for in the same way as any other large provincial city—Manchester, for example, or Leeds or Birmingham, places that had grown to be cities in the same period as Melbourne, and where much the same culture was to be found; the same grand buildings, the same plays and operas (Melbourne saw its first performance of Gounod's *Faust* just six months after the London opening), the same books in the public libraries and reading-rooms, the same serialisations of new novels by Dickens or Mrs Gaskell or George Eliot to be breathlessly awaited and passed around.[101]

By the late 1860s, Melbourne would also have within its bounds a circle of writers—including, in addition to Gordon, Marcus Clarke, George Gordon McCrae, and Henry Kendall—eventually recognized as some of Australia's founding literary figures. In 1868, these men together founded the Yorick Club, a literary clique with high aspirations for Melbourne's emerging print culture.

According to Andrew McCann, local writing in Melbourne had up to this point been overlooked in favor of imports from Britain and America; colonial publications, primarily in the form of circulating periodicals, were viewed as "mass produced and ephemeral," whereas books published in England by Tennyson and Matthew Arnold, for example, were of "enduring cultural value."[102] The books lining the shelves of the newly constructed public library would have been almost entirely European and American in origin. Clarke, who took over editing the *Colonial Monthly* in 1868, aimed to overturn this dynamic and to establish Melbourne as a colonial literary capital.

His task was a tall one. If we take the reception of Gordon's poetry as representative of the period in which he wrote it, what emerges is a patchwork of contradictions. For all the romanticism attached to 1860s Melbourne, those trying to earn a living by the pen generally failed in their endeavors. Melbourne's literary bohemia, writes McCann, was "an underworld—a space haunted by poverty, death, alcoholism, drug abuse and above all, literary failure."[103] The two volumes Gordon published in 1867—one a lengthy closet drama, the other a collection of lyrics—were mostly ignored, and dismissed by those few colonial newspapers that chose to review them.[104] Clarke himself trumpeted Gordon as "the most Australian of our literary aspirants," and by the end of the nineteenth century, in the decades when Australia was looking for national heroes, he came to be regarded as a foundational Australian poet: "Australia's hero, as well as her poet," according to Douglas Sladen.[105]

Spectators who knew Gordon as a horse racer thrilled to poems such as "How We Beat the Favourite," which captured the rhythms of riding horseback and anticipated Banjo Paterson's later bush ballads (discussed in chapter 6). Gordon "felt Australia in his veins," writes Sladen, "the glittering Australian climate, the champagne-like air, the long days in the saddle, the shooting of extraordinary game . . . the excitements of raging floods and raging bush-fires."[106] All that said, Gordon himself lived the last years of his life in a state of "restlessness, depression and ill-health," and literary scholars have more or less discounted his work.[107] He earns just two quick mentions in Paul Kane's *Australian Poetry* (1996); Judith Wright is more generous, but even she deems Gordon "no more than mediocre": "a kind of secondhand Byron, with modern overtones, a legend rather than a poet."[108]

Wright is especially critical of Gordon's imitative capacities: his poem "From the Wreck," she writes, "is so close to its [Robert] Browning original that it is practically an infringement of copy-right."[109] The "Browning original" Wright refers to is "How They Brought the Good News from Ghent to Aix," part of Browning's *Dramatic Romances and Lyrics* (1845), and there can be no doubt that Gordon had the Browning poem in mind. Gordon's contemporaries, too, worried at his imitative tendencies. Just three months after his suicide, the *South Australian Register* wrote that "[the poet] is one who makes. To make he must be original, and the warmest of Mr. Gordon's admirers must admit that originality was not his leading characteristic."[110] Oscar Wilde, writing of Gordon in the *Pall Mall Gazette* in 1889, suggested that "From the Wreck" is "a sort of Australian edition of" Browning's poem.[111] Wilde blames Australia for Gordon's derivativeness, not the poet himself: "On the whole, it is impossible not to regret that Gordon ever emigrated. His literary power cannot be denied, but it was stunted in uncongenial surroundings, and marred by the rude life he was forced to lead. Australia has converted many of our failures into prosperous and admirable mediocrities, but she certainly spoiled one of our poets for us. Ovid at Tomi[s] is not more tragic than Gordon driving cattle, or farming an unprofitable sheep-ranch."[112]

Wilde's assessment returns us to the opening of this chapter and the broader nineteenth-century connections among Australia, criminality, and unlicensed copying. One might read Gordon's rewriting of Browning's poem as yet another "crisis of authenticity," a failure of the emigrant poet to stake out truly original territory. But this would be a misreading, first, of Gordon's poem, and second, of the literary moment in which he was writing. Gordon's poem is not a work of "slavish imitation," nor is his engagement with Browning passively derivative. Like the parodic shipboard poems examined in the first chapter of this study, Gordon's "From the Wreck" uses old materials to establish a genuinely new work. The poem is as much a critique of Browning's lyric as it is a galloping account of the Australian outback and the challenges it posed for European emigrants.

In Browning's original poem, three horsemen famously ride out "into the midnight" to deliver news from Ghent to Aix:

> I sprang to the stirrup, and Joris, and he;
> I galloped, Dirck galloped, we galloped all three;
> "Good speed!" cried the watch, as the gate-bolts undrew;
> "Speed!" echoed the wall to us galloping through;
> Behind shut the postern, the lights sank to rest,
> And into the midnight we galloped abreast.[113]

The specific news Browning's horsemen carry remains a mystery, and Browning himself insisted that the premise of the poem was fictive and not based in any historical reality: "I was in a sailing vessel slowly making my way from Sicily to Naples in calm weather. I had a good horse at home in my stables, and I thought to myself how much I should like a breezy gallop. As I could not ride on board ship, I determined to enjoy a ride in imagination; so I galloped all through the night with the steed Roland."[114] Browning transports himself imaginatively by means of both the poem's theme and its anapestic galloping rhythm—a prime example of meter serving, in Yopie Prins' words, as "a technology for poetic transmission."[115] The experience of reading Browning's poem is meant to resemble, and even embody, a vigorous horse ride.

Gordon, a horse racer and trainer, would have been drawn to Browning's poem for obvious reasons. But Gordon clearly also needed to distinguish himself from Browning's original, effectively one-upping Browning in the difficulty of his ride and the suffering it entailed. Like "How They Brought the Good News," "From the Wreck" opens with three riders heading out to a distant town with important news:

> Between the tall gum-trees we gallop'd away—
> We crashed through a brush fence, we splash'd through a swamp—[116]

The immediate differences between Browning's and Gordon's poems are as significant as the similarities. Gordon especially highlights the rough Australian landscape his riders must navigate—crashing through a brush fence, splashing through a swamp—as opposed to the road between Ghent and Aix, which Browning's poem seems to take for granted. Like a set of parallel horseraces, Gordon competes with Browning at every stride:

> Still galloping forward we passed the two flocks
>   At M'Intyre's hut and M'Allister's hill—
> She was galloping strong at the Warrigal Rocks—
>   On the Wallaby Range she was galloping still—

And over the wasteland and under the wood,
   By down and by dale, and by fell and by flat,
She gallop'd, and here in the stirrups I stood
   To ease her, and there in the saddle I sat. (130)

Browning's riders carry unspecified "good news" from Ghent to Aix; Gordon's riders bring news of a shipwreck off the South Australian coast. The ship *Admella* was wrecked on 6 August 1859, breaking into two pieces on a reef and scattering passengers into the sea. Those that survived were marooned for eight days, until they were finally rescued by a lifeboat from shore.[117] Gordon's poem follows the riders who hope to inform authorities in time for some of the passengers to be rescued:

Look sharp. A large vessel lies jamm'd on the reef,
   And many on board still, and some wash'd on shore.
Ride straight with the news—they may send some relief
   From the township; and we—we can do little more. (126)

In no way could Gordon have been unaware of his indebtedness to Browning: the poem's structure and theme are explicitly, patently imitative. To accuse him of plagiarism, or a failure of originality, misreads Gordon's clear critique of the original poem.

The implicit overlapping of European and Australian scenes makes all the more explicit the differences between their content and the apparent competitiveness Gordon brought to his revision. Wilde erroneously insisted that Gordon remained always "distinctly English" and that "the landscapes he describes are nearly always the landscapes of our own country."[118] To the contrary, Gordon's distinctly Australian scene seems to wag a finger at privileged European readers: *here in Australia*, the poem suggests, *we ride hard, and without the luxury of roads, without the absurdity of an unspecified purpose*. Like Simson's revision of Hemans's "The Homes of England," which imagines Canadian mobility and opportunity in contrast to English stasis, Gordon's revision of Browning demonstrates colonial pride in a rougher, more urgent outback lifestyle. To borrow Caroline Levine's notion of formal *affordances*, we can say that imitation with a difference affords the colonial poet a clear structure for critique.[119]

If "From the Wreck" is an "Australian version" of "How They Brought the Good News," then it is one with a critical agenda. Browning closes his poem with the lone surviving horse drinking "a measure of wine" in celebration of having successfully brought the news to Aix. Gordon's poem instead ends mercilessly with the horse's death: "A short, sidelong stagger, a long, forward lurch, / A slight, choking sob, and the mare had gone down." As if to emphasize the absolute brutality of the Australian scene, Gordon's rider concludes by wondering "What was she worth?" and "How much for her hide?" (131). Readers who understand these lines simply as an imitation of Browning's lyric miss all the signals to the contrary. Gordon resists as much as he borrows from Browning.

Conclusion

We've seen through this chapter three varieties of colonial reproduction. Stapleton's *Poetry of the Cape of Good Hope* reproduces British and American poetry without attribution, omitting or altering stanzas that would have identified their origins. Like the South African periodicals from which he took most of his poems, his anthology reproduces Anglo-American culture en masse, offering colonial readers a version of culture nearly indistinguishable from what would have been found in Britain or the United States; his is a copy-and-paste model for one sort of colonial cultural reproduction.

Dunlop, Leakey, and Hill composed original poetry within the genre of the sentimental lyric, allowing popular Anglo-American structures of feeling to circulate in colonial Australia and adapting those structures of feeling to their particular locales: Dunlop's New South Wales, Leakey's Tasmania, and Hill's Adelaide. Their model of reproduction transports genre and affect from home to abroad and might as easily have been found in Canada, as we saw in Letitia Simson's poem, and elsewhere.

Finally, with Gordon we turn to critical rewriting and adaptation, a distinct shift from an original English lyric to something grittier and more in keeping with the harsh Australian outback. Gordon borrows a great deal from Browning, but he also adapts "How They Brought the Good News" to his own purposes, ultimately devising a new poetic mode for his colonial scene.

Rather than stages of development, these versions of colonial poetry were instead overlapping strategies that produced for colonial readers different affective modes. Unattributed reproduction says in effect, *you can feel here exactly what you might have felt elsewhere*. Sentimental imitation says *you can feel here in a way similar to what you might have felt elsewhere, but with some important differences*. Critical revising, finally, says *you can feel here in a way that resembles what you might have felt elsewhere, but in fact your experience will be quite different.* All three strategies contributed significantly to emerging nineteenth-century Anglo-colonial print cultures, and none should be viewed through the lens of "crisis." Indeed, we do both the poems and colonial print cultures a disservice when we read these works as anxious about their own authenticity.

The colonial cultures of South Africa, Canada, Australia, and New Zealand all participated in a global culture of enthusiastic reprinting, borrowing, and adaptation, in which such practices would have been both expected and welcome. In chapter 3, I extend this argument by turning to the more specific example of Scottish culture and the ways Scottish bardic voice was transported to the Cape colony, New Zealand's Otago province, and Canada. I intend chapters 2 and 3 to be read together in suggesting alternate models for understanding British cultural reproduction in the colonies.

CHAPTER 3

Sounding Colonial
Dialect, Song, and the Scottish Diaspora

Scottish Bards in Colonial Spaces

From 1810 to 1821, the fledgling town of Sydney was governed by Lachlan Macquarie, the Scottish general responsible for transforming a makeshift penal colony into a fully functioning city. The signs of Macquarie's influence are still readily visible throughout modern-day Sydney: stroll down Macquarie Street, a main thoroughfare the Scottish governor had built, and you will pass by the Hyde Park Barracks, which Macquarie constructed in 1819 to house working convicts; note as well the Sydney Mint, built between 1811 and 1816 to generate the colony's first coinage, and the Sydney Hospital, built at Macquarie's behest in the same period and known as the "Rum Hospital"; admire the botanical gardens that the governor established in 1816, and then meander down Mrs. Macquarie's Road to a peninsula jutting out into Sydney harbor; there sit in "Mrs. Macquarie's Chair," a sandstone seat carved by convict laborers in 1810 and from which the governor's wife, Elizabeth, is said to have admired the panoramic views.

For all of Macquarie's structural influence over the city, however, modern-day Sydney cannot be said to have an especially Scottish flair. A statue of Robert Burns outside the Gallery of New South Wales, unveiled in 1905, stands as one of few explicit signs in Sydney of what the historian Michael Fry calls the "Scottish Empire," the pervasive contributions made by the Scottish people toward Britain's imperial and colonial efforts.[1] That Macquarie transformed Sydney is well known, but Macquarie's Scottish origins rarely figure significantly in accounts of the period.

In many ways this should not be surprising. By the time Macquarie arrived in Sydney, Scotland had been part of the United Kingdom for over a century. The leading intellectuals of the Scottish Enlightenment, including

David Hume and Adam Smith, were Unionists, believing that the long-standing animosity between England and Scotland had reached an end. Walter Scott, too, according to Magnus Magnusson, held that "all the old divisions had been healed: Highlander and Lowlander, Jacobite and Hanoverian, Presbyterian and Anglican, Scotsman and Englishman"; all these "had all been assimilated into a single, peaceful and civilised united kingdom."[2] Scott was more optimistic than the circumstances warranted, overlooking tensions that persisted, as Katie Trumpener has argued, between the interests of the United Kingdom as a whole and those of Scottish nationalism. In literary terms, these tensions manifested as conflicts between "the forces of linguistic normalization" and "those of vernacular revival" and between "a London-centered, print-based model of literary history [and] a nationalist, bardic model based on oral tradition."[3] In the global context of the British Empire, however, the Scots abroad—including Lachlan Macquarie—had shown themselves "enthusiastically loyal to the British crown," in particular during the American War for Independence and the subsequent Napoleonic wars. According to T. M. Devine, the Scottish "contribution in blood" during these years of war "cemented the Union."[4]

At just this moment of apparent political consolidation, Britain entered a profound and enduring economic downturn, which eventually sparked an unprecedented "enthusiasm for emigration" throughout the nation; by the mid-1820s, according to historian H. J. M. Johnston, "public concern about pauperism was translated into increased interest in the emigration remedy."[5] From 1775 to the 1810s, the British government had pursued an anti-emigration policy, largely in response to the war in America.[6] But in the aftermath of the 1819 massacre at Peterloo, the government began to imagine emigration as a solution to the threat of working-class radicalism. The British prime minister, Lord Liverpool, supported in limited measure assisted emigration to South Africa's Cape colony and to Upper Canada, and in Glasgow unemployed weavers gathered by the tens of thousands to petition the government for funds to leave.[7] Highland agriculturalists similarly pleaded for emigration assistance.[8]

Scottish emigrants had populated what were to become the Canadian Maritime provinces before the 1820 turning point, beginning with the 1773 sailing of the *Hector* from Loch Broom, Scotland, to Pictou, Nova Scotia; between 1773 and 1815, more than ten thousand Scots arrived in Nova Scotia and Prince Edward Island. From 1815 to 1838, however, those numbers more than doubled, with twenty-four thousand Scots arriving in Nova Scotia alone.⁹ Even more significantly, after 1820 the "Scottish Exodus" expanded from its transatlantic compass to become a global phenomenon.¹⁰ Legions of Scots emigrants set out, first to South Africa, then to Australia (beginning in the mid-1830s and reaching a high point during the gold-rush years of the 1850s), and eventually to New Zealand.

This chapter examines strains of Scottish culture in the poetry of these increasingly global Scots emigrants. Scotland serves as a case study to highlight the diversity within British emigrant culture and the ways more particular forms of cultural identification were or were not maintained by emigrants absorbed into the global *British* diaspora. When historians generalize about the culture of British emigration, insisting on patterns of British cultural reproduction in the colonies, they risk overlooking the diversity of cultures replicated in those spaces. Bernard Porter has argued that even within the United Kingdom, the British "were virtually foreigners to one another," divided primarily along class lines, but also by religion, sex, region, and language.¹¹ These differences translated to colonial spaces in complex ways that are often overlooked, sometimes intentionally, as when James Belich uses the word *Anglo* in the subtitle to his study of British emigration to mean "simply shorthand for Anglophone or English-speaking, whatever the ethnicity." Belich identifies as problematic the reducing of all English speakers to one monolithic culture, but for the most part he nonetheless looks to the commonalities among Britain's Anglo emigrants and the "neo-Britain[s]" they shaped around the globe.¹² Indeed, Belich's thesis about cultural reproduction in many ways depends on a flattening out of how "British" or "Anglo" culture might be understood, concentrating as it does on larger, structural mechanisms, such as politics and the law, rather than finer, more regional indicators of culture, such as song or dialect.

I offer two preliminary theses, which subsequent sections of this chapter will elaborate. First, for many Scottish emigrants, their own varied regional dialects served as generic markers for "Scotland," forms of "portable property" that were transportable from Scotland to anywhere on earth.¹³ Though the majority of Scots abroad adapted to standard spoken English, emigrants throughout the nineteenth century continued to use dialect to mark a general sense of Scottish culture. Back home in Scotland, a debate had emerged in the later-eighteenth century about the value of the Scots "broad dialect"; poet and philosopher James Beattie, for example, wrote that he did not "think the Broad Scotch a language worth cultivating, especially as it tends to corrupt a much nobler one, the English."¹⁴ Beattie's "nobler" shows how the language of class inflected accounts of Scottish dialect. Robert Burns, on the other hand, saw dialect serving as a channel for "a distinctly Scottish idiom," a vernacular connection to traditional Scottish culture having more to do with place than class.[15] In his preface to *Poems, Chiefly in the Scottish Dialect* (1786), Burns writes of "our language" and "our nation," distinguishing a specifically Scottish literary tradition tied to Scotland itself, as both a land and a nation.[16] In the colonies, Scottish dialect sounded more often in this latter register, facilitating distinct nostalgic attachments to the homeland. Understood as generic, dialect served a greater purpose in colonial spaces than it did in Scotland itself, fabricating for Scots abroad a homogenized and readily portable sense of "Scotland" and Scottish identity, even as standardized English remained the language of class mobility and exchange.

Second, insofar as songs and ballads in the nineteenth century were associated with national cultures *tout court*, poetry was an especially vital component of portable culture.[17] James Mulholland notes that collective singing in the poems of the mid-eighteenth century Scottish poet James Macpherson, for example, "is figured as an act of remembrance"; in works such as *Fingal* (1761), which Macpherson claimed to have translated from the Gaelic, "bardic voice functions as a custodian of traditions."[18] Such forms of oral tradition offer ways of thinking about culture and portability that resonate with Catherine Robson's recent work on poetry and memorization. Robson herself understands poetic memorization and recitation, a compulsory part of grade school curricula throughout the nineteenth century, as mechanisms for establishing "collective identity."[19] Nineteenth-century writing on ballads often presented British oral culture in similar terms, as "song which is peculiarly national," as William Motherwell puts it in the introduction to his 1827 *Minstrelsy, Ancient and Modern*, "that body of poetry which has inwoven itself with the feelings and passions of the people, and which shadows forth, as it were, an actual embodiment of their Universal mind."[20] Ballads signify collectivity, the belief in shared feeling, giving communities the sense of being connected.

An important component of the shared culture Scottish emigrants believed they carried with them to the colonies would have been oral in nature and poetic in form, either literally or figuratively: that is, spoken, sung, or printed so as to invoke a speaker or singer. Whether these poems were recited by emigrants to themselves or to others, whether they were published and circulated in book form or scrolled by hand in journals or commonplace books, whether they were copied down dutifully or rewritten in critical or parodic registers, the memorized poem and its oral performances served emigrants as a powerful tool for maintaining and adapting Scottish culture abroad. Poetry, as Michael Cohen argues, is "a mode of socialization," and it was all the more so in nineteenth-century colonial spaces, where the work of cultural identification was under especial strain.[21]

In what follows, I examine Scots poetry and dialect in three colonial locales: South Africa's Cape colony in the 1820s, and both New Zealand's Otago province and Canada's Toronto region in the 1850s and '60s. Each of these colonial spaces saw the rise of at least one Scottish emigrant poet and, in the works of those poets, the careful negotiation of Scottish and British-colonial culture. The circulation of these poems, I argue, complicates notions of homogenous cultural replication and pushes us toward an understanding of a more heterogeneous "neo-British" colonial space. I argue moreover that dialect in these nineteenth-century colonial spaces was itself *generic* in its function as shared, recognizable, and portable. Like the sentimental tradition typified by Hemans's poetry, the use of Scottish dialect was a strategy for emigrants to feel at home together, a tool for overcoming feelings of dislocation and isolation.

Two notes before proceeding: first, other colonial spaces—Cape Breton, Nova Scotia, for example—saw the printing and circulation of Gaelic poetry, but I focus here on English-language Scots poetry because my interests are primarily located in multicultural communities: places where Scots immigrants would have had to negotiate cultural and linguistic differences.[22] Second, I follow J. K. Chambers and Peter Trudgill in not distinguishing between "dialect" and "accent." As Chambers and Trudgill write, "we are used to talking of accents and dialects as if they were well-defined, separate entities: 'a southern accent', 'the Somerset dialect'. Usually, however, this is actually not the case. Dialects and accents frequently merge into one another without any discrete break."[23]

Sounding the Local in Thomas Pringle's South Africa

There could be no better example of dialect's complex position in British colonial spaces than the work of Scottish poet Thomas Pringle (1789–1834). I focus here on a series of ballad-like poems he published in Scotland and in South Africa, showing how both dialect and the ballad form allowed Pringle to navigate among varying ideas of Scotland and home.

Pringle came from humble origins, raised on a farm near Kelso, about forty miles to the southeast of Edinburgh. Injured while still an infant, Pringle for his lifetime required crutches to walk and was therefore unfit for agricultural work; he turned instead to literary studies, eventually earning the attention of James Hogg and Walter Scott.[24] Though he worked as an editor for a range of Scottish journals, including the *Edinburgh Monthly Magazine* (the precursor to *Blackwood's Edinburgh Magazine*), and though he managed to publish a volume of his own poetry, *"The Autumnal Excursion" and Other Poems* (1819), Pringle failed to achieve security in either his literary or financial circumstances. The year 1820 was a crucial turning point, as the British government moved to fund an emigration scheme to South Africa, "a political [maneuver] by the Tory Government," that was "desperate" in the aftermath of the Peterloo Massacre "to demonstrate public concern for the unemployed in order to stave off pressures for more radical reform."[25] Pringle joined the effort, along with his wife and extended family, setting sail for the Cape colony on 15 February 1820.

Historians estimate that Scottish emigrants made up only about 10 percent of the four thousand to five thousand original "1820 Settlers."[26] Yet in Pringle's account in his *Narrative of a Residence in South Africa* (1834), the British settlers are firmly Scottish, and they are even pulled ashore on landfall by dutiful Highland soldiers who rush to ease their arrival. This "carefully staged scene of Scottish national recognition," as Katie Trumpener puts it, is the first of several that shape Pringle's memoire.[27] Pringle writes:

> I spoke to [the Highland soldiers] in broad Scotch, and entreated them to be careful of their country folks, especially the women and children. It was delightful to witness the hearty outburst of nationality and kindly feeling among these poor fellows when I thus addressed them. "Scotch folk! are they?" said a weather-beaten stalwart corporal, with a strong northern brogue—"never fear, sir, but we sal be carefu' o' *them*!" and dashing through the water as he spoke, he and his comrades hauled the boats rapidly yet cautiously through the breakers; and then surrounding the party, and shaking them cordially by the hands, they carried them, old and young, ashore on their shoulders, without allowing one of them to wet the sole of his shoe in the spray. Being Highlanders, these men had no connection with our native districts; but the name of "Auld Scotland" was a sufficient pass-word to their national sympathies.[28]

In Pringle's recounting of their landing, which itself appears in standardized English (Pringle does not transcribe his own use of dialect), the broad Scotch dialect transforms the foreign South African beach into a scene of reunion, perhaps even of homecoming. The scene is notable in no small part because the Broad Scotch dialect was not one that would normally have been spoken by Pringle or by the Scots Borderers traveling with him, who would have spoken a version of Lowland Scots. The Highland soldiers themselves would likely have spoken Gaelic as their first language. Pringle settles on Broad Scotch, then, as a common ground for all those on the South African shore, a "national" language overriding local dialects. Pringle's enthusiasm toward the Highland soldiers challenges Devine's view that Highlanders and Lowlanders outside Scotland would not normally have sympathized much with one another: "There was precious little sign of ethnic solidarity . . . [between] Catholic Highlanders, who mainly supported Toryism, [and] . . . Protestant Lowlanders, many of whom were committed to a more reforming agenda."[29]

To the contrary, Pringle's Broad Scotch "outburst of nationality and kindly feeling" captures precisely what Benedict Anderson has called "unisonality," the phenomenon whereby the shared sounds of language and song instantiate "the echoed physical realization of the imagined community."[30] In this instance, the identification with Scotland—"Scotch folk! are they?"—unifies Pringle's emigrants and the Highland soldiers, the sounds of dialect acting as affective glue to hold them together. We see in Pringle's account part of a larger phenomenon whereby markers of local or provincial identity come to stand in for a more generalized national identity once one moves outside the nation. "Scottish culture" becomes roughly homogenized abroad, allowing for a sense of collectivity among Scots emigrants who, back in Scotland, more likely would have understood themselves as belonging to distinct local and regional cultures. Robert Burns's own poetry exemplifies this shift from the local to the broadly national. Burns's original publications show the poet "positioning himself as bard of his locality."[31] However, the places specific to Burns's birthplace, Ayrshire, immortalized in poems such as "Tam O'Shanter"—"Auld Ayr, wham ne'er a town surpasses / For honest men and bonnie lasses"[32]—ultimately come for Burns's global readers to stand as universal signs of Scottish identity and culture: that is, they become generic. Through Burns's poetry, especially as it circulates among nineteenth-century Scots abroad, local places such as Ayr's Brig o' Doon (the bridge over the River Doon) signal a universalized "Scotland," even for those born far afield from Ayrshire.

Pringle was in many ways primed to think in terms of a broad Scottish fraternity. He came of age in an era of ballad-collecting and ballad-like metrical romances that contributed to what Ian Duncan calls Scotland's "new nationalist ideal of a mystic secular totality": a post-Enlightenment "epoch" epitomized by Scott's novels and the essays John Gibson Lockhart and John Wilson later published in *Blackwood's*.[33] Pringle's first significant publication included a ballad in Alexander Campbell's 1816 *Albyn's Anthology: A Select Collection of the Melodies and Local Poetry Peculiar to Scotland and the Isles*. Matthew Gelbart has shown that Campbell's volume focuses on "the similarities rather than the differences between the traditional Highland and Lowland music, collecting them together in a single work and asserting that both owed a greater debt to other Celtic music than to any English influence."[34] Campbell makes explicit in his introduction this argument about Scottish homogeneity: "the melodies of the Scoto-Gael, and those of the Scoto-Saxons . . . do not essentially differ; and their shades of difference are really so imperceptible, as frequently to elude discrimination. The truth is, that the present Editor made repeated trials of this fact during his late journey to the Highlands and Western Isles, by singing to the natives several of the Lowland melodies, and some of the Border airs; when these tunes were immediately recognised as old Hebridean and Highland melodies."[35]

Strikingly, Campbell finds similarities not just within music from around Scotland, but between Scottish and Chinese music, too, fully supporting Maureen McLane's claim that "Scottish song distresses any stable concept of cultural or national authenticity and distresses as well the category of literature itself."[36] If Highland and Chinese music resonate with each other, to what degree could either be considered "national" in origin? Campbell's introductory essay seemingly deconstructs his volume's commitment to the local, the "local poetry peculiar to Scotland and the Isles" of his title, finding instead broad universalities both throughout Scotland and between Scotland and the outside world. Pringle's understanding of Scottish fraternity works in a similarly universalizing register, allowing him to identify warmly with the Highland soldiers in South Africa. The soldiers' "outburst of nationality and kindly feeling" thus reflects a principle of shared Scottish nationalism that had become foundational to the Scotland Pringle left behind.

Enthusiastic as his Highland greeting appears, we find very little dialect in Pringle's published poetry. "The Banks of Cayle; or, the Maid of Lerden's Lament," one of the poems in the 1816 *Albyn's Anthology*, offers a rare and important exception:

> In Warwick halls while minstrels gay
>   Delight the festive band,
> Awake, my lute, the melting lay
>   Of Teviot's lovely land!
>
> *O, bonny grows the broom on Blaikla knowes,*
>   *And the birk in Lerdan vale;*
> *And green are the hills o' the milk-white ewes*
>   *By the briery banks o' Cayle.*[37]

As a dialect poem, "The Banks of Cayle" takes a distinctly oral form. *Albyn's Anthology* includes music, "A Border Melody" (figure 7), to accompany the "little ballad," making explicit its nature as song; a later reprinting of the poem in *The Autumnal Excursion* indicates simply that the air "The Demon Lover" might serve as a model for the poem's song.[38] Music here encourages what Yopie Prins calls "generic recognition," signaling to readers the oral, sung origins of the ballad form.[39] The dialect itself appears in the form of a "melting lay."

The poem's narrative tells the story of an "orphan heiress" who was, in Pringle's own words, "compelled by King Edward the First, in one of his desolating incursions [into Scotland], to give her hand to an English Knight of his retinue."[40] The unfortunate Scottish heiress is brought unwillingly to England's Warwick Castle, where she pines nostalgically for her native Teviotdale: "*O bonny grows the broom on Blaikla-knowes*" is her repeated lament. That Pringle was himself born on Blaiklaw Farm must be significant to the poem's sense of place; the dialect song specifically laments the heiress's distance from what would be (centuries after the present time of the poem's story) the site of Pringle's own birth. Pringle's most significant turn to dialect thus corresponds with an account of the particular local landscape of the poet's own childhood.

We will return to "The Banks of Cayle," but for now let me note that nearly all the remaining poems published before Pringle's emigration avoided any dialect whatsoever. As Matthew Shum has shown, the poems of *The Autumnal Excursion* were written almost exclusively "in a mannered, often cramped, and always decorous neo-Augustan register," suggesting the poet's self-consciousness "of the necessity to write within linguistic norms and stylistic conventions" and thereby "distance himself from a Scottish regionalism."[41] Though he locates his poems in the Border region of his birth, Teviotdale, his style privileges standardized English as the best instrument

Figure 7. "The Bank o' Cayle," from the *Albyn Anthology*, ed. Alexander Campbell (Edinburgh: Oliver & Boyd, 1816). Music Library, University of North Carolina, Chapel Hill.

for communicating via the printed page. Pringle points out in a footnote that Teviotdale, located on the southeastern border between Scotland and England, has "had the rare good fortune to have given birth to . . . a greater number of distinguished poets than probably any other district of the British empire."[42] Nonetheless, Shum notes, for all his pride in his home county, Pringle's poetic models would have been not Burns or James Hogg, the "avowedly vernacular poets" of southern Scotland, but instead Thomas Campbell and James Thomson, poets "whose work successfully entered the English mainstream and gave little indication of its Scottish provenance."[43] Pringle thereby participates in the larger project of universalizing English that Aamir Mufti has addressed as "fraught" with "scenarios of linguistic and literary acquisition, assimilation, and dissemination."[44]

The sounds of Scottish dialect figure importantly in Pringle's *Residence in South Africa*, but rarely in the written text itself. After their adventurous

Highland welcome to Algoa Bay, Pringle and his compatriots encounter a "Scotch gentleman," Mr. Hart, who had been living in the South African colony for two decades. Long removed from the sounds of his home soil, Pringle describes Hart as intensely moved by the speech of his compatriots. "The Scottish accent," writes Pringle, "seldom entirely lost even by the most polished of the middle ranks of our countrymen, was heard from every tongue; and the broad 'Doric dialect' prevailed, spoken by female voices, fresh and unsophisticated from the banks of the Teviot and the Fields of Lothian. Hart, a man of iron look and rigid nerve, was taken by surprise, and deeply affected. The accents of his native tongue, uttered by the kindly voice of woman, carried him back forty years at once and irresistibly . . . to the scenes of his mother's fire-side" (*Narrative* 28). Following such enthusiasm for dialect, one might reasonably expect the "accents of his native tongue" to play a prominent role in the poetry Pringle composed while in South Africa, but this is not the case. John M. MacKenzie suggests that the absence of Scots dialect is perhaps due to Pringle's desire for the widest possible readership.[45] But the issue may also have been one of genre.

Both before and after his emigration to South Africa, Pringle associates Scots dialect primarily with song and spoken language rather than the more expository and "literary" poems, such as "Afar in the Desert," his most anthologized work (discussed in chapter 2). The difference, that is, seems to be between notions of oral and printed culture, with Scots dialect in all its permutations siding firmly with the oral (this explains why the unfortunate maiden in *Albyn's Anthology* sings her lament in dialect). Pringle's vociferous welcome to the Highland soldiers at Algoa Bay, and his description of Mr. Hart's pleasure, make sense within this framework of an oral, sounded culture. Pringle's printed description of these scenes, however, takes the form of standardized English; he registers the effect of Scots dialect in his printed text, but rarely the dialect itself.[46]

The story of "The Banks of Cayle" and its relation to dialect, place, and national identification does not end with Pringle's emigration. One of Pringle's first published poems in South Africa, "An Emigrant's Song" (1824), calls to mind "The Banks of Cayle" both structurally and thematically, but with some important twists. Published in Cape Town's *South African Journal*, which Pringle edited with his friend John Fairbairn, the poem features an English woman in South Africa lamenting her distance from the landscape of her birth:

By the lone Mancazana's margin grey,
    A heart-sick Maiden sung,—
And mournfully poured her melting lay,
    In England's gentle tongue:—

O! lovely spreads th' Acacia grove,
    In Amakosa's glen;
But fairer far the home I love,
    And ne'er must see again![47]

Like "The Banks of Cayle," "An Emigrant's Song" invokes the idea of song. Situated in a South African landscape, on the "margin" of the Mancazana River, the nostalgic maiden sings of her homeland much as, in "The Banks of Cayle," the Scottish heiress sang of hers. A footnote to the poem informs readers that the poem had been "sent . . . by an esteemed Correspondent . . . from the English Settlements on the Eastern Frontier," where emigrants from the 1820 settlements "suffered most severely." Contrary to what the footnote suggests, Pringle himself authored the poem and no doubt intended its publication to help raise funds for those on the frontier (his volume *Some Account of the Present State of the English Settlers in Albany, South Africa* was also published in 1824; by the end of 1825 more than £10,000 had been raised to support the unfortunate emigrants, among whom were several of Pringle's own relatives).[48] Pringle's English maiden thus serves the explicit political purpose of raising sympathy and funds for long-suffering settlers, English and Scottish alike.

We know Pringle wrote "An Emigrant's Song" because his later poetic volumes—*Ephemerides; or, Occasional Poems, written in Scotland and South Africa* (1828) and *African Sketches* (1834)—include versions of that original 1824 poem. These later versions, titled respectively "The Scottish Exile's Song" and "The Exile's Lament," notably replace the original English maiden with a Scottish one:

By the lone Mancazana's margin grey
    A heart-sick maiden sung;
And mournfully pour'd her melting lay
    In Scotland's Border tongue—[49]

"Scotland's Border tongue" here replaces "England's gentle tongue," but the differences between "An Emigrant's Song" and "The Scottish Exile's Song" have only just begun. In place of the 1824 song "O! lovely spreads the' Acacia grove," Pringle substitutes none other than the dialect song from his 1816 "Banks o' Cayle":

> O, bonny grows the broom on Blaikla knowes,
>   And the birk in Lerdan vale;
> And green are the hills o' the milk-white ewes
>   By the briery banks o' Cayle.

Pringle's Scottish maiden thereby pines nostalgically from South Africa for the specific place of Pringle's own birth. More than that, she pines in an explicitly musical register; Pringle indicates that the printed words on the page should be sung to the air "The Banks o' Cayle," the music printed originally in *Albyn's Anthology*. Through that ballad song, the poem oscillates between two river banks, Scotland's Cayle and South Africa's Mancazana. The poem also moves temporally between two specific moments: the present of Pringle's South Africa and the past of fourteenth-century Scotland, where the original "Banks of Cayle" is set. The ballad links the Scottish emigrant in South Africa, singing in the poem's present moment, to a Scottish past she "mournfully" imagines, a Scottish past she ventriloquizes through "The Banks of Cayle."

The conceit of Pringle's 1816 "The Banks of Cayle" is that the poem printed on the page was overheard while someone sang it, and it was subsequently transcribed, committed to ink and paper; the conceit of the later South African poem is that the Scottish emigrant knows the same ballad from oral tradition—either that, or she learned it from Pringle's original volume. Assuming the former, likelier interpretation, Pringle's South African poem approaches ballad poetry as part of what Paula McDowell calls "a living oral practice" that is also mediated by print.[50] For Pringle, dialect signals that process of oral transmission through the medium of the printed page: "an encounter," as Meredith McGill writes about ballads in general, "between orality and literacy"; this encounter, argues McGill, is "the central drama of the ballad" as a genre.[51]

More broadly, the song echoed in "The Banks of Cayle" and "The Scottish Exile's Song" suggests that recollections of home—and cultural identifications with the place of one's birth—manifest most powerfully via this encounter between print and oral tradition. The poems that precede "The Scottish Exile's Song" in the *Ephemerides*, in particular "Evening Rambles," are marked instead by names of vegetation and animals particular to the South African landscape, all of which Pringle footnotes for the unacquainted

British reader: *spekboom* and *erythrina* (local plant life), *reebok* and *duiker* (antelope and gazelle).[52] Pringle seems keen to distinguish the South African landscape and its inhabitants from the Scottish landscape of his youth, noting the differences between the "swart [Khoikhoi] Shepherd" of South Africa and "Fair Scotland's jocund swains."[53] In the absence of those jocund swains and the comforts of a familiar landscape, Pringle turns to the internalized song of his earlier poetry, the "portable property" that—memorized, internalized—offers comfort, perhaps, in the way his friend Hart was "deeply affected" by the sounds of "Teviot and the Fields Lothian," carried back "at once and irresistibly ... to the scenes of his mother's fire-side."

Back home in Scotland, much of what emigrants abroad found unifying might have been disparaged as inauthentic, "defined by a mystified—purely ideological—commitment to history and folklore," as the authors of *Scotland and the Borders of Romanticism* put it: "a series of kitsch, fake, more or less reactionary 'inventions of tradition,' from Ossian and Scott to Fiona MacLeon and *Brigadoon*."[54] Once outside Scotland, emigrants were more likely to indulge in a bit of romance, valuing kitsch alongside dialect as vehicles for transforming foreign spaces into home and simultaneously for understanding fundamental ties among Scots settlers. In Svetlana Boym's terms, kitsch "domesticates every possible alienation," satisfying the needs of homesick exiles the world over.[55]

Pringle no sooner steps ashore at Algoa Bay than he begins imagining the South African landscape as a scene of especial welcome to the Scottish immigrants: "the grandeur and the grace" of the mountainous coastline, "majestic and untamed," inspires in Pringle and his compatriots "stirring recollections of their native land."[56] The sincerity of Pringle's connections here matters more than reality. Even more powerful than those visual connections are the *sounds* of Scotland's past: the dialect and ballad song that, through scenes of nostalgic recognition (invented though that recognition may be), bring together Highland soldiers and Borderer emigrants. No surprise, then, that the Scottish exile of Pringle's later poem overhears a ballad in dialect as she wanders mournfully along the South African river. The overheard ballad, as Pringle orchestrates the scene, is part of the exile's internalized soundscape of home. That her home is specifically the place of Pringle's own birth, Blaiklaw Farm, highlights the work of the ballad in "domesticat[ing]" the emigrant's "alienation."

Nearly a decade after Pringle's juxtaposing of Scottish and South African ballad song, John Stuart Mill would argue that "poetry is *over*heard": "All poetry is of the nature of soliloquy."⁵⁷ The songs of both the Scottish heiress and the South African emigrant might well be characterized as overheard; readers likely imagine these isolated women singing to themselves. But their songs arrive for our eyes and ears through complex processes of textual and oral mediation, the work of transmission that, as scholars of the ballad have long shown, was under scrutiny at the turn of the nineteenth century.⁵⁸ The nature of poetry is for Mill, as it was for Wordsworth, an individual pouring his or her feelings out onto a page: the attention rests with the act of production.

Ballad poetry instead turns our attention to modes of circulation—the mediation of print and oral cultures—and to the invocation of community foundational to the genre. Through the ballad genre, the local particulars of Pringle's Teviotdale transform into broad markers of Scottish nationality, just as in Campbell's *Albyn's Anthology* the specific sounds of Scottish music elide into a mostly unified totality.⁵⁹ Like the earlier identification between Pringle's emigrants and the Highland soldiers, whose sense of identity within Scotland would have been distinct (antagonistic, even), "Teviotdale" and the Borderland song of "The Scottish Exile's Lament" point to a shared Scottish sensibility made possible through an idea of oral culture. Though the overheard dialect and the particulars of the landscape in Pringle's poem signal a specific Scottish region, the exile's song ultimately functions at the level of genre. That is, at the point of remove from Scotland, the specificity and regionalism of dialect evaporate and the sounds of Scotland become *generic*—and, as a result, shared and portable.

Dialect and Difference in Scottish New Zealand

Scotland's poetic culture resonated proudly throughout colonial New Zealand, far more so than in South Africa. An 1862 *Descriptive Sketch of the Province of Otago, New Zealand* shows 4,760 assisted emigrants "dispatched" from Scotland to Otago between 1857 and 1861, compared to only 1,137 from England between 1855 and 1861: roughly four assisted Scottish immigrants for every one English.⁶⁰ According to Belich, nineteenth-century New Zealand was "roughly twice" as Scottish as the British Isles, due to the disproportionate number of Scots who emigrated there.⁶¹ We see cultural evidence of these numbers with the colony's first printed volume of poetry, William Golder's 1852 *New Zealand Minstrelsy*, the title of which clearly points back to Walter Scott's *Minstrelsy of the Scottish Border* (1802).

Writing from Hutt, just north of Wellington, Golder foregrounds in his preface his aspiration for building communal and ultimately nationalist sentiment in New Zealand, explaining that he hopes his poems will "endear our adopted country the more to the bosom of the bonâ fide settler; as such, in days of yore, has often induced a people to take a firmer hold of their country, by not only inspiring them with a spirit of patriotic magnanimity, but also in making them the more connected as a people in the eyes of others."[62] As Brian Opie has argued, the poems of *New Zealand Minstrelsy* show Golder's indebtedness to the cultural, philosophical, and poetic traditions of his birthplace, the Scottish Lowlands, firmly connecting the circulation of poetry to the birth of national enthusiasm.[63] Through his volume, Golder aspires for a broader New Zealand nationalism and culture, modeled on Scotch nationalism but not limited to Scottish emigrants. The *New Zealand Minstrelsy* charts a colonial version of the nationalist enthusiasm prominent in Scotland through the early decades of the nineteenth century.

A decade after Golder's volume, we find a somewhat more complex meditation on the relationship between Scotland and New Zealand in the poetry of John Barr (1809–89), an 1852 Scottish emigrant from Paisley, just outside Glasgow, to the Otago province of New Zealand, near Dunedin. As we've seen, Thomas Pringle's dialect poems framed nostalgia for Scotland through an oral, sounded tradition. In other contexts, Scottish colonialists used dialect to mark positive differences from their homeland; John Barr falls into this latter, more politically abrasive category. In the preface to his 1861 *Poems and Songs*, Barr presents himself as a laborer emigrant, "busily employed upon his ground, clearing with his axe" and turning to poetry as the "greatest recreation after his day's labour."[64] His poems were published in local newspapers such as the *Otago Witness* and the *Saturday Advertiser*, and Barr became the representative poet of the Otago region.

Barr was eventually an active member of the Caledonian Society of Otago, established 1862, and references to Barr's participation as a laureate-like figure appear regularly in Otago newspapers. The *Otago Daily Times*, for example, on 16 February 1869, describes Barr toasting "the immortal memory of Robert Burns" at a Burns anniversary dinner.[65] Burns remained an important figure for New Zealanders, as he did for Scottish emigrants worldwide; poets such as Barr stood in as colonial surrogates, revising Burns's work for colonial readers. As the *North Otago Times* testified in 1870, "the shepherd on Australian or New Zealand plains . . . the sailor on the deck of his ship, the soldier in his barracks, the colonist on the banks of the St. Lawrence and by the shores of the great American Lakes—in short wherever men of British descent are to be found, there are the admirers of the great Scottish Poet."[66]

Burns's humble origins—his birth "in a clay hovel"—may have been especially inspiring for immigrants looking to make a life for themselves through agriculture in New Zealand.[67] Even for someone as removed from emigration as Arthur Hugh Clough, the English poet, New Zealand seemed from afar a space to live out a solid working-class life. The conclusion of Clough's long 1848 narrative poem, *The Bothie of Tober-Na-Vuolich*, finds the protagonist and his bride heading to the antipodes for a life of highly romanticized farming. "They are married and gone to New Zealand":

> There he hewed, and dug; subdued the earth and his spirit;
> There he built him a home; there Elspie bare him his children,
> David and Bella; perhaps ere this too an Elspie or Adam;
> There hath he farmstead and land, and fields of corn and flax field.[68]

In Barr's poems from Otago, we find a similar emphasis on the status of labor. Two poems from Barr's 1861 *Poems and Songs* especially point to the complex relationship between Scotland's laboring classes and the lives of Scottish immigrants in New Zealand. Take as a first example the first and fourth stanzas of "There's Nae Place Like Ane's Ain Fireside":

> There's nae place like ane's ain fireside,
> In humble cot or ha';
> There's naething like ane's ain fireside
> When frosty winds do blaw.
> Nae place can warm the heart sae weel,
> If peace and love preside;
> It's there a man feels like a man,
> Wi' a' a father's pride.
>
> Otago boasts her valleys green,
> Her hills and fertile plains,
> Where scenes like this are often seen,
> Spread o'er her wide domains;
> Where happy hearts make happy homes.
> Where plenty reigns supreme,
> 'Tis worthy of the painter's eye,
> And of the poet's theme.[69]

The first three stanzas of the poem imagine a rural, domestic space marked as Scottish by the poet's use of dialect. Barr's poem also echoes a well-known song by the Scottish poet David Macbeth Moir, whose collected poetical works were published in Edinburgh the year Barr sailed for New Zealand. Moir's song, "The Rustic Lad's Lament in the Town," voices the sorrows of a working-class young man in the city, overwhelmed by nostalgia for his rural home: "There's nae hame like our ain hame—/O I wush that I were there!"[70] Moir's poem circulated through Scottish emigrant spaces, too, appearing in the Nova Scotia *Acadian* in 1827.[71] Nostalgia for a rural Scottish home, as Kirstie Blair has shown, was central to nineteenth-century Scottish poetic culture, even for those Scots who never ventured far from their places of birth.[72] Barr's formulation, then, was entirely generic, a form of portable nostalgia that relied on dialect as its primary vehicle.

Like so many poets before him, Burns included, Barr links both dialect and nostalgic sentiment to rural and working-class culture. Poetry such as Burns's helped create a generic and readily identifiable rural poetry that was easily transported and adapted to colonial scenes, even though it is true, as Elizabeth Helsinger warns in *Rural Scenes and National Representation*, that such rural and working-class cultures cannot be generalized with any degree of historical accuracy: "No image of rural life" in nineteenth-century England "could be counted on to produce consensus or a common national nostalgia out of what were understood to be the different and competing relations to rural places, and to 'the nation,' of landowners and laborers ... city dwellers and countrymen, northerners and southerners, natives and immigrants, English and Irish or Scottish or Welsh, British emigrants and the empire's subject natives, men and women."[73] In the Otago colony, and especially in a poem composed in Scottish dialect, "the rural" clearly signals a universalized and imagined version of Scottish bardolatry, brought to New Zealand in the spirit of Burns, that concerns itself with the lives of common people. Even the *Dundee Courier and Daily Argus*, a Scottish newspaper, identified Barr's poetry as being "chiefly in the Scottish dialect," a phrase borrowed directly from the title of Burns's 1786 volume; Barr's *Poems and Songs*, then, were explicitly read within Burns's bardic tradition in both New Zealand and Scotland.[74] In the context of New Zealand, that bardolatry called attention to the hardships of working-class life in Scotland and the opportunities for a better life in Otago.

The difference between Scottish suffering and New Zealand opportunity manifests formally in Barr's poem as a turn from dialect to standard English, or "Received Pronunciation." Otago offers its immigrants "fertile planes" and "happy homes"; what starts in the opening three stanzas as nostalgia for Scotland, written in "the Scottish dialect," turns to anticipation for a better life. "There's Nae Place Like Ane's Ain Fireside" stands as the eighth poem in Barr's volume, and the fourth stanza, printed above, is the first entirely in standard English. The stanza also marks the first explicit mention of Otago; all the preceding poems express generic perspectives on life—courtships, excessive drinking—that might have transpired anywhere on earth. In articulating via standard English the better life for Scottish emigrants in New Zealand, Barr points at least in part to the mixed cultures of the Otago colony and the degree to which upward mobility required leaving behind absolute identification with the Scottish homeland. The Dunedin colony was founded in 1848 by evangelical Scots, but even in the 1850s it was only one-half Scottish in origin; by 1864, roughly one third in the Otago province were Scottish-born.[75] Immigrants from around Great Britain called Otago home, and spoken English there would have reflected this diverse mix.

If Barr's dialect conjures a domestic space that replicates a generic Scottish homeland, his turn to Received Pronunciation complicates the narrative of cultural cloning, pointing to the emerging multicultural community of colonial New Zealand. Barr's turn to Received Pronunciation additionally makes sense within the larger global move toward standardized English: for example, Thomas Babington Macaulay's argument in his 1835 "Minute on Indian Education" that in India, "English is the language spoken by the ruling class.... It is likely to become the language of commerce throughout the seas of the east."[76] Standardized English in Dunedin would have been imagined not only to promote the upward mobility of its Scottish immigrants but also to facilitate communication across the empire and more firmly establish the Otago province as part of that global network. Barr's poems capture a moment in which the Scots dialect was superseded by what Aamir Mufti calls "the cultural system of English," but they also demonstrate that Scots dialect remained an important part of Dunedin's linguistic tapestry.[77]

A second poem, "There's Nae Place Like Otago Yet," clarifies even further the differences between Scotland and New Zealand and the relative positions of dialect and standard English in the colony (I again offer the poem's first and fourth stanzas):

> There's nae place like Otago yet,
>   There's nae wee beggar weans,
> Or auld men shivering at our doors,
>   To beg for scraps or banes.
> We never see puir working folk
>   Wi' bauchles on their feet,   *[a shoe worn down at the heel]*
> Like perfect iciles wi' cauld,
>   Gaun starving through the street.
>
> My curse upon them, root and branch,
>   A tyrant I abhor;
> May despotism's iron foot
>   Ne'er mark Otago's shore:
> May wealth and labour hand in hand
>   Work out our glorious plan,
> But never let it be allowed
>   That money makes the man.[78]

Barr once more opens his poem in dialect and then shifts in the final stanza to Received Pronunciation. Here dialect takes the form not of nostalgia but instead of blatant anger at Scotland's social inequities. The Scottish class system, under which the poor suffered in the cold, begging for scraps of food, comes up against the more egalitarian progressivism of the New Zealand colony. "Home" in this verse is an ideal Scotland built on antipodean shores, a version of Scotland that would not have been possible in Scotland itself. Dunedin was named after the Gaelic word for Edinburgh, and the town's vibrant rolling landscape conjured memories of home for most Scottish emigrants.[79] Nonetheless, Barr makes it clear that Otago differed from their original home in affording far superior economic opportunities to working-class Scots. This privileging of working-class quality of life is no doubt why the *People's Journal*, a radical working-class newspaper published in Dundee, Scotland, reprinted Barr's poem on 11 February 1860.[80]

Barr had originally published "There's Nae Place Like Otago Yet" in October 1859, in the *Otago Witness*.[81] The poem might have found its way to Dundee's *People's Journal* through any number of channels. With the three- to four-month journey from New Zealand to Britain, we can imagine a ship returning from Otago to Scotland and a passenger then passing along a copy of the *Otago Witness* to an editor at the *People's Journal*. Barr himself or an emigration agent may have sent the poem, or an emigrant in Otago may have cut out the poem and sent it to Dundee in a letter.[82] Whatever the specific mechanism, the move between New Zealand and Scotland represents what Trumpener calls a "transcolonial consciousness," an identification between colonial spaces on the peripheries of empire.[83] The lessons learned in one colonial periphery, Otago, are picked up by progressive Scots in Dundee as inspiration for motivating change at home.

According to the *Otago Witness*, Barr's poem was eventually responsible for encouraging "puir working folk" back in Scotland to abandon the "despotism" of Scotland's class structure in favor of New Zealand's fair shore. On 19 May 1860, the colonial newspaper printed a letter from a British emigration agent enthusing on the effects of Barr's poem on Scottish emigration to New Zealand: "Mr. John Barr's effusion, 'There's nae place like Otago yet,' has *told*. It comes home to Scotchmen's hearts; it was a *capital advertisement*, and appeared in several of our papers."[84] Otago seems to have taken hold of the working-class Scottish imagination, as suggested by the numbers of assisted immigrants heading from Scotland to New Zealand's southern island; even a decade later, in 1871, we find the *People's Journal* encouraging emigration to Otago (figure 8), advertising assisted emigration for "agricultural labourers, shepherds, tradesmen, fishermen, and their families, and female domestic servants," all "on most favourable terms."[85]

Thomas Pringle's dialect poems invoked a communal Scottish sentiment founded on the idea of a shared oral tradition. Barr's poems at first work in a similar register but then pivot toward a more radical critique of Scottish working-class life; Pringle's own judgment against English colonization—in his poetry, at least—was far more subtle and less attuned to the dynamics of class. Moreover, dialect in Barr's poetry signals a shared space of present suffering (his stanzas in dialect consistently catalogue the ills of working-class urban life), rather than an idealized communal history. Barr uses dialect to solidify for his readers—and for his auditors, as the case may have been—a shared Scottish past, all the more to imagine a shared, improved new home for Scots emigrants in New Zealand.

The Canadian Burns: Alexander McLachlan

Nostalgia for Scotland thrived in nineteenth-century Canada, with particular force in the Maritime Provinces. The 1860s, the period of John Barr's

> **EMIGRATION TO**
> **OTAGO, NEW ZEALAND**
> ASSISTED PASSAGES GRANTED TO
> AGRICULTURAL LABOURERS, SHEPHERDS, TRADESMEN, FISHERMEN, AND THEIR FAMILIES, AND FEMALE DOMESTIC SERVANTS,
> For whom there is a great demand in the Province.
>
> To those classes the Home Agent of the Provincial Government is prepared to grant Assisted Passages on most favourable terms, by Messrs P. Henderson & Co.'s well-known Line of Packets from GLASGOW.
> Parties eligible to receive assistance, and others intending to pay their own Passage Money, will receive full information on applying to
> GEO. ANDREW, Secretary; or
> ROBERT STEWART, 9 St Andrews Street, Dundee.
> Otago Home Agency, 3 Hope Street, Edinburgh.

Figure 8. "Emigration to Otago, New Zealand," *People's Journal* (Dundee), 14 January 1871, 3. Circulation of 118, 290: "Being the largest circulation of any weekly paper printed out of London" (4 February 1871), 2. This advertisement appeared regularly in the journal in the early 1870s. Dundee Central Library. With permission from DC Thomson & Co., Ltd.

rise to prominence in Otago, was especially enthusiastic in reflecting Scottish sentiment in colonial Canada. In 1867, the year of Canadian confederation, John Le Page (1812–86) published *The Island Minstrel* in Charlottestown, Prince Edward Island, and a year later in Saint John, New Brunswick, one Professor Lyall published lyrics such as "Scotia's Classic Streams" and "Moonlight on the Trosachs" in the local journal *Stewart's Literary Quarterly*.[86] William Murdoch (1823–87), an emigrant from Paisley, Scotland, to Saint John, included in *Poems and Songs* (1860) "Verses, Suggested by the Recollection of a Scottish Spring," among other nostalgic, locodescriptive lyrics.[87] Murdoch's title page features an epigraph from Burns—"I am nae poet, in a sense,/But just a rhymer, like, by chance"—and the vocabulary and cadences of his poems would have been familiar to any devotee of the Scottish bard. Unlike the political framing of Barr's New Zealand poems, Murdoch's recollections of Scotland seem unabashedly positive:

> Land of my love, land of my joy,
> Land where my life began;
> Land where I rambled when a boy,
> And sojourn when a man.[88]

John Barr's poetic critique of Scotland was used to encourage emigration to New Zealand; Alexander McLachlan, called "the Burns of Canada," was himself an emigration agent.[89] Born in 1817 in Johnstone, Scotland, just three miles from Barr's home of Paisley, McLachlan emigrated to Canada in 1840, a little more than a decade before Barr set sail for Otago. Elizabeth Waterston describes McLachlan as a "big, rough-bearded tailor," who "settled just west of Toronto, there to raise a big family and a big reputation as a poet."[90] McLachlan's Canadian poetry works in similar registers to Pringle's and Barr's: first, in its invocation of an imagined emigrant community established by an idealized (fictive) "unisonality" of dialect; second, in its foregrounding of dialect as a part of oral culture, primarily associated with spoken language and song; and finally, in its use of dialect as a form of internalized, portable property. McLachlan's work highlights even more than Pringle's and Barr's the musical nature of Scottish dialect poetry and the political, communal ramifications of that musicality.

While still in Scotland and apprenticed to a Glasgow tailor, McLachlan "associated with other young men who shared his interest in Scottish history and traditions, and who were writing poetry in the style of Robert Burns"; these men were also involved throughout the 1830s in the emerging Chartist movement.[91] Jonathan Rose has shown that Scotland's working-class communities, and especially those in the southwest of the country, tended to be more literate than those in the rest of Britain: there were at least fifty-one working-class libraries in southwestern Scotland by 1822, whereas "few such libraries existed in England at the time"; by 1796–97, there were already "thirty-five reading societies, mostly in and around Glasgow and Paisley, many of them based in weaving communities."[92] Poetry, according to Florence Boos, "was the principal mode of nineteenth-century working-class literary expression," and without question Chartist poetry was circulating throughout Scotland's reading societies.[93] Alexander Smith, working-class fabric designer and author of the best-selling poem *A Life-Drama* (1853), attended one such literary society in Glasgow in the 1840s.[94] John Barr may well have circulated among this cohort in the years prior to his emigration to New Zealand, and McLachlan likely would have remained part of it had he not left for Canada in 1840.

No doubt encouraged by the symbiosis of poetry and working-class politics in Victorian Glasgow, McLachlan's Canadian work is haunted by the sounds and communal sympathies of his Scottish homeland, more so than most other emigrant writing. As in chapter 2, I invoke the word *haunted* here in a positive sense, and in a way similar to Susan Stewart, who writes of ballad singers as being "radically haunted by others," overhearing both formally and thematically the sound of other voices in their own work.[95] McLachlan is haunted just so by Burns, hearing always the earlier poet's Scots dialect, along with his cadences and rhymes. More broadly, McLachlan is haunted by the notion of a folk poetic tradition, important to Chartists throughout the United Kingdom.[96] Insofar as the ballad is "a song... on the lips of the people," as Henry Wheatley wrote in 1876, McLachlan's poetry seems especially conscious of the embodied, sung nature of traditional balladry.[97] Whereas Thomas Pringle overhears a ballad song, a faint echo of the "border melody" that resonates in "The Scottish Exile's Song," McLachlin foregrounds in his poetry literal singing voices. In these voices we hear not just the sounds of emigrant nostalgia but also a persistent working-class embrace of community and resistance to structures of power.

Ballads and sung lyrics fill most of McLachlan's first full-length volume printed in Toronto, his 1858 *Lyrics*.[98] Three years later, McLachlan's longest work, *The Emigrant* (1861), characterizes embodied voices and song as foundational to the development of Canada.[99] In the second chapter of that poem, the passengers aboard the ship *Edward Thorn* pass the transatlantic journey from Scotland to Canada telling stories of "the land they loved so dear" and the "tale[s] of deep distress" that inspired them to emigrate (27). McLachlan punctuates the chapter with two songs, one on the colonial outrages England enacted on Scotland and the other on "Scotia's bonnie woods and braes" (29–32). The shipboard crowd of emigrants in "mournful groups around him hung,/Sadly sighing as he sung," a community of emigrants brought together by the affective experience of song (29). In McLachlan's third chapter, the emigrants sing "in concert" while camping in the Canadian woods, and in chapter 5 the emigrants wait out the long winter both telling stories and singing old ballads while huddled in their log cabin (34, 57–60). These songs and ballads appear mostly in standard English, punctuated only by occasional sparks of dialect: "big were the tears frae / My e'en that did fa' "; "bonnie wee birds sing" (31, 62).

McLachlan left *The Emigrant* incomplete, publishing only seven chapters in 1861. The final, seventh chapter focuses on a Highland emigrant called Donald Ban: "The perfect type of man,/ And Highland bards had sung of him,/ As stalwart Donald Ban" (74). Ban has an internalized "voice of other days," which he carries with him, "treasured in his heart," and he "loved to sit and sing" that "balladical lore" (75). A repository of Old World knowledge, Ban knows by heart the folk stories and songs emigrants like McLachlan worried would eventually be lost among the New World generations. Though Highland Ban would seem an ideal source of dialect poetry, instead we experience through his words just occasional fragments of dialect song, mostly smoothed over such that any English-speaking reader would understand perfectly well. Ban sings, for example, that

> Each cairn has its story, each river its sang,
> And the burnies are wimplin' to music alang,   [small brooks are rippling]
> But here nae auld ballad the young bosom thrills,
> Nae sang has made sacred thae forests and rills,
> And often I croon o'er some auld Scottish strain,
> 'Till I'm roving the hills of my country again. (79)

Ban eventually loses his sight and ends his days wandering the Canadian backwoods settlements, singing nostalgic songs of Scotland, leaving the ultimate message of McLachlan's poem ambivalent. Although "all the neighbours gather round" to listen to Ban's songs, and "many a young heart leaped for joy," still Ban reflects dismay at the loss of Highland tradition: "O sad was the heart of the old Highland piper" (82–83). McLachlan shows ballad poetry to be, as Motherwell put it, "inwoven . . . with the feelings and passions of the people," but it remains unclear how McLachlan's Scottish traditions will adapt in the New World.

Throughout *The Emigrant*, McLachlan shifts into dialect at those moments that most vividly invoke the idea of sounded performance. This makes sense, given that Burns remained in the middle decades of the nineteenth century "a patron saint of collective poetry," recognized as such by working-class journals like the *Northern Star* and the *Chartist Circular*.[100] More than that, the oral suggestiveness of Burns's lyricism, along with the cultural resonances of ballad culture, made spoken or sung dialect an especially powerful manifestation of working-class Scottish identity. In Scotland itself, as William Donaldson has shown, the working-class *People's Journal* began printing vernacular Scots in the late-1850s; additionally, Scots remained the language spoken "in many schools."[101] Far from being "a literary and cultural myth," then, as Brian Maidment suggests of Britain more generally, dialect still retained power both in Scotland and among Scotland's emigrant communities.[102]

The most notable example of McLachlan's connections among dialect, orality, and working-class politics appears in a poem apparently delivered in person at the 1859 "Scottish Gathering" at the Crystal Palace grounds in Toronto. McLachlan was an impressive public speaker, according to Edward Hartley Dewart's 1864 *Selections from Canadian Poets* (the first anthology of Canadian English-language poetry): "He has the gifts of an orator as well as those of a poet."[103] Titled "Song," the poem McLachlan recited stands out in his 1861 volume, *The Emigrant*, as one of few composed in a hearty Scots dialect. One can imagine the poet enjoying his public recitation on 14 September 1859, before a crowd of Toronto emigrants:

My heart leaps up wi' joy to see
    Sae mony Scotchmen here,
Sae I maun sing about the laun,   [land]
    The laun we lo'e sae dear;
We a' hae climbed her heathy hills,
    And pu'd the gowden broom,   [picked the yellow flower / daisy]
And wandered through her bonnie glens,
    Wi' gowans a' in bloom.   [daisies]

But oh we ne'er again shall see
    Her burnies wimplin by,   [small brooks rippling]
Nor hear the blackbird on the tree,
    Nor laverock in the sky;   [lark]
But tho' we've left the hame o' youth,
    And wandered far and wide,
In every lake and stream we hear
    The murmurs of the Clyde. (159)

The year 1859 was the centennial of Burns's birth, and celebrations were held across the globe to honor the poet's birthday, January 25. According to the *Chronicle of the Hundredth Birthday of Robert Burns* (1859), an account of 872 Burns celebrations held the world over, McLachlan was present for the festivities in Toronto, giving an "eloquent and feeling address on the life and character of Burns," which concluded with "a very beautiful poem composed by him for the occasion."[104] McLachlan's subsequent address to the "Scottish Gathering" in September of that year suggests the poet was still thinking of Burns and his significance to Scottish-Canadian emigrants.

After his opening gesture to Wordsworth's "My Heart Leaps Up," McLachlan's "Song" becomes an echo chamber of Burns's lyrics: "pu'd the gowans fine" appears in the third stanza of "Auld Lang Syne," and "burnies wimplin" comes from "Elegy on Capt. Matthew Henderson": "Ye burnies, wimplin' down your glens" (Highland Ban, quoted above, also mentions the burnies wimplin').[105] Both Burns poems tie memory to the natural world, and specifically the Scottish landscape. "We twa hae run about the braes,/And pu'd the gowans fine," from "Auld Lang Syne," recalls running about the flower-covered Scottish hillsides, and the rippling brooks of Burns's "Elegy" add a sonic component to McLachlan's reflections. The rippling brook, daisies, and larks of Burns's poetry represent lived Scottish experiences that McLachlan and his fellow Canadian emigrants would never again encounter, except as memory. That these nostalgic memories appear in the form of dialect, and via the genre of "Song," is important. McLachlan suggests first the ephemerality of lived experiences and the ways the communal experience of dialect, song, and shared memories of Scotland might help push back against nostalgia and loss. In recognizing their shared heritage, McLachlan's Scottish emigrants come to recognize idealized aspects of home in their present Canada: "In every lake and stream we hear/The murmurs of the Clyde."

Glasgow's Clyde at midcentury was an industrialized waterway feeding a major city, and it certainly would not have "murmured" like a Canadian stream.[106] McLachlan's connection between colony and metropole was patently false, and his emigrant readers would have known it. His point had less to do with accuracy and more with a global Scottish diasporic community linked by patriotic and nostalgic attachments to their homeland: attachments mediated in part by idealized memories of that home.

If Scotland were ever to be threatened, McLachlan writes, then

> brither Scots owre a' the earth,
>   Will stretch a haun to save,   *[hand]*
> They're no the chiels wad sit and see   *[children]*
>   Their mother made a slave;
> The spirit of covenant,
>   Wi' every Scot remains,
> The blood o' Wallace and o' Bruce
>   Is leaping in our veins. (161)

This sense of a unified Scottish community, Trumpener's "transcolonial consciousness," was explicitly the goal of the global Burns centenary. The planners of the celebration aspired to create "a lasting bond of union between the inhabitants of Caledonia and those of every country and clime who sincerely adopt as their creed—'A man's a man for a' that.' "[107] Significantly, this goal frames the reception of Burns foremost in terms of a shared political sentiment, a version of egalitarianism that would have been familiar to any attendee of Glasgow's 1840s Chartist reading societies. Ann Rigney suggests additionally that each of the Burns celebrations was "both imagined and rooted in embodied experience": "imagined" in its global scope, a community of Burns devotees united in a worldwide celebration, and "embodied" via each individual celebration, the collectives of readers localized in Toronto, Melbourne, Sydney, London, Chicago, Glasgow, or wherever they happened to find themselves.[108]

McLachlan's performance before the Toronto crowd at the Scottish Gathering of 1859, and in particular his turn to a form of Scots dialect littered with the well-worn phrases of Burns's poetry, suggests his strategic, political deployment of sound in the interest of community building. Though he embraced his identity as a Canadian Burns, most of his printed poetry did not take the form of Scottish dialect. One scholar has suggested that "the Scots dialect has been washed out" of McLachlan's work "by the new local content," because to write in the Scottish vernacular might have demonstrated a "stubborn patriotism" that would have alienated many of his Canadian readers.[109] This view seems not exactly right, given the enthusiastic dialect poetry one occasionally finds in McLachlan's volumes. We should instead understand dialect throughout McLachlan's work as an indication of oral performance: the vehicle for an embodied and performed voice. Dialect for McLachlan is ephemeral rather than printed, in the mouth of a speaker or singer and in the ear of an auditor rather than in the mind of a reader. At those moments when McLachlan needed to signal a genuine speaking or singing body and a genuine community drawn together by poetry, he was more likely to return to a version of Scots dialect.

New Scotlands

Oxnam, Scotland, is to this day a rural community of country roads and rolling farmland about fifty miles south of Edinburgh. From there in 1818, the blacksmith Andrew Shiels emigrated to Nova Scotia, the "New Scotland," settling eventually on a farm of his own just across the harbor from Halifax, in Dartmouth.[110] At a time when, according to the *Halifax Monthly Magazine*, "the poetical volumes of Nova-Scotia—as may be expected—

would occupy but a narrow shelf in the library,"¹¹¹ Shiels published an ambitious poetical work, *The Witch of the Westcot; A Tale of Nova-Scotia, in three cantos; and other Waste Leaves of Literature* (1831). Shiels telegraphs his Scottish pride on the title page of his volume, quoting from Burns's "Second Epistle to Davie":

> Leeze me on rhyme; its aye a treasure,
> My chief—amaist only pleasure,
> At home, a field, at wark or leisure;
>   My muse, poor hizzie,
> Tho' rough an' raploch be her measure,
>   She's seldom lazy.¹¹²

Like Barr in Otago, Shiels finds himself a Scotchman in the midst of a multifaceted emigrant community, the "inhabitants [of the Halifax region] being," as he writes in his preface, "a remnant of many nations." Given these demographics, Shiels opts to compose his poems in standard English, asking his reader "to exculpate at least a part of [his] rhyming delinquencies" because the "sudden change from the vernacular tongue of an outlandish borderer, to pure English, is (at least was to [Shiels]) rather an awkward transit."¹¹³

Scottish emigrants often followed Shiels's path in leaving behind the dialect of their origins, turning to standardized English as a way of communicating to the diverse communities in which they found themselves abroad. Catherine Helen Spence, an 1839 emigrant from Melrose, Scotland, to Adelaide, South Australia, published a series of lyrics in the *South Australian* in 1845, all showing degrees of nostalgia for her Scottish homeland without recourse to even a hint of dialect:

> when my eyes were turned to look
> Upon the sparkling, rippling brook,
>   They filled with tears.
> Wild Caledonia's mountain scenes,
> Her cataracts, and deep ravines,
>   Rushed to my mind;
> Her castles, abbeys, haunted ground,
> Where elves and sprites long since were found—
>   Where rivers wind.¹¹⁴

Spence's poem eventually leaves nostalgia behind and claims Australia as a place of opportunity, where "tales of wild romance" have yet to be told, and where "ideas in [the] mind" have yet to be awakened. In her autobiography, written at the age of eighty-four, Spence recalls that she and her siblings "took hold of the growth and development of South Australia, and identified ourselves with it."[115] The novels for which Spence is better known, such as *Clara Morison: A Tale of South Australia During the Gold Fever* (1854), similarly eschew nostalgia for Scotland and instead celebrate Australia as a land of opportunity, especially for women. "They grieved that I had been banished from the romantic associations and the high civilization of Melrose to rough it in the wilds," writes Spence about friends and family left behind in Scotland, "while my heart was full of thankfulness that I had moved to the wider spaces and the more varied activities of a new and progressive colony."[116]

Both Shiels and Spence understood themselves to be upwardly mobile—Shiels went on to be a justice of the peace and a magistrate for Halifax County, and Spence was Australia's first woman to run for political office—and their turn to standardized English makes sense from the perspective of class. For emigrants with fewer opportunities for upward mobility, dialect held more of a staying power. Henry Lawson's story "The Songs They Use to Sing," from his collection *On the Track* (1900), recalls the dialect songs of Australian gold diggers, circa 1880, in the Dubbo district of New South Wales. Lawson recounts diggers in a tavern with "a fresh back-log thrown behind the fire," taking out their pipes and calling, "Give us a song, Abe! Give us the 'Lowlands!'" Abe's voice, writes Lawson, "used to thrill me through and through, from hair to toenails, as a child."[117] As the man begins to sing, the whole public house rises, "toe and heel and flat of foot begin to stamp the clay floor.... Heels drumming on gin-cases under stools; hands, knuckles, pipe-bowls, and pannikins keeping time on the table."[118] The evening concludes with "Auld Lang Syne," "and hearts echo from far back in the past and across wide, wide seas."[119]

Communal song and balladry was also alive and well in Nova Scotia at the turn of the twentieth century. In 1932, a full century after Shiels's *Witch of Westcot*, folklorist Helen Creighton visited the region just east of Dartmouth, Nova Scotia, where Shiels had settled, to record songs and ballads from the oral culture of local fishermen and lumbermen. Creighton's *Songs and Ballads from Nova Scotia* quotes a fisherman who explains how the local vernacular tradition survived into the early twentieth century: "Men in

Halifax County fish in the summer and go into the lumber woods in winter. When fishermen have time to put in away from home they sing, and in the lumber woods they stay in camp for two or three months and this is how they entertain themselves. This means songs are always being exchanged, and that is what has kept them alive."[120] The songs Creighton records are not exclusively Scottish in origin; they include as well English, Welsh, and local ballads, such as "Barrack Street," which details the goings-on of a Halifax street market. Creighton notes however that the origins of this particular poem might be traced to the traditional Scottish ballad "Jack Hawk's Adventure in Glasgow," which is "very similar, even to the remarks of other people about the ill-fortune the hero is to suffer."[121] The folk traditions of Nova Scotia, then, carried forward and adapted to their local environs the long-established customs of Scotland, even into the early decades of the twentieth century.

Such a range of responses to dialect shows the degree to which oral culture was a tricky business in British colonial spaces. T. L. Burton and K. K. Ruthven have addressed what they call the "second-rateness of dialect," the ways that "historically the English class-system has ensured that regional difference denotes social inferiority."[122] In a similar way, nineteenth-century colonialists connected a more globalized and standardized English with both physical and social mobility. That's not to say that the poets addressed in this chapter abandoned the positive ideas of home associated with Burns and dialect poetry: their careful adaptation of dialect shows this not to be true. But for John Barr and his fellow Scottish immigrants, Otago's green valleys and fertile plains would be both an echo of home and something importantly new, something ultimately to be expressed in the Received Pronunciation, just as Alexander McLachlan's Highland bard eventually dies, leaving younger Scottish emigrants to a more standardized English-Canadian culture.

The "unisonality" of Scottish emigrant culture, then, shows itself to have been always polyvocal, divided by colonial region and, even more important, by class. Scots dialect functioned throughout the nineteenth century as a generic marker of "Scotland" and as a shorthand indicator of shared nostalgia for home. To argue that dialect is generic is in no way meant to detract from its power, but instead to suggest the significance of the generic and its force as an affective glue for far-flung emigrant communities. Genre was among the most powerful tools for imagining connections—both national and class-based—across vast spaces. Especially at early moments in the colonial process, such as Pringle's arrival on the shores of Algoa Bay, Scottish emigrants depended on the fiction of their own cultural homogeneity. Only gradually would they settle with comfort into the new multicultural communities in which they found themselves, accepting standardized English as the lingua franca of British settlement and upward mobility.

CHAPTER 4

Native Poetry

Forms of Indigeneity in the Colonies

Native-Born Poets

Not long after the January 1788 arrival of the First Fleet in Botany Bay, a new sense of the word *native* emerged for those convicts and officers first encountering the local Australian flora and fauna. Arthur Phillip, the original governor of what was to become the colony of New South Wales, wrote on 15 May 1788 that "five ewes and a lamb had been killed in the middle of the day, and very near the camp, I apprehend by some of the native dogs."[1] *The Oxford English Dictionary* quotes from Phillip as the first instance of a special sense for *native* particular to Australia and New Zealand: "Prefixed to the name of an animal or plant to form the name of an indigenous Australian or (less commonly) New Zealand animal or plant that is related to it or thought to resemble it in some way."

The Australian *native*, then, is both distinct to the Australian landscape—it is *indigenous* to Australia—and, at the same time, has a relationship to something familiar from back home, the United Kingdom. The dogs Phillip believes to have killed his ewes and a lamb are not British dogs, although those familiar with a London cur would recognize the native Australian dog, a dingo perhaps, as having a relationship to the species. A letter on "Native Flowers" from the 15 July 1856 *Sydney Morning Herald* invokes *native* in just this way: "native roses" and "native heaths," says the author, far surpass the "rubbish" English flowers brought over by "new arrivals from England."[2]

Other, more familiar uses of *native* persist alongside this special sense. An 1855 *Sydney Morning Herald* article writes of Māori unrest in New Zealand as "native disturbances."[3] Sepoy soldiers in India are "native troops."[4] According to Alan Lester, in the early nineteenth century South African context "the word 'natives' was taken to mean Afrikaners"—white settlers of Dutch descent—"as much as it did Africans."⁵ The word thus holds a complex place in the colonial lexicon, signaling both "indigenous" and second-generation colonial. Rudyard Kipling, born 1865 in Mumbai, identified himself as "native born." His 1894 poem "The Native-Born" evaluates the condition of white colonialists born throughout the British Empire, those who "learned from [their] wistful mothers / To call old England 'home'."⁶

What Kipling took to be the role of these "native-born" has been the subject of some debate. John McBratney suggests that Kipling saw them—himself included—as foundational to the "rehabilitat[ion]" of an empire that had developed a "sickly imperial core."⁷ Tricia Lootens, however, cautions against reading Kipling's poem without a serious dose of skepticism: the "suggestive ... quotation marks around 'home'" are only the first indication that the "Native-born" for Kipling are alienated both from the colonial space of their birth *and* from the English "home" of their mothers.⁸ Kipling makes clear that "native-born" colonialists will never fully assimilate to English culture, even as he asserts their loyalty to a global British Empire united through fraternal identification (a notion we encounter again in chapter 6):

> *From the Orkneys to the Horn*
> *All round the world (and a little loop to pull it by),*
> *All round the world (and a little strap to buckle it),*
>   *A health to the Native-born!*⁹

Second- and third-generation immigrants across nineteenth-century British colonial spaces found themselves, like Kipling, torn between "native" and "British" forms of identification.¹⁰ As the authors of *The Empire Writes Back* note, "White European settlers in the Americas, Australia, and New Zealand faced the problem of establishing their 'indigeneity' and distinguishing it from their continuing sense of their European inheritance."¹¹ Second- and third-generation immigrants were additionally taxed with the burden of perceived cultural and educational inferiority, not having had what were understood to be the cultural and educational advantages of a childhood in Britain.¹²

Colonial indigeneity (locating one's identity from within the colony) inverts the practice of British cultural cloning (importing one's identity from the metropole). For obvious reasons, second-generation colonialists were more likely than their parents to feel a sense of belonging in the colonies.

They also more likely resisted British culture foisted on them involuntarily.[13] Both second- and third-generation colonialists acted instead to establish their own "native" presence in Australia, New Zealand, and Canada: a sense of their own indigeneity (colonialists in South Africa, we will see, were less likely to imagine a natural connection to the land). In Terry Goldie's words, white "Australians, New Zealanders, and Canadians have, and long have had, a clear agenda to erase [the] separation of belonging."[14] Wishing not simply to occupy space, but to belong, British settlers adapted to the lands in which they found themselves. This yearning to belong helps to make sense of the myriad lone, meditative poets we find throughout the British colonies: writers seeking in different ways a "native" relationship with the land they inhabit and reflecting, as Mary Ellis Gibson notes with respect to India, "forms of unhomeliness" that were "expressed with particular intensity in poetry."[15]

Though these forms of unhomeliness manifest variously around the globe, they most often bear some relation to ideas of the native. Alex Calder identifies this phenomenon in colonial New Zealand as "Pakeha turangawaewae": *Pakeha* being the Māori term for an outsider (generally a white person), and *turangawaewae* "a sense of belonging, of having a place to stand." Pakeha turangawaewae, then, is literally a place for an outsider to stand.[16] In suggesting the difficulty of finding such a place, Calder writes both historically and from his own perspective in the twenty-first century, indicating the persistence of the feelings experienced by his Victorian ancestors: "We Pakeha are at home here, we identify as New Zealanders," he writes, "and yet . . . there is another degree of belonging that we do not have that is available to Maori."[17] Margaret Atwood captures a similar feeling of being out of nature, or not belonging, in her 1970 rewriting of Susanna Moodie's 1832 arrival in Canada: "The moving water will not show me / my reflection. / The rocks ignore."[18] Moodie, as Atwood imagines her, has no place in the Canadian landscape, nor is she recognized as belonging in any fashion.[19]

In both Calder and Atwood, we see that pronouns and voicing signal key differences in the experience of colonial belonging. Optimism radiates from colonial poems about community: poems with an obvious "we" voice. From "Come into the Boats, My Lad" (chapter 1) to the dialect poems of Barr and McLachlan (chapter 3), those poets who write in the plural "we," or who imagine a communal context for their poems' performance and circulation, are more likely to express confidence in where they stand, their right to speak from newly inhabited land. Even though he acknowledges belonging in a way different from the Māori, Calder's invocation, "We Pakeha," signals a form of belonging *through community*: "We Pakeha are at home here." With the singular "I" voice, by contrast, comfort turns to ambivalence. This is apparent both in poems written on emigrant ships (I'm thinking here especially of "A Dream" and its elegiac resonance with Ovid's *Tristia*) and poems of simple nostalgia, like Catherine Helen Spence's "South Australian Lyrics" (from chapter 3: "when my eyes were turned to look/Upon the sparkling, rippling brook,/They filled with tears"). Atwood's solitary Moodie remains appropriately invisible in the Canadian stream.

To put this another way: the failure of colonial poetry in the first-person singular is the failure of a particular poetic mode, a mode M. H. Abrams was to label the greater Romantic lyric. These poems, as Abrams describes them, feature "a determinate speaker in a particularlized, and usually localized, outdoor setting, whom we overhear as he carries on, in a fluent vernacular which rises easily to a more formal speech."[20] Colonial communities had less use for poetry such as this—the poems John Stuart Mill had in mind when he wrote in 1833 that poetry is "overheard" and not "heard," that "eloquence supposes an audience; the peculiarity of poetry appears to us to lie in the poet's utter unconsciousness of a listener."[21] To the contrary, British colonial poetry was conspicuously communal, dependent on the circulation of feelings understood as shared and familiar. Each of the three preceding chapters showcases a different facet of this communality: the parodic revisions of emigrant shipboard poetry, the sentimental lyrics of early colonial spaces, and the performances of colonial dialect poetry. These poems all posit the necessary presence of a community of shared cultural knowledge: parodies whose references make sense, sentimental feelings that resonate, and dialect that need not be translated.

The poems of "native" colonial poets, by contrast, often retreat into more interior spaces. In this turn inward, we see more clearly the generic conflict between individual and community, overheard and heard. I argue in what follows that this tension comes into particular focus in poems about colonial indigeneity: poems that establish a relationship between the "native" (as second-generation colonialist) and the "Natives," the Indigenous peoples of British colonial spaces. My subject in this chapter is not poetry *about* Indigenous peoples, but instead poetry that questions how notions of lowercase indigeneity depend on a complex relationship to the capital-*I* Indigenous.²² Above all, this chapter examines how poetry formally and generically highlights the ambiguities of settler belonging.

Henry Kendall's Natives

In 1862, a young Henry Kendall, soon to emerge as one of the most influential nineteenth-century Australian poets, sent the editors of the *Athenaeum* a sheaf of poems, imploring the London journal to publish work from "a native of a country yet unrepresented in literature."²³ In the decades to follow, Kendall came to sign his poems "N. A. P."—Native Australian Poet—to indicate his "special creative capacity and an ordained mission" with respect to Australia, the place of his birth.²⁴ As a third-generation Australian, Kendall understood himself as *native* in much the same way the native roses and heaths identified in the *Sydney Morning Herald* were thought to be native: he was of the Australian continent, but recognizable (as a poet, and perhaps as a man as well) primarily in relation to Britain, a place he never in his life set foot. In 1882, the year of Kendall's death, Alexander Sutherland reflected that Kendall had been more an "Australian poet" than Adam Lindsay Gordon because he was Australian by birth; immigrant poets like Gordon only "caught the impression of Australian life and scenery . . . in their maturer years."²⁵

Kendall's family had arrived in the southern hemisphere early in the nineteenth century. His paternal grandfather, Thomas Kendall, sailed to New Zealand with financial support from the Christian Missionary Society of London and in 1815 founded a school for Māori children. In pursuing his religious mission to bring Christianity to the Māori people, Thomas Kendall found that he needed first to understand the Māori language, culture, and religion. As Michael Ackland suggests, this process brought Kendall closer to the Māori than he likely had anticipated, and it resulted in forms of genuine sympathy and affection for them (too much affection, it turned out, as he later had a disastrous affair with his teenage servant, daughter of a Māori chief).²⁶ His publications nonetheless laid a groundwork for future European-Māori relations: first *A Korao no New Zealand; or, The New Zealander's First Book; being An Attempt to compose some Lessons for the Instruction of the Natives* (1815) and then, more significantly, *A Grammar and Vocabulary of the Language of New Zealand* (1820). "To the end," writes Ackland, Thomas Kendall "retained his fascination with native people and his recognition of them as the custodians of an independent and complex culture."²⁷

Henry Kendall was born in 1839 near Ulladulla, Australia, a coastal area roughly 140 miles south of Sydney settled by his grandfather, Thomas, after his departure from New Zealand. Writing from the end of the nineteenth century, Sutherland describes Ulladulla as an Edenic landscape in which "neighboring mountains seem to shut the township and its little harbour out from the world, and shelter the district so completely that the vegetation is of distinctly tropical character, and the scenery rich beyond description."[28] Accounts of the area from the time of his childhood also permit us to imagine the young Kendall surrounded in all facets of life by Indigenous people. When Joseph Phipps Townsend visited the Ulladulla region in the mid-1840s, for example, he noted approvingly the ways Indigenous Australians were "to be found on the premises of every settler in the bush, forming, in fact, a part of his household."[29] Townsend's sketches of Indigenous life in Ulladulla resemble Henry Mayhew's contemporaneous ethnographic writing on *London Labour and the London Poor* (1851) in their detailed attention to their subjects, though his tone shifts unclearly between sympathy and caricature:

> That black-looking dame, with a pipe stuck between her protruding lips ... is Mrs. Paddy, the elder wife of yonder fine-built man, whose costume consists of a shirt and pea-jacket only. Her usual resort is the back kitchen, where she washes dishes, and also employs herself in roasting parrots and magpies for her own particular benefit.... Yonder lively, active, clever fellow, is called "Charley." He is very fond of riding, and that as fast as his horse can scamper. When the maize is ripe, his duty is to shoot the cockatoos, parrots, and magpies that infest it; and in this employment he delights. He patronises Paddy's elder wife aforesaid, and presents his feathered spoils to her. It is to be observed, that he has a very fine, bright eye.... About Ulladulla were many smart, active, young black men, who occasionally made themselves useful, especially in reaping, and in felling timber; and in the former employment they were very expert.[30]

Historian Grace Karskens has argued that the time has come "to shake off the idea that [colonial] Sydney was a 'white' city, that Aboriginal people simply faded out of the picture and off the 'stage of history': it is simply untrue." Townsend's account suggests of Ulladulla what Karskens has shown with respect to Sydney, that "Aboriginal people became urban people very quickly."[31] Integrated into several walks of colonial life, then, Kendall would have known Indigenous Australians as part of his childhood community.

Kendall's adult writing makes explicit the ways he understood colonial culture as having originated in acts of gross violence against Indigenous peoples. In this way, he joins Marcus Clarke, who wrote of the "Weird Melancholy" of the Australian bush, a melancholy emerging in part from the suffering of its Indigenous peoples.[32] Unlike Clarke, whom Patrick Brantlinger has called "pitiless" and "racist," Kendall positions himself in bizarre and sympathetic relation to Australia's original inhabitants.[33] Four years after first contacting the *Athenaeum* and identifying himself as a "native" Australian, Kendall sent a second bundle of poems to the London journal, writing that he was "very anxious for the existence and recognition of an indigenous native literature."[34] By this he means not a literature of Australian's Indigenous peoples, but of those such as Kendall, the "indigenous native[s]" of the continent. A year prior, in 1865, Kendall had written in a letter, "When I face the face of things, through the eyes of [poetry], I am as it were, an *Aboriginal* Man. I look about me, as one might have looked on the first morning of Creation, with a surpassing wonder."[35] Kendall would undoubtedly have understood the strain in his use of these terms to refer to a British colonialist: *native, indigenous, aboriginal*. His abiding wish to be of the Australian continent conveys primarily an ambivalent relation to the land of his birth, but it also points to the ways he understands himself as a poet: the ways being native, indigenous, and aboriginal would have granted him a stronger ground from which to speak—an Australian version of "Pakeha turangawaewae."

We find this ambivalent sense of belonging rendered thematically in Kendall's poetry through his eerie depictions of the Australian landscape. His 1869 *Leaves from Australian Forests*, for example, features "alien" sounds, "black ghosts of trees, and sapless trunks" (HK 68, 69). In "A Death in the Bush," an oncoming storm brings "snaps and hisses ... // Which ran with an exceedingly bitter cry / Across the tumbled fragments of the hills," presaging the death of a settler in his isolated hut (HK 34). Since the poem's first circulation, Kendall's readers have drawn attention to its "morbid melancholy"; those specific words belong to Richard Hengist Horne, who chose "A Death in the Bush" as prize-winner of an 1868 poetry competition administered through the *Sydney Morning Herald*.[36] Horne worried that the author of such a poem might be led "by slow but certain degrees, into loss of sympathy with mankind," yet he singled out "A Death in the Bush" for its "fresh" and "first hand" descriptions of the Australian bush: "They are not in the least like American forest scenery, and still less like English or other

European scenery. They are expressly and wholly Australian."[37] The *Athenaeum*, too, in its 1866 response to Kendall's manuscript, valued his poems "on indigenous subjects" and dismissed "two allegorical poems about America," which "anybody might have written."[38] Melancholic as his landscapes appeared to be, then, his contemporaries attached value to their being *Australian*, marked by the continent of Kendall's birth.

In "The Wail in the Native Oak," a poem from *Poems and Songs* (1862), Kendall signals his ambivalent sense of the Australian landscape not just thematically but formally as well, in its voicing of an isolated lyricism. The poem is an Australian example of Abrams's "greater Romantic lyric," and it proceeds in clear relation to Charles Harpur's "The Voice of the Native Oak" (discussed above, in my Introduction):

> Where the lone creek, chafing nightly in the cold and sad moonshine,
> Beats beneath the twisted fern-roots and the drenched and dripping vine;
> Where the gum trees, ringed and ragged, from the mazy margins rise,
> Staring out against the heavens with their languid gaping eyes;
> There I listened—there I heard it! (HK 5)

What he hears within this distinctly Australian landscape (note the quintessential "gum trees, ringed and ragged") is a "melancholy sound": mysterious "hollow, hopeless tones" that sometimes appear to be "muffled sobbing" (HK 5–6). Harpur's 1851 poem similarly points to "Mournful things," but the tone of the earlier poem remains conspiratorial, as if conjuring a community of auditors: *listen, everyone, to the strange sounds around you*. Kendall instead isolates himself, sinking into abject horror: "There I listened—there I heard it!"

"The Wail in the Native Oak" offers several possible explanations for its overheard sound, attempting to make sense of the unfamiliar: perhaps it comes from a spirit of long ago, wandering the Australian forest; or perhaps the source is a living man once exiled and now searching "for familiar faces, friends for whom he long had yearned" (HK 6). Whatever the explanation, the sound comes almost certainly from a living or dead Indigenous Australian:

> here his people may have died,
> Or, perchance, to distant forests all were scattered far and wide.
> So he moans and so he lingers! (HK 6)

Eventually, an actual, living Indigenous man appears in the landscape, "a wild man through the gloom," sparking a desperate need for clarification and perhaps an equally desperate need for human companionship: certainly this man must know the source of the melancholy wailing. But the Indigenous man refuses to engage, and ultimately

> he rose like one bewildered, shook his head and glided past;
> Huddling whispers hurried after, hissing in the howling blast! (HK 7)

The wail of the native oak thus goes unexplained, and the poem captures instead a general feeling of unease, displacement, and isolation. If Kendall thought of himself as native, indigenous, or aboriginal, his poem articulates instead deep misgivings about belonging in and understanding the Australian landscape. "The Wail in the Native Oak" also figures overheard lyricism—in the form of the forest's indistinct wailing—in the eeriest of registers.

Just over a decade later, Kendall returned to the same subject in a poem titled "The Voice in the Native Oak," published in the *Australian Town and Country Journal* in 1874.[39] Kendall notes under the poem's title that he composed it "in the Shadow of 1872," a period of mental instability and alcoholism that followed his eighteen-month stay in Melbourne. If psychologically and physically challenged by Melbourne, Kendall was also enlivened by the city's emerging literary culture, which included fellow poets Clarke and Gordon (discussed above, in chapter 2). "Finding friends in Bohemia," he wrote in an 1871 essay, "I was baptized, and became one of the glorious brotherhood who live on their wits."[40]

Nonetheless, his 1874 "Voice in the Native Oak" finds him abandoning hope as a poet of Australia:

> Twelve years ago, when I could face
>   High heaven's dome with different eyes—
> In days full flowered with hours of grace,
>   And nights not sad with sighs—
> I wrote a song in which I strove
>   To shadow forth thy strain of woe,
> Dark widowed sister of the grove—
>   Twelve wasted years ago. (HK 113)

The song of the forest—the "wail of the native oak"—eluded him in 1862, and in 1874 he admits full defeat:

> But I who am that perished soul
>   Have wasted so these powers of mine,

> That I can never write that whole
> > Pure, perfect speech of thine.
> Some lord of words august, supreme,
> > The grave, grand melody demands:
> The dark translations of thy theme
> > I leave to other hands. (HK 114)

Kendall's abiding frustration and deep pain rests in his sense of having overheard a song—the voice or wail of Australia—that he cannot translate into poetry. In Kendall's estimation, Charles Harpur, another native-born Australian, may have done better; years after Harpur's 1868 death, Kendall wrote that the earlier poet "sleeps in the august forest.... Over this last home of his, the wild oak ... iterates its mysterious music year after year. The air is full of the sounds that have passed into his poetry."[41] But such music eludes Kendall's own poetry. Also missing from Kendall's 1874 "Voice of the Native Oak" are any indications of Indigenous Australians; even the "native" of the poem's title has become a less suggestive "wild" by 1880. That said, the inarticulate "wail" of the 1862 poem has become in 1874 more distinctly a "voice." If Kendall cannot speak or sing the Australian landscape, if he cannot translate into language the "mysterious music" he overhears, he nonetheless continues to acknowledge a "whole/Pure, perfect speech" emanating from that space.

Kendall himself, according to his own estimation, could not rise above his own personal trials and the antagonisms of colonial life: "We are not in a country, like England, mossed with beautiful traditions; we are in a new land that has all its traditions to form, excepting those which have been steeped in the colours of sin and shame."[42] An 1875 prose essay Kendall published in the *Australian Town and Country Journal*, "Arcadia at Our Gates," points to some of the ambiguity and emotional strain endemic to second- and third-generation immigrant identity—ambiguity and strain that Kendall clearly felt personally. Kendall addresses his imagined reader as an immigrant, not a native-born Australian, in the picturesque landscape around Gosford, the coastal region just north of Sydney, where the poet spent his later years: "Nature has here and there furnished this creek with bits of background having all the grace and delicacy of an old world scene.... In the hollow of a tree like this you hid yourself, reader, when you were playing the truant from school.... In a fair smooth sapling like this you whittled a certain name." Kendall concludes the first part of his essay with nostalgia for the old world of this imagined childhood, a childhood Kendall himself never experienced: "On meeting such reminders, when the hair is dashed with a sorrowful grey, our old thoughts come back to us with a certain alien majesty."[43]

Identifying here with all the clichés of what a privileged childhood in England might have been like, Kendall's "alien majesty" is all the more alien to him for his having an entirely imaginative relationship with that past. Emerson's original use of the phrase "alien majesty" in "Self-Reliance" (1841) captures a similar sense of recognition in something to which one has only an imaginative relation: "In every work of genius we recognize our own rejected thoughts; they come back to us with a certain alienated majesty."[44] If memories of an English childhood "come back" to Kendall, the experience can only be notional, in the way one might "recognize" one's own ideas in an Eliot novel or a Turner painting—or, better, in the way one sees a dingo as an English dog, only different. Common to all these experiences is an internalized belatedness, a feeling of coming late to the game, of recognizing one's distance from the original.

Why a man who signed his poems "N. A. P."—a man keen on identifying *not* as English, but as a native Australian—wished to invoke such an English childhood becomes clearer in the second part of "Arcadia at Our Gates," published the following week. The essay concludes rhetorically with a similar deictic pointing to the landscape around Gosford, only Kendall's attention turns to the violence brought to Australia by European settlers. In place of an idyllic English childhood, Kendall presents resolute settler colonialism and the destruction of Australia's Indigenous communities:

> "Here," they may say, "was the camp where the poor blind blackfellow, 'Pannican,' was shot down by the soldiers like a vulture." . . . . "Here Jem Wells lived, the bushman who had all the notions and accomplishments of a blackfellow." "There, on that slope, stood the lone hut of Jack Hayes, the brave old cripple who lived by himself and worked till there was no work left in him." "At the head of this Popran Creek, Billy Fawkner, the last of the blacks, killed his mate, Long Dick." "Over yonder is the cave where Tom Desmond slept, the giant convict who tied the savage that speared him to a tree, and then cut his hands off."[45]

Rhetorically and structurally parallel to the earlier nostalgia for an English childhood, this final turn in Kendall's essay substitutes playful idyll for tragic violence, Britain for Australia. The essay as a whole paints the Gosford region as an "Arcadia at our Gates," a bucolic escape from an increasingly industrialized Sydney, but the actions of both colonialists and Indigenous Australians mar the landscape. Slopes, creeks, caves, and trees become markers of death by gunshot, exhaustion, and spearing; the substitution of one for the other makes explicit the ways colonialist nostalgia comes at the expense of Australia's Indigenous populations.

Kendall's place among this violence seems unclear: he identifies neither as a British immigrant carrying fond memories of an English boyhood nor as a murderous colonialist. Newly arrived British emigrants happily projected onto the Australian bush a nostalgic connection to England, seeing in Australia "all the grace and delicacy of an old world scene." But as Kendall knew too well, that projection came at a cost of violence to the Indigenous peoples already there. As a "native," Kendall seems powerless: he can neither sing the indigenous Australian landscape nor identify with the British emigrants around whom he lives. Native, indigenous, aboriginal: a lifetime of straining toward connection with the place of his birth finds Kendall ultimately detached and isolated, convinced that Australia possesses a "majestic lay" that yet "Remains a mystery!"—and that he certainly will never sing himself (HK 116).

Arguably, Kendall's replacement of actual Indigenous Australians with his own self as "indigenous" is itself a form of erasure, part of the larger phenomenon Patrick Brantlinger has called "dark vanishings."[46] Kendall's account of Indigenous loss in "Arcadia at Our Gates" suggests the poet is himself aware that such acts of substitution—"Native" for "native"—have more than just linguistic implications. His 1869 poem "The Last of His Tribe" showcases the pervasive assumption, examined most thoroughly by Brantlinger, that "primitive peoples . . . were doomed to extinction and that there was nothing even the most vigorously humane intervention could do to save them."[47] Kendall's poem asks whether the last remaining Indigenous man "will go in his sleep from these desolate lands,/Like a chief, to the rest of his race" (HK 39). The poem immediately following in *Leaves from Australian Forests*, "Arakoon," hails yet another isolated Indigenous man: "Arakoon, the black, the lonely!/Housed with only/Cloud and rain-wind, mist and damp" (HK 39).

Readers of Kendall's volume likely imagine the poet's necessary distance from such figures. Just as he cannot, in "The Wail in the Native Oak," understand the sounds of the Australian bush, surely Kendall cannot identify in any serious way with the Indigenous figures of "The Last of His Tribe" and "Arakoon." And yet Kendall very much did—or, at least, he tried to. In 1868, when he sent his poems to the *Sydney Morning Herald* to be judged by Richard Hengist Horne, Kendall signed them with the name "Arakoon"; Horne writes that "who 'Arakoon' may be I know not; but his poems bear the unmistakable stamp of a recluse of the far-off bush."[48] According to "Aboriginal Names," a 1921 article in the *Sydney Morning Herald*, Arakoon, "really 'Ahra-coo-on,' was from Ahra, a rock, and *coo-on*[,] the voice, literally the 'voice of the rock,' an expression often used for an Echo."[49] Kendall positions himself, perversely, as exactly the sort of "wail" or "voice" from the Australian landscape—a "voice of the rock"—which, according to his poems' content, he consistently failed to capture.

Paul Kane notes that Kendall wrote "in many modes and moods," and yet his predominant, recurring motif is "negativity."[50] To the degree that I take Kendall at his word and believe that he in some way failed, I understand that failure specifically in relation to his isolated, first-person lyricism. The generic tension between individual and community signals in Kendall's poetry a lost community of Indigenous Australians and a corresponding failure of connection between the colonial poet and the Australian landscape. Kendall's self-identification as *native*, *indigenous*, and *aboriginal* could never fully be dissociated from the actual Indigenous peoples of the Australian continent, and his vocation as poet could never escape the limitations he understood to arise from that foundational connection. His discomfort and sense of dislocation—his failure to belong—thus manifests most powerfully as a generic mode: a bleak and overheard lyric wail.

Canadian Land Clearings: Oliver Goldsmith

Kendall's dislocation from the landscape was common among nineteenth-century Australian emigrants. Warwick Anderson, in his study of race and medicine in Australia, notes that the foreign climate, along with the continent's new diseases, introduced questions about how "doctors [might] transform Britons from sojourners into settlers, how [they might] make them feel at home in such a strange place," and how they "would . . . ever acclimatize such alien whites."[51] One key question, in other words, was whether doctors might aid in making natives out of foreigners. Kendall, arguably, was struggling to answer a similar question from his perspective as a poet. A different but related set of concerns confronted British immigrants in Canada, a land whose climate was more familiar to the European-born and therefore somewhat less alienating.

European settlers had been frustrated by the Australian landscape from the beginning. The original convicts sent to Botany Bay found the soil disappointingly thin, just barely covering the vast sandstone plateaux of the Port Jackson region. "The appearance of infertility," wrote Darwin on his 1836 visit, "is to a certain degree real"; the ground's porous sandstone absorbed and carried away the nutrients that otherwise could have sustained farming.[52] Agricultural hope shifted west from Sydney to Parramatta shortly after the arrival of the First Fleet, and by 1792 farms there "were slowly extending their frail patchwork into the ancient gray-green chaos of the bush."[53] Even the region around Parramatta, though, was "recalcitrant, leached-down and grudging."[54] Australia offered many things to nineteenth-century emigrants, including vast tracks of land for sheep and cattle, but farming of the sort practiced in Britain was not readily available; the future of New South Wales "lay with grazing, not with agriculture."[55] As a result of this focus on livestock and not farming, forests such as those covering the Blue Mountains west of Sydney remained largely uncleared, leaving in place the spaces that were to haunt Henry Kendall in the middle decades of the nineteenth-century.

In Canada, by contrast, forest clearing was well under way by the start of the nineteenth century. The industrial revolution only hastened the growth of an already robust industry, bringing "emigrants in [the] thousands" from Britain to Canada to join the lumber trade: "by 1805 fifty ships a year were needed to carry 300,000 cubic feet of squared timber from Pictou [Nova Scotia] to Britain."[56] At the turn of the nineteenth century, timber and the agriculture enabled by land clearings overtook the once dominant fur trade of Lower Canada as the colony's primary exports.[57] This was the economy into which the poet Oliver Goldsmith (1794–1861) was born and to which his 1825 poem *The Rising Village* makes clear reference. The son of British Loyalists who had retreated from the American colonies to New Brunswick at the time of the Revolutionary War, Goldsmith was the first native-born, English-language Canadian to earn serious literary attention—this owing in part to his being the grandnephew of Oliver Goldsmith, author of *The Deserted Village* (1770).[58]

In *The Rising Village*, Goldsmith explicitly links the "gloomy shades" of the wooded Canadian landscape to personal discomfort, and he positions an idyllic settler future in relation to the felling of local forests:

> When, looking round, the lonely settler sees
> His home amid a wilderness of trees:

How sinks his heart in those deep solitudes,
Where not a voice upon his ear intrudes;
Where solemn silence all the waster pervades,
Heightening the horror of its gloomy shades;
Save where the sturdy woodman's strokes resound,
That strew the fallen forest on the ground. (ll. 59–66)[59]

Goldsmith's "lonely settler" resembles Kendall's emigrants in being overwhelmed by the "wilderness of trees" and the isolation he feels there. He experiences what Northrop Frye calls the "primeval lawlessness" of Canada's vast landscape.[60] The felling of trees allows a shift from anxiety to comfort; once the trees are burnt and the land cleared, agricultural crops take the place of the intimidating wilderness:

Soon from their boughs the curling flames arise,
Mount into air, and redden all the skies;
And where the forest once its foliage spread,
The golden corn triumphant waves its head. (ll. 69–72)

The complicated process of clearing the land encouraged the settler to feel in "possession of the soil" (l. 104).[61] Catherine Parr Traill's 1836 memoir *The Backwoods of Canada* similarly traces the move from "dark forests . . . and no garden at all" to "a comfortable frame-house, and nice garden, and pleasant pastures." "Depend upon it, my dear," her husband tells her shortly after arriving at their settlement near modern-day Peterborough, Ontario, "your Canadian farm will seem to you a perfect paradise by the time it is under cultivation; and you will look upon it with the more pleasure and pride from the consciousness that it was once a forest wild."[62] Figure 9 positions the sun on a horizon overlooking a deforested field and what is clearly meant to be an idyllic scene.

Land clearing led to other perceived benefits as well: according to Goldsmith, lack of tree cover inspired Native Americans to "seek their prey beneath some other sky" (l. 108). Travis Mason argues that Goldsmith assumes throughout *The Rising Village* that the Canadian landscape will be increasingly "modified . . . to resemble that which [his British] literary forefathers had been describing for centuries."[63] The poem's heroic couplets, from Mason's perspective, anticipate a cleared and ordered terrain, free from any Indigenous presence, on which both British crops and British culture might be planted and sustained. British North America, in other words, will become

Figure 9. "Newly Cleared Land," in Catherine Parr Traill, *The Backwoods of Canada*, 4th ed. (London: Charles Knight, 1839), 129. The sun rises optimistically over a field of tree stumps. Princeton University Library.

increasingly like Britain, both physically and culturally. It becomes as well a land for immigrant *communities* rather than "lonely," individual settlers.

Henry Kendall struggled to understand the "strain of woe" he overheard in the Australian forest—woe he clearly linked both to isolation and to the suffering of Australia's Indigenous population. Goldsmith by contrast writes of how "sweet" it is "to hear the murmuring of the rill" and "the note of the Whip-poor-Will" as they resound through the cleared Canadian landscape (ll. 475, 477). He explains in a footnote that the "Whip-poor-Will . . . is a native of America," and just a few lines later he identifies himself as a native of that land, too:

> Sweet tranquil charms, that cannot fail to please,
> Forever reign around thee, and impart
> Joy, peace, and comfort to each native heart. (ll. 482–84)

Such peace and comfort, according to the poem, are available to European settlers because they have adapted the land to their own needs and because Native Americans, by the turn of the nineteenth-century, had been killed, removed, or pushed westward: "some few years have rolled in haste away,"

Goldsmith writes, "since savage tribes, with terror in their train,/Rushed o'er thy fields, and ravaged all thy plain" (ll. 503, 501–2). On this second point, Goldsmith's view is clearly a settler fantasy. Recent scholarship demonstrates instead that British North America "remained substantially unsettled" by Europeans up to 1820, "and most indigenous groups retained access to, if not government-recognised control over, their traditional land."[64] Even in the years leading up to the 1867 Canadian Confederation, as settlers took increasing control of land in the Maritime colonies and around the St. Lawrence River, local colonial governments consistently held an Indigenous legal right to the land.[65]

In contrast to such legal truths, *The Rising Village* participated in the late eighteenth- and early nineteenth-century framing of Native Americans as nomadic wanderers with no concept of land ownership or land usage.[66] In the Australian context this view was called *terra nullius*, the notion that until Europeans arrived on the continent the land there belonged to no one and therefore was open for the taking (legally this doctrine was not overturned until the 1992 *Mabo v. Queensland* case, which at last recognized native title in Australia).[67] As in Australia, European settlers in Canada understood themselves absolved of responsibility for claiming land rights, since they believed Native Americans had never possessed the land, nor wished to.

In reality, after 1820 Native Americans did their best to adapt to European agricultural practices; the Algonquians of Upper Canada (now southern Ontario), for example, planted "wheat, oats, peas, potatoes, and other crops, and often [sold] these products to settlers."[68] Such shifts in Indigenous practice seem to have had little effect on Goldsmith, who remained committed to a Canadian landscape cleared of both primeval forest and Native Americans. Drawing on land-clearing language from John Young's 1822 *Letters of Agricola on the Principle of Vegetation and Tillage*, as D. M. R. Bentley has shown, Goldsmith presents the "wilderness" of Nova Scotia as "repugnant to the human heart." When the land has been properly cleared, according to Young, then "it will win our affections, and consolidate our patriotism."[69]

Land clearing might be understood as the Canadian settler's response to "Pakeha turangawaewae." Young and Goldsmith bulldoze over the sort of existential dread felt by New Zealanders like Alex Calder, aggressively altering the North American landscape until it feels like home: land on which they belong because they've marked it so violently as their own. Absent existential dread, Goldsmith lacks sympathy for the Indigenous peoples displaced by European settlerism. Henry Kendall's soul-searching misery has no place in *The Rising Village*, which frames the Canadian settlement in Nova Scotia as a land of "noblest conquerors," who have "spread ... glory" and "thunder hurled" (ll. 538, 540). The shift in sentiment runs parallel to a shift in genre, from lyric isolation to odic collectivity. Goldsmith's heroic couplets and their rousing, communal sentiment—"The land of heroes, generous, free, and brave,/The noblest conquerors of the field and wave" (ll. 537–38)—anticipate not just a cleared landscape but a unified and triumphant settler community.

Isabella Valancy Crawford and the Native Canadian

Five decades later, in the years immediately following Canadian Confederation, the terms of settlement elaborated in Goldsmith's poem remained mostly in place: specifically, "native" continued to signify Canadians of European descent, and the clearing of forested land continued to enable feelings of settler belonging in British North America. These motifs from *The Rising Village* play out, with slight variation, in *Malcolm's Katie*, an 1884 narrative poem by Isabella Valancy Crawford (1846–87). Crawford's work shows the degree to which poems about indigeneity had themselves become generic, in part following the massive popularity of Longfellow's *Hiawatha* (1855). Virginia Jackson argues that Longfellow's poem established "the fiction that poetic writing may be ... indigenous" and in so doing become familiar, "an inscription of national character."[70] Crawford thus follows Longfellow in domesticating Indigenous Canadian culture to signal both that culture's decline and the rise of a new settler indigeneity.

Crawford had emigrated from Dublin with her family around the author's tenth birthday, settling in the small backwoods village of Paisley, Ontario.[71] Though not "native-born," Crawford nonetheless participated in the rhetoric of native cultures, and literary scholars have long considered her one of the most important nineteenth-century Canadian poets. In *Malcolm's Katie*, the protagonist Katie recounts how the land on her family's farm was originally cleared by plough and then by fire:

> with mighty strains
> They drew the ripping beak through knotted sod,
> Thro' tortuous lanes of blacken'd, smoking stumps.[72]

Crawford's poem is a romance, tracing the eventual union of Katie with Max, a backwoods logger. The titular Malcolm is Katie's father and the owner of an estate that Katie and Max will eventually inherit. Like Goldsmith's poem, *Malcolm's Katie* presents the cutting down of trees in positive terms, allowing settlers to proclaim possession of the land around them: "Mine own!" (52).

The poem has little to say explicitly about Native Americans, aside from one peripheral character described as a "half-breed" with "deep Indian eyes / Lit with a Gallic sparkle" (50). Canada's Indigenous peoples instead find their way into the landscape through a series of long and regularly anthologized passages in which Crawford imagines nature through Native American tropes, what Terry Goldie calls "a general system of indigene-linked terminology."[73] In other words, Crawford's Native American has been domesticated to the point of becoming entirely generic. Here, for example, is the arrival of spring:

> The South Wind laid his moccasins aside,
> Broke his gay calumet of flow'rs, and cast
> His useless wampun, beaded with cool dews,
> Far from him, northward; his long, ruddy spear
> Flung sunward, whence it came, and his soft locks
> Of warm, fine haze grew silver as the birch.
> His wigwam of green leaves began to shake;
> The crackling rice-beds scolded harsh like squaws. (45)

Language like this differs significantly from Goldsmith's poem in that Native Americans do not appear as sources of danger. But the absence of actual Native Americans in Crawford's wilderness also positions *Malcolm's Katie* as a participant in the "dying Indian" narrative. In the world of *Malcolm's Katie*, figurative moccasins and wampuns are all that remain of a once-thriving culture; they conjure a bittersweet and safe nostalgia (white readers know themselves not to be at any genuine risk) similar to that which had turned Longfellow's *Hiawatha* into such a popular success.[74]

Crawford's poetry shows the extent to which Native American tropes had become communal property for North America's white settlers. Frye describes Crawford's "mythopoeic" language as "first, taming the landscape imaginatively, as settlement tames it physically," and then "deliberately re-establishing the broken cultural link with Indian civilization."[75] But "re-establishing" no doubt overstates the case, given the absence of a genuine "link" between European and Native American cultures. Crawford's metaphors instead suggest a notional and ultimately fictive relationship between her poem and actual Native American life and culture. The real point of *Malcolm's Katie* is to better establish settler indigeneity through the domesticated tropes of Native American culture.

Kendall's "Wail in the Native Oak" opined that European settlers could never truly understand the sounds of the Australian outback. By comparison, Crawford's poem seems presumptuous in its interpretation of the Canadian landscape. Crawford demonstrates little of Kendall's sensitivity to cultural difference, instead borrowing the iconography of Native American cultures without more than casual knowledge. A similar critique has been leveled against Crawford's 1873 novel *Winona; or, The Foster-Sisters*, in which the heritage of the title character, a Native American woman, remains unexplored, "suggest[ing] distinct limitations in Crawford's personal knowledge of Native peoples."[76] In *Winona*, Crawford instead concentrates on the lineage of her white protagonists and defers much of Winona's characterization to material apparently gleaned from *Hiawatha*: "In her brighter moods," Crawford notes of Winona, "one could have fancied her an embodiment of Longfellow's ideal Indian maiden, the lovely Minnehaha."[77]

The end of *Malcolm's Katie* finds the poem's lovers, Max and Katie, united and living in a man-made "Eden" through which "r[ings] out the music of the axe" (68). Absent throughout Crawford's poem is the tension of Kendall's ambivalence, his struggle as a man of European descent to establish a sense of his own Australian belonging or "indigeneity." Crawford's protagonists experience setbacks, but they always triumph in the end. Max is even crushed by a falling tree, caught by its "piercing branches" as "in a death-throe" (71), and Katie nearly drowns in "frantic waters" (83), but each perseveres and overcomes the apparent wrath of the natural world. They persevere in part because they understand and accept that their relationship to the natural world is antagonistic—up until the point at which they tame it. Kendall, by contrast, aspires for more than just wresting control of the natural world: he wants for himself the idealized consonance he imagines between Indigenous Australians and the Australian landscape. Like the Indigenous Australians about whom he writes, he too wants to understand "the voice of the rock," the ever-elusive sounds of the natural world.

We can understand the differences between these writers—Goldsmith and Crawford on one hand, Kendall on the other—as a difference of genre. Goldsmith and Crawford each write in broad gestures meant to suggest a population of European settlers, whereas Kendall captures a more particularized and individuated voice. Crawford's landscapes default to the categorical: sweeping gestures in language that could describe nearly any temperate locale—"Down the rich land / Malcolm's small valleys, fill'd with grain, lip-high" (80). Goldsmith strikes a similar note with "crops of grain [that] in rich luxuriance rise, / And wave their golden riches to the skies" (ll. 455–56). Reading Goldsmith and Crawford, one imagines British life literally transplanted to Canadian soil. Kendall differs in remaining uncomfortable with vastness, perhaps because the act of encompassing the Australian landscape seemed itself an act of colonial violence: more appropriation than adaptation. To the extent that Kendall's poetry is also generic, it borrows from a different tradition: an interiorized, Romantic lyric never quite at home in the Australian context.

That feeling of unhomeliness resonates throughout Kendall's poetry. "The Wail in the Native Oak" presents a space of dream-like "mazy margins" in which an outsider could only feel disoriented and lost (HK 5). Later Australian writers would follow suit, in fiction as well as in poetry. Turn of the century author Barbara Baynton's "Squeaker's Mate," for example, part of a 1902 collection of short stories, focuses on the trials of life in the Australian outback. Unlike Crawford's Max, who recovers from his accident in the Canadian woods, Baynton's protagonist suffers a broken spine when a "thick worm-eaten branch snapped at a joint" and crushes her.[78] For the remainder of the story, she wastes away in frustrated isolation, part of a strong Australian counter-narrative to the dominant settler mythology. The novelist John Mulgan shows the staying power of these counter-narratives in his 1939 *Man Alone*, in which the rural spaces of New Zealand offer settlers only grotesque indifference: "There was . . . [a] man whose axe slipped into his leg below the knee one day when he was out at the back, splitting fence posts. He bled to death, and lay for a week before anyone thought of looking for him, and when they found him the blood was black and dry where he had crawled half-way up the track to home, and there were flies on him."[79] Like Kendall's poems, both "Squeaker's Mate" and *Man Alone* connect the feeling of displacement to physical isolation and individualism.

In attempting to write poetry specific to the Australian landscape, both its sublimity and its indifference to humans, Kendall found himself consistently falling short of his aspirations. Goldsmith and Crawford shared a different set of goals; their work instead aims to replicate British culture in a manner similar to that of the poets discussed above, in chapter 2. Like Eliza

Hamilton Dunlop and Caroline Leakey, Goldsmith and Crawford enthusiastically repurposed and adapted genres, motifs, and styles, bringing to the colonies versions of established British culture—and pieces of successful American culture as well. *Malcolm's Katie* accordingly can be read from one perspective as a revision of familiar Anglo-American narrative poems. At the same time, the poem clearly articulates its Canadian situatedness, much as Dunlop's "Aboriginal Mother" attaches the genre of the sentimental lyric to the particulars of Australian racial politics. Max claims that the wood he chops in the Canadian forest will "build up nations," and so too Crawford's poetic lines—building blocks like Max's logs—aspire to be a structure for supporting culture in the new Canadian nation (66). Both Goldsmith and Crawford succeed to the extent that their poems invoke communities rather than individuals.

Significantly, both Goldsmith and Crawford also make explicit that their emerging colonial culture depends on the usurpation of Indigenous peoples. Passages such as Crawford's arrival of spring suggest the twinned triumphalism of politics and aesthetics: the poem itself develops as it incorporates Native American culture, turning local traditions into familiar—and thereby unthreatening—kitsch. Kendall by contrast remains explicitly an outsider to Indigenous Australian culture, longing deeply for but never accomplishing a greater sense of belonging. In looking broadly at colonial "native" poets, then, Kendall emerges as an outsider to the more common trend of easy appropriation and adaptation.

Ambivalent Indigeneities

South African poetry offers a variation on the ideas so far explored in this chapter. For reasons about which we can only speculate, English-speaking poets in nineteenth-century South Africa tended not to think of themselves as "native" to that land. When Thomas Pringle, who stayed in South Africa for only seven years, writes of his "Native land" in "Afar in the Desert," he means Scotland. In "The Bechuana Boy," on the other hand, a local Bantu child has an African "native home" that Pringle never claimed for himself. South Africa attracted far fewer British emigrants than Australia and Canada, and the colony was itself far more internally diverse, with a population that included the Afrikaner descendants of Dutch colonists; slaves and freed slaves taken originally from the Dutch East Indies (now Indonesia); the Khoisan and Xhosa people; and the British themselves, along with increasing numbers of mixed-race children.[80] In 1870, Cape Town's population of 50,000 was roughly one-half white.[81] Trollope was skeptical that Britain had a place in South Africa, suggesting that it was an "unnatural extension of [British] colonization,—unnatural when the small number of English emigrants who have gone there is considered."[82] British emigrants like Pringle would have struggled more than those in other colonial locales to maintain the illusion that the South African landscape was naturally theirs.

Even a second-generation colonialist like William Roger Thomson (1832–67) used "native" solely in reference to the Khoisan and Xhosa. Thomson was born in the Cape Colony, son of a minister at the Kat River Settlement, and he eventually served on a "Commission of Inquiry" charged to examine "the relations of the Colony with the Native Tribes residing within and upon its borders."[83] Thomson thought of Pringle as a hero for his work as an emancipator (Pringle had become secretary of London's Anti-Slavery Society after leaving South Africa), and he wrote in an 1864 letter that "there is sad wrong done in our intercourse with the coloured classes. There is something radically wrong with our colonial system; you must come to the Frontier to see that."[84]

Like Kendall, then, Thomson understood the violence of colonialism, and he aspired for progressive changes in Britain's colonial policy. His ballad "Amakeya" offers a sympathetic view of the Xhosa chief, Maqoma, and his daughter Amakeya, both dispossessed of their "native land" following the Eighth Frontier War (1850–53):

> Poor Amakeya! years shall pass,
> And white men still shall come
> Across that sea, and still press on,
> And take thy new-found home![85]

Thomson highlights the violence against the Xhosa and the pain of their displacement, but he seems not to worry over his own place in the South African landscape: he is distinctly not part of it. By midcentury the early enthusiasm of the "1820 settlers" for claiming South Africa had passed, and it was increasingly evident that the Cape would not be a significant destination for British emigrants. Until the influx of settlers to the Kimberley diamonds fields, which began in the early 1870s, the region remained significant for Britain primarily because of its shipping route around the Cape of Good Hope.[86] Unlike Kendall, who resided in Australia for the duration of his life,

Thomson attended university in Scotland and seemed mostly to identify as European, not South African.

Mobility between Europe and the colonies was thus a significant factor for settlers in determining their sense of home and belonging. Charles Tompson (1807–83), son of a convict transported to Sydney in 1804, lived his entire life on the Australian continent, and he lays easy claim to being a "native" of that land. Indeed, Tompson was the first Australian-born writer to publish a volume of poetry, the title of which invokes his "native" status: *Wild Notes, from the Lyre of a Native Minstrel* (1826). Like Kendall, Tompson overlooks the awkward distinction between his own identification as a "Native Minstrel" and the "Natives of Australia" he references. Tompson however exhibits neither Kendall's sensitivity nor his critique of colonial violence. He instead suggests a divine purpose first in overtaking the landscape—"our Austral clime"—and then in educating the Indigenous peoples there out of their "unenlightened state."[87]

Printed just one year after the Canadian Goldsmith's *Rising Village*, Tompson's volume also makes reference to Oliver Goldsmith's 1770 *Deserted Village*. Echoing Goldsmith's original elegy, Tompson's "Blacktown" concerns the remains of the Parramatta Aboriginal Native School, which had been built, according to the poem's introduction, "for the purpose of civilizing the aboriginal Natives of Australia, and teaching them the art of agriculture, &c."[88] The school failed and, notes Tompson, "at the time I wrote the following Elegy, the Chapel and Cottages were deserted, the latter in ruins, and the whole scene exhibited the strongest marks of desolation." Tompson's Australian revision of *The Deserted Village* differs significantly from Goldsmith's Canadian *Rising Village* in imagining a place for Indigenous Australians within white Australia, circumscribed as that place clearly was. Paul Kane points to the poem's "conventional tropes and sentiments" and proposes reading "Blacktown" as "a screen for the poet's own anxiety about the futility or impossibility of founding any lasting [European] enterprise in Australia, including an Indigenous [white] literature."[89] We can see Tompson's colonial ambivalence—his desire for a meaningful colonial life in Australia crossed with his sense that such a life may be impossible—in his oscillation between triumphalism ("Go on, Britannia!") and resignation ("Ill-fated Hamlet!").

Nearly eighty years later, in turn-of-the-century New Zealand, the poems of Dora Wilcox (1873–1941) exhibit a similar tension between belonging and discomfort. A native-born New Zealander, Wilcox's 1900 poem

"Onawe," reprinted in her 1905 *Verses from Maoriland*, opens by considering a New Zealand landscape carpeted with "English grass":

> Peaceful it is: the long light glows and glistens
> > On English grass;
> Sweet are the sounds upon the ear that listens;—
> > The winds that pass
>
> Rustle the tussock, and the birds are calling,
> > The sea below
> Murmurs, upon its beaches rising, falling,
> > Soft, soft, and slow.—⁹⁰

The Ōnawe peninsula, just southeast of Christchurch, was once the land of the Ngāi Tahu, the dominant Māori group of New Zealand's southern island. Wilcox presents the Māori as "a nation /Doomed, doomed to pass" (3), but her poem suggests more than just the British usurpation of traditional lands.⁹¹ Wilcox identifies the grass, literally transplanted from Britain to New Zealand, but she also mentions "weird sounds" associated with the memory of the Māori haka, or war dance (2). In Wilcox's present, a disturbing "weird wild wailing" of a gull takes the place of Māori voices, and the colonizing Pākehā are welcomed, seemingly by the land itself, with a Māori greeting: "Tena koe Pakeha!" (3). What seems at first a simple lyric turns out to be highly ambiguous, torn between discomfort arising from historical consciousness—awareness, like that experienced by Henry Kendall, of the violence perpetrated against the land's original inhabitants—and the desire to belong to the land: in this case, the Christchurch land on which Wilcox herself was born.

As the different poems examined throughout this chapter have suggested, Wilcox's ambivalence was itself generic, a position common among second-generation colonialists. According to Jane Stafford and Mark Williams, the period in New Zealand between 1880 and the late 1910s was marked by "both modernity and nostalgia": a turning away from the original violence associated with colonization and a simultaneous effort to document those historical moments as they receded into the past.⁹² Wilcox accordingly asserts her modernity—those beautifully groomed lawns of English grasses—even as she ponders the weight of history. Historical loss seems even more apparent in "The Last of the Forest," winner of the New Zealand Literary and Historical Association's prize for "best New Zealand poem" in 1901.⁹³ Here again Wilcox writes of a threatening and audible natural scene: "screaming... night birds" and "shrieking/Wild voices" (7). The poem wonders whether these sounds emanate from

> Ghosts of Earth, and Air, that cry,
> Moaning a requiem, in their utter desolation,
> For old worlds passing by. (8)

Wilcox's poem resonates with Kendall's earlier work in relating a "voice that mourns the vanished Forest" (8). Like Kendall's "Wail of the Native Oak," Wilcox's "The Last of the Forest" does not claim to understand the haunted sounds of the landscape, but the overall message of loss is clear. Wilcox's poem stands out as "best New Zealand poem" from 1901 perhaps because of its vantage from the other side of desolation; to be a Pākehā New Zealander at the turn of the twentieth century meant carrying an awareness both of Māori loss and of shared complicity in that loss.

Such awareness did not, however, translate into a sense of belonging, or "Pakeha turangawaewae," for British settlers. Absent triumphalist narratives such as those of the Canadian Goldsmith, Victorian settler poetry most often testified instead to feelings of near-absolute dislocation from the land. Indeed, among the primary experiences of second- and third-generation immigrant poets was the existential challenge of being *from* a geographical place but not *of* that place. Henry Kendall's impossible desire to be "Arakoon"—the "voice of the rock"—makes sense as part of the fundamental human desire to have been of a place, from *somewhere*, as do the somersaults performed by Crawford, Wilcox, and others to negotiate their strained relationship to indigeneity. Like countless other second- and third-generation poets around the globe, Kendall, Crawford, and Wilcox were well aware that, at some necessary existential level, they did not belong to the land on which they lived. Their poetry testifies time and again to that underlying and persistent experience of dislocation.

Colonialism was necessarily communal, as Lorenzo Veracini argues, owing to the ways settlers understood their rights of land ownership as "corporate" and "pluralistic."⁹⁴ Rarely could an individual divorced from notions of community, nation, and empire assert a claim to possession. I have been arguing that this historical framework, the communality of settler colonialism, manifests generically within poetry of the British nineteenth century. To invoke a community was, in colonial poetry of the era, to indicate success: triumph over a hostile environment, the founding of a new homeland. To speak as an individual, as a voice manifest most clearly as an individuated lyric, was most often to fail: to fall victim to the landscape, to remain in a position of existential dread or uncomfortable ambivalence. Colonial authenticity and belonging, the qualities most relevant to claiming "native" status, emanated directly from and remained in necessary relationship to genre.

CHAPTER 5

Colonial Laureates
Navigating Settler Culture

Laureates Abroad

Teach me how to feel at home here. This, in effect, was the directive for British colonial laureates: poets tasked with maintaining tradition and ritual for settler communities. To the extent that British colonies invested in cultural replication, colonial laureates were their necessary accomplices.

Sydney's Governor Macquarie appointed the convict Michael Massey Robinson (1744–1826) to the laureate position in 1810. His tasks included composing two odes per year, to mark the birthdays of King George III (June 4) and Queen Charlotte (January 18). "So highly did his poetic efforts please Macquarie," the story goes, that "in 1818 and 1819, he was granted two cows from the Government herd 'for his services as Poet Laureate.'"[1] John Barr, the Scottish emigrant in Otago, was called the "Poet Laureate" of the colony's Caledonian Society, just as Alexander McLachlan, "the Robert Burns of Canada," became a laureate-like figure for Scottish emigrants in the colony.[2] Thomas Pringle, the Scottish poet in Cape Town, was without question a representative poet for the British colonialists of South Africa. The politics of Robinson's birthday odes differed significantly from those of writers like Barr, McLachlan, and Pringle, all of whom were Scottish and, to varying degrees, outsiders to the colonial establishment. Nonetheless, a set of shared qualities allow us to group their work together as representative laureate poetry.

Laureate poems are distinct in both form and function. Valerie Pitt reminds us in her classic study of Tennyson as a laureate figure that such poems "are necessarily rhetorical; the pleasure of them is not in the startling brilliance or profundity of their thought, but in the skill of their expression." Poems about coronations, royal birthdays, battles, weddings, and deaths serve a public duty, bringing "dignity and solemnity" to events and setting them "in the perspective of a common order": allowing the multitude a shared perspective on matters of public interest.[3] In other words, laureate poetry is fundamentally communal in nature. Like the dialect poetry of chapter 3, laureate poetry by nature invokes a community rather than an isolated individual voice.

Laureate poetry also embodies the pomp of imperial ceremony that David Cannadine calls "ornamentalism," but with an especially communal frame of reference.[4] Colonial laureates had the great responsibility of maintaining ceremony in far-flung colonial spaces. Take as a point of reference the landed gentry in early colonial Sydney, who preferred eating smoked or dried fish imported from England rather than the abundant fresh fish to be found in Sydney harbor.[5] In a similar way, Michael Massey Robinson's laureate odes address the king's birthday and the colonialists' enduring loyalty to the crown, not the lived experiences of the Australian outpost. The genre requires the backward glance. Both Robinson's laureate poems and the dried English cod are indicators of conservative cultural replication, the work of reproducing British culture abroad.[6] Robinson's first poem on George III's birthday, published 9 June 1810 in the *Sydney Gazette and New South Wales Advertiser*, makes explicit the dynamic of reproduction:

> Tho' far from ALBION's hallow'd Coast,
> OCEAN's first Pride, and NATURE's Boast:
>   Whose Fame the sacred Bards of old
>   In Strains prophetical foretold:
>   Though, wafted by the refluent Tides,
>   Yon watery Waste her Sons divides,
> Still shall the Muse prefer her tribute Lay,
> And *Australasia* hail her GEORGE's Natal Day!
> Auspicious Morn! To BRITONS dear:
> The Pride of each revolving Year![7]

Robinson foregrounds Sydney's distance from England, all the more to insist on the colony's loyalty to the king. The "Bards of old" may be far from Sydney's shores, but poems on the king's birthday, composed in recognizably odic stanzas, still resound through the penal colony.

Laureate poems in British colonies served more purposes than honoring royalty. They were more broadly significant in their ideological work of training settler colonialists to see foreign spaces as extensions of Great Britain.

The different chapters of this book have so far tested the hypothesis, promoted most enthusiastically in James Belich's work, that British colonies succeeded to the degree that they replicated culture from home to abroad. Propagating varieties of British culture often included the ideological yoking of poetry to patriotic sentiment and national belonging. As Tricia Lootens has suggested, following Benedict Anderson, "Victorian poetry is inextricably linked to the project of imagining" the British nation.[8] Meredith Martin's work in *The Rise and Fall of Meter*, subtitled "Poetry and English National Culture, 1860–1930," demonstrates the extent to which ideas of nation were interwoven with nineteenth-century aesthetic and pedagogical practices: as British school children were taught the intricacies of English rhythm and meter, so too were they taught what it meant to be a British citizen. Catherine Robson's *Heart Beats: Everyday Life and the Memorized Poem* suggests the ways the recitation of memorized poems gave both British and American schoolchildren frameworks for understanding their own relationship to the state.

In settler colonial spaces, one significant variety of laureate poetry aimed to reproduce national sentiment and British culture, taking advantage of the already established ideological connections between poetry and national belonging. Such poetry, in the mode of Robinson's birthday odes, has led scholars to view colonial poetry as necessarily conservative in its agenda. Norman Newton, for example, suggests that nineteenth-century Canadian poetry invariably replicates the ideology of the "Establishment" rather than ideas from "common life." The result, Newton argues, was a century of mediocre efforts to maintain an "aristocratic idea, deprived of its local roots" and a community of readers generally uninterested in the work of its poets.[9] This narrative, however, represents only part of the story. A second, equally important form of laureate poetry worked against the aristocratic tradition to adapt British culture to settler-colonial life, aspiring not simply to reproduce but to make new.

We have already seen hints of these divisions between old and new: for example, in the gap between reprinting and parodying canonical works of British and American poetry (examined in chapters 1 and 2). In chapter 3 we saw how emigrants carried abroad the specific sounds of Scottish poetics, recreating bardic culture in far-flung locales *while also* finding ways to critique the oppressive class-based societies from which they came.

The poets of the present chapter are divided as well, between those who saw poetry as a tool for cultural replication, in the style of Michael Massey

Robinson's birthday odes, and those who took more imaginative approaches, using poetry to make new sense of the emigrant experience. As a category, laureate poetry aimed to naturalize the processes of emigration and colonialism, so on the surface it tends to appear in a conservative guise. But the politics of that naturalization as practiced in colonial spaces differed significantly between conservative reproduction and the progressive possibilities opened by more imaginative approaches.

Laureate by Profession: Melbourne's R. H. Horne

Richard Hengist Horne's poetic aspirations were tragically unmatched by his abilities. His status as a "laureate" of colonial Melbourne had more to do with persistence than talent. Driven by one part financial need and another part starry-eyed ambition, Horne also styled himself an educator: like Prometheus, about whom he wrote, Horne would bring enlightenment to the masses.

A friend of Dickens, Browning, and other prominent mid-Victorian authors, Horne first arrived in Melbourne in 1852. His life prior to Australia had been more colorful than most. In addition to authoring the 1843 epic poem *Orion*, Horne fought in the war for Mexican independence from Spain and served on a royal commission to investigate the conditions of children working in mines. In Australia, beginning shortly after his arrival, he stood as commander for troops in a privately owned gold escort, ran for public election (and lost, to an illiterate Welshman), attempted to start one of Australia's first vineyards, and had plays performed in Melbourne's burgeoning theater scene.[10] Horne left Britain for Australia largely for financial reasons; like so many in the 1850s, he couldn't resist the temptation of Victoria's gold rush.

Horne was keen at first to distinguish his Australian endeavors from his career as a poet, and he insisted he had absolutely no poetic ambitions in the colony: "I never thought of coming out to Australia as a man of letters, but as one possessing active energies and a very varied experience. I did not wish to exercise any abstract thinking, nor to write either poetry or prose, but to *do* something." Even as he published this letter, though, Horne was already writing both poetry and prose for journals in England—some of his work from Australia was published in Dickens's *Household Words*—and publishing reprints of his earlier poetry in Melbourne newspapers, including the *Argus* itself. Horne insisted that "this Colony does not desire literature or the fine arts at present, and I do not desire to contribute to them," all the while taking the first steps toward becoming Melbourne's resident laureate.[11]

Horne was likely hoping to be drawn out as a colonial literary celebrity. Three days before his letter protesting authorial intent, the *Argus* had published a report on the roads and mining communities in and around Sawpit Gully, a region to the northeast of Melbourne, that mentioned Horne and bemoaned his fellow colonialists' lack of appreciation for the English poet:

> Having heard that the author of "Orion" had been appointed to the command, I had the curiosity to inquire of one of the men whether it was the poet Horne that I saw close at hand. . . . "It is Mr. Horne," was the brief rejoinder, "but he is no poet that I am aware of." I thought the reply an appropriate one. It was the accidental echo of the Colony of Victoria. Victoria knows that she has had for the past six months a great man within her border, one of the triumvirate of living English bards. Yet she has made no sign that she is cognizant of his existence, much less that she is sensible and appreciator [sic] of his genius.

The *Argus* contributor wishes Horne well in gold-digging so that he might return with speed to England, "the land where thy noble epic was read with swelling heart and deep emotion, where thou may'st receive the grateful incense so honorably thy due, where thou may'st consort with kindred spirits, here, alas! existing not."[12] Horne's return to England was not to come until 1869, and his seventeen years in Australia never resulted in the financial security to which he aspired (his mining efforts were predictably disappointing). He may well have been "Melbourne's official literary spokesman," as Ann Blainey writes, "the unofficial Laureate of Victoria,"[13] but in the end this failed to translate into financial success. His efforts nonetheless reveal a good deal about Melbourne's midcentury literary culture and the function of a laureate figure in the colony.

In early 1853, just a few months after his arrival, Horne began a campaign to publish an Australian edition of *Orion*. The *Argus* published an excerpt from the poem in late January, calling it "The Lights of the World," subtitled "Public Benefactors and Their Treatment." In the context of the Australian newspaper, the lines suggest an indictment of colonial culture, even as Horne was ostensibly attempting to build it *sui generis*:

> The wisdom of mankind creeps slowly on,
> Subject to every doubt that can retard,
> Or fling it back upon an earlier time,

So timid are man's footsteps in the dark,—
But blindest those who have no inward light.
One mind, perchance, in every age contains
The sum of all before, and much to come;
Much that's far distant still; but that full mind,
Companioned oft by others of like scope,
Belief, and tendency, and anxious will,
A circle small transpierces and illumes:
Expanding soon, its subtle radiance
Falls blunted from the mass of flesh and bone,
The man who for his race might supersede
The work of ages, dies worn out—not used.
Yet lives he not in vain; for if his soul
Hath entered others, though imperfectly,
The circle widens as the world spins round,—
His soul works on, while he sleeps 'neath the grass.[14]

Horne undoubtedly wished to imagine himself one of the lights of the world, a mind that might understand history and human nature and that might anticipate "much that's far distant still." Unappreciated and, at the time of the poem's publication, not yet recognized in the Melbourne colony for his contributions as a "public benefactor," the excerpt suggests resignation to dying "worn out—not used," and yet still having an effect on the world he's left behind.

When the Australian edition of *Orion* finally came out, in October 1854, Horne introduced it as "the first Poetic Work ever published in this Gold-trading Colony."[15] Both Barron Field's 1819 *First Fruits of Australian Poetry* (the first book of poetry published in Australia) and Fidelia Hill's 1840 *Poems and Recollections of the Past* (discussed below) had been published in Sydney. Though *Orion* is a reprint, and though its subject had nothing to do with the Australian continent, Horne claimed the honor of publishing the first poetic volume in Victoria, as well as the first epic poem published in Australia. "I little imagined on leaving England," he writes in the preface, "that the next edition of 'Orion' as an 'experiment upon the mind of a nation' (in embryo, though this nation is) would be called for in Melbourne."[16] Horne quotes here from his own prefatory note to the original 1843 *Orion*, in which he had imagined his poem as not "a mere echo or reflection of the Past," but a vital, living work, with the power to influence the spirit of the age:

an "experiment upon the mind of the nation."[17] The original *Orion* had been sold for just one farthing, earning Horne the dubious title of "farthing poet," and this publicity scheme is in part the experiment to which he refers. How curious, Horne suggests in his 1854 edition, to think of his poem now influencing the development of a colony so distant from the land of its original composition.

Though originally written as a reflection on Britain's class relations, Horne's account of the Orion myth was well suited for Australia. Orion, the mythological giant, was meant in Horne's poem to represent the working man. Orion comes by the end of the epic to appreciate his intellect in addition to brute strength; he discovers the "serene delights / Of contemplation."[18] Back in England, Horne had imagined his farthing volume an inspiration for working-class readers, and for a time through the mid-1840s he succeeded, finding himself a "fashionable rage."[19] But the response in Melbourne appears to have been restrained, at least in the press. On receiving Horne's book, the *Argus* focused mostly on the quality of the volume's printing, not its content: it "is very well got up. . . . Its success will be as gratifying as its very appearance is a matter of interest." The volume, the newspaper concluded, is "a very creditable specimen of colonial typography."[20] Simply having published a bound volume of poetry was more important to Melbourne's reviewers than the nature of the poetry itself.

Horne was not one to rest in the face of indifference, though he must have been disappointed at *Orion*'s colonial failure. In early 1855 he helped to establish the Garrick Club, an amateur theater company whose first performance, according to the *Argus*, "would have been favorably received in any town in the mother country . . . and some of the leading characters would put many professionals of long standing to the blush."[21] In a manuscript from this period, Horne notes that the "attempt to found a Guild of Literature and Art in Victoria . . . is not premature." Gesturing most likely to the newly constructed Melbourne public library, he continues, "the tide of books has now set in; before another year has passed, not only the majority of the best works of ancient genius and learning will be found in the city, but most of the standard work of European literature."[22] Horne's first major contribution to this library of European literature was his epic drama, *Prometheus the Fire-Bringer* (published 1864 in Edinburgh, 1866 in Melbourne).

If the mythological Orion represented the working-class man, Horne's Prometheus is none other than Horne himself, an isolated, self-pitying, and unappreciated bringer of enlightenment to the masses. The poem is patently outside the laureate genre insofar as its subject is the suffering individual. The preface to the 1854 *Orion* had described the "barren and isolated district" outside Melbourne in which Horne was then living: "the very Siberia of the Gold-fields—a sort of exile within an exile—where the rains of winter are a constant flood, while the heat of summer reminds one of Africa, without its fruits and flowers, and the prodigality of the insect-life is a constant torment beyond description."[23] Echoing a long tradition of writers in exile, Horne finds poetic composition at odds with his frontier experiences. Similar language accompanies *Prometheus the Fire-Bringer*, which was composed outside Melbourne, on Blue Mountain: "In this savage solitude—this Blue Mountain of dark forests, rain, and hurricanes— . . . without books—without any society—impressed, at times, with a sense of the precariousness of human life, amidst horse-accidents, the fall of massive trees, or the evil chances of dark nights in localities abounding in waterholes and deep mining shafts in unexpected places, always left quite unprotected,—this Lyrical Drama was composed, in the intervals of labours of a very different kind, and written for the most part during the night."[24]

In framing his drama as such, Horne likely had in mind both his own surroundings and the setting of Aeschylus's original Greek drama, on "a bare and desolate crag": a space of exile if ever there were one. Aeschylus's opening lines—"This is the world's limit that we have come to; this is the Scythian country, an untrodden desolation"[25]—resonate through Horne's introduction. One might think as well of Shelley's *Prometheus Unbound* (1820), which Horne had admired for decades: "torture and solitude, / Scorn and despair,—these are mine empire."[26] As Horne's biographer has suggested, the unhappy poet seems to have recognized his own experiences in the suffering Greek hero.[27] The volume's introductory note indicates that "Prometheus should . . . be regarded as the friend and instructor of humanity," and we can easily imagine Horne stepping imaginatively into Promethean shoes, becoming the friend and instructor of a generally uneducated, though literate, emigrant population.[28] He had written in 1859 that the young men of Australia "have no relish for learning, or philosophy, or science, no idea of the distinction between verse-spinning and poetry, painting and daubing, the music of Mendelssohn and the brass-band in a boozing bar, no taste for reading anything but trash, or seeing anything on the stage but burlesque . . . and no ruling impulse with respect to literature, the fine arts, manners, the respect and delicacy due to ladies, and personal habits in regard to the bath, and some self-command in drinking and smoking, no ruling impulse, let me say, but one, and that one is desecration."[29]

Into this unlikely milieu stepped Horne himself. He set his drama, unlike Aeschylus and Shelley, *before* Prometheus's great act of rebellion, his giving of fire to humankind. The poem's choruses articulate various forms of human suffering, including hunger and lack of proper clothing and shelter: "our blood/Ran cold about our bones,/Like winter-rills through stones." It remains for Prometheus to teach the chorus members to fend for themselves, to fight for what they need: "Only a slavish mind can be enslaved . . . //For tyrants thrive best on man's dreamy fears,/Thus liberty is lost" (21). Read as an allegory for the Australian colony, Horne sees himself bringing light to exiled colonialists and ultimately transplanting the origins of Western civilization to the southern hemisphere.

Reviewers in both Britain and Australia responded favorably to Horne's poem. Though the *Westminster* worried that "Mr. Horne is too classical to become popular," the reviewer yet noted that "a few students . . . are sure to welcome his drama, and the poet must find his reward in the fitness of his audience."[30] The *Atlas* suggested that "Australia ought to be proud of such men as Mr. R. H. Horne. They are the literary progenitors of future generations."[31] More enthusiastic still, Australia's *Bell's Life in Victoria* anticipated that Blue Mountain would "become the Parnassus of Australia," and the *Spectator* celebrated the poem as "amply vindicat[ing] Mr. Horne's claim to the high position as a poet which the majority of critics have been disposed to accord him."[32] Each journal imagined Horne as the central poet of a projected, future colonial literary scene. He appeared to his reviewers in much the same light as Prometheus at the close of Horne's poem:

> Yet had he left the seeds of a great mind,
>   To germinate through ages slow,
>   And flourish in futurity,—
> Realized visions of the martyr'd dreamer!
>   For all things now,
>   To us poor mortals, rich in hope,
>   Whom also faith and love inspire,
> Are placed within our work's expanding scope,
>   By the pure gift of Fire! (55)

Like the unappreciated visionary of *Orion*, and like Horne himself, Prometheus is a "martyr'd dreamer," isolated and struggling to subsist.

Martyr or not, Horne persisted in his effort to be a laureate-like poet for the colony. What we see distinctly is a shift in Horne's style, from the obscure and recondite work of his earlier poems to a form of public poetry more in keeping with the laureate function. Horne seems gradually to have realized that a classically styled poem would be doomed to a severely limited colonial function. He ventured the first of his less erudite efforts with an 1863 account of Robert Burke and William Wills's attempt to traverse the Australian continent from Melbourne to the Gulf of Carpentaria. The men had died in 1861, and in January 1863 they were given a state funeral in Melbourne. Horne's poem, "Australian Explorers," was published a month later in the *Sydney Morning Herald*, a notable shift in both style and content from his earlier poetry.[33] Horne clarifies his break in style with a footnote: "Nothing of what is understood as imaginative poetry is offered in the above story, which is simply an attempt to *condense the whole narrative*, divested of all its prose details and technicalities, and to give a few touches of local scenery."[34]

Most of the 301-line "Australian Explorers" remains true to the footnote's promise, following the erstwhile Burke and Wills across the Australian desert with clear, straightforward language:

> Month treads on month; dangers and pangs are borne,
> Of scanty water—oft with none at all—
> Tenfold more terrible than hunger's fangs.

Toward the end, however, Horne breaks from narrative to return to his familiar theme, finding Burke and Wills martyrs to the cause of Australian exploration:

> THE WORLD PROGRESSES BY ITS MARTYR'D MEN:
> Let none deplore the means whereby it moves
> To higher knowledge and to larger acts.

That the poem was published in Sydney and not Melbourne raises questions about its role in Horne's emerging laureate status. Blainey makes no reference to the poem in her Horne biography, but she identifies the early 1860s as a period of extreme financial hardship for the poet.[35] "Australian Explorers" may have been an effort simply to raise money, but it suggests as well the role Horne imagined he might play as a colonial laureate.

His first real opportunity for a laureate poem came in 1866, when Melbourne hosted an intercolonial exhibition. The event was held under an enormous carapace that recalled London's Great Exhibition, showcasing the agriculture and industry of Victoria, New South Wales, South Australia, Queensland, West Australia, Tasmania, and New Zealand (figure 10). Horne contributed a poem for the exhibition's opening ceremonies, *The South-Sea Sisters, A Lyric Masque*, performed with incidental music composed by Charles Edward Horsley. The poem tells in brief the history of Australia, from its origins as a "primeval wilderness" to its glories as the seat of the British empire: "empire's central tower."[36] In recounting the growth of Australia into a mercantile center of empire, Horne fulfills the role of laureate precisely. Unlike Henry Kendall's sensitive meditations on Australia's Indigenous peoples, Horne describes pre-European Australia as a "hopeless wilderness" characterized by "unspeakable sadness" (3). The opening molto adagio music shifts to andante pastorale with the arrival of "civilized man," who come "to claim—redeem—and use the land" (4). The final chorus of *The South-Sea Sisters* apostrophizes the various Australasian colonies as central to the empire's economic growth,

>   circling east, west, north!
> Unite in Federal bonds for one fixt power,
>   So shall ye find no sudden evil hour
> Darken your future—check your prosperous growth. (12)

When we consider that Horne's non-"laureate" Australian poetry bemoans his exile from civilization, his loneliness and despair, the celebratory ode on the International Exhibition strikes one as disingenuous. Taking on the mantle of a colonial laureate meant shelving his disdain for colonial life and performing instead both enthusiastic optimism and ideological kowtowing. More of the same soon followed.

Shortly after the exhibition, Horne changed his middle name from *Henry* to *Hengist*, perhaps the most obvious sign that he wanted a new role for himself in the colony. In taking the name of the fifth-century Saxon invader, considered one of the founders of England, Horne positioned himself—imaginatively, at least—as part of a long colonizing lineage. His most explicit laureate poem came out the following year, with the arrival of Prince Alfred, the Duke of Edinburgh, in Melbourne. Notably archaic and explicitly conservative in its yoking of Melbourne to the British monarchy, Horne's address is emblematic of what many subsequent readers have found most distasteful in colonial poetry:

Figure 10. Melbourne Intercolonial Exhibition. *Illustrated London News* (2 March 1867), 216. Princeton University Library.

> Our hearts' belov'd—our ever heart-true Queen—
> We recognise in thee
> The seaboard branch of that dear island Tree,
> Sacred to Science—Art—and Liberty—
> Queen and Queen Consort! Chronicled must be
> Thy Royal Mother's Throne—
> Like a pure star that shines alone—
> The most beneficent reign
> In Britain's history.[37]

Horne's debut was for the most part a failure. The *Argus* was harsh in its review, pointing to the "ruggedness and abruptness of the language."[38] Moreover, the duke himself managed to avoid the performance altogether: according to the *Age*, "his Royal Highness never 'showed up,' to use the vulgar phrase, from first to last."[39] Horne's efforts as a genuine colonial laureate, complete with an imperial middle name, could not have been satisfying.

What was wanting, both here and elsewhere in Horne's work, was an innovative principle that might have genuinely inspired colonial readers and auditors: something to give settlers new perspective on their lives in the colony. The fate of the "Odaic Cantata" points not only to Horne's failure in the colony but also to the fragility of arguments about colonial cultural replication. What was being rejected—or, at best, treated with indifference—in Melbourne was the replication of a conservative, monarchist ideology in a space where such values had increasingly little hold. Indeed, the decades to follow witnessed the move toward Australia's eventual 1901 federation, accompanied by an increasing call for a distinctly "Australian" form of poetry (see chapter 6).

A year and a half after Prince Alfred's Melbourne visit, Horne left Australia in mild defeat, returning to England in 1869 aboard the *Lady Jocelyn*. A fellow passenger, writing in a newspaper published aboard the ship, tellingly identified him first as "the friend and associate of many of the master minds in the literature of the present age—of Leigh Hunt, Thackeray, Wordsworth, Carlyle, Dickens, Browning, and Tennyson," and only then, and with the whiff of faint praise, as "author of several works bearing the impress of originality and great literary ability."[40] This assessment might have been different had Horne recognized what his Melbourne readers most desired. In writing about the concert staged to honor the prince, the *Age* indicated that the audience that evening demanded an encore performance of Horne's "Corroboree Chorus" from the earlier *South Sea Sisters*, a song based roughly on Indigenous Australian musical traditions.[41] Their enthusiasm for the local, or that which passed as local, considerably outweighed their investment in the conventional, the traditional values transported from Britain and manifested in the ode to the duke. In a public speech during his visit in the colony, Prince Alfred insisted that Melbourne "[clung] with affection to England and English institutions."[42] While no doubt true with respect other institutions (the law, religion, the education system), midcentury Australia desired innovation in its poetry, not the staid replicas of British culture on display in most of Horne's colonial poetry.

Genteel Laureate: Susanna Moodie and the Rebellion of 1837

Susanna Moodie (1803–85), born Susanna Strickland in Suffolk, England, emerged as a laureate-like figure for Canada in the late-1830s. As with Horne, her frame for viewing the world was generally conservative, inspired in part by her firmly middle-class status. Her first engagement with Britain's colonial affairs came while she was still in London and working for the Anti-Slavery Society there. The society's secretary at the time was Thomas Pringle, who had returned from Cape Town following his frustrating experiences with the colonial government. Strickland (not yet Moodie) worked with Pringle to transcribe and publish the memoir of Mary Prince, *The History of Mary Prince, A West Indian Slave* (1831). In 1830 she met her future husband, John Moodie, at Pringle's home; John Moodie had spent ten years in South Africa, 1819–29, and had known Pringle while there. Strickland and Moodie married in 1831, and they set sail for Canada as emigrants in 1832.[43]

The move was a hard one for the newlywed couple. Like Horne, Moodie maintained a profound distaste for colonial life, inspired in large part by the change in social status attendant on emigration. Educated and genteel, Horne and Moodie each turned increasingly conservative with distance from England. Horne complained in *Household Words* that "luxury ... has no place here [in Melbourne]; even comfort ... is impossible." Worse still, from Horne's perspective, Melbourne in the 1850s lacked the clear distinctions among social classes that shaped London culture: "There is a mixture of the highly educated with the totally uneducated, the refined with the semi-brutal (many a convict with his bull-dog being among us), all dressed roughly, and faring precisely alike."[44] In her 1852 memoir *Roughing It in the Bush*, Moodie recounts similar horror at the scenes of working-class life she witnessed on her 1832 arrival in Canada, in particular with respect to Irish and Scottish emigrants. Even the "chiefly honest Scotch labourers" on board Moodie's own ship turned for the worse on arriving in port: "No sooner [had they] set foot upon [Canadian soil] than they became infected by the same spirit of insubordination and misrule, and were just as insolent and noisy as the rest."[45]

Rule and order in British North America were of paramount concern for Moodie from the beginning. Even before departing England, her poetry was enthusiastically loyalist. Her 1830 volume *Patriotic Songs*, edited with her sister, Agnes Strickland, crosses earnest love for Britain with rhapsodic avowals of liberty and freedom.[46] No wonder the raucous scenes of settler Canada rattled Moodie: "The vicious, uneducated barbarians," she writes of Irish emigrants bathing outdoors, "each shouting and yelling in his or her uncouth dialect, and all accompanying their vociferations with violent and extraordinary gestures, quite incomprehensible to the uninitiated" (20).

The Moodies eventually settled in the Douro township of Upper Canada, roughly ninety miles northeast of Toronto. According to historian Robert Bothwell, Upper Canada in the early 1830s largely mirrored the "privilege and inequality" of Great Britain, with an elite political hierarchy meant to "preserve British rule and repel republicanism."[47] When in 1837 the colony erupted in revolutionary violence directed explicitly against that political hierarchy, both John and Susanna Moodie were drawn into the fray. The 1837 rebellion was orchestrated by the Scottish-born William Lyon Mackenzie, a printer and politician infuriated by Upper Canada's top-down governance. In his incendiary "Proclamation" to the inhabitants of Upper Canada, clearly modeled on the American Declaration of Independence, Mackenzie railed against being ruled "not according to laws of our choice, but by the capricious dictates of... arbitrary power.... We are wearied of these oppressions, and resolved to throw off the yoke. Rise, Canadians, rise as one man, and the glorious object of our wishes is accomplished."[48] Mackenzie's proclamation anticipated by thirty years the 1867 Canadian Confederation. From the vantage point of 1883, John Seeley understood the "Canadian Rebellion" as "a war of nationality in the British Empire, though it wore the disguise of a war of liberty."[49] Mackenzie's blustery rhetoric and violent tactics were unsuited for the general Canadian public. The Moodies, though isolated "in the depths of... old primeval forests," and therefore at a distance from the rebellion, never questioned which side they would support. John Moodie left to join the British loyalist forces in Toronto, and Susanna set to writing fervently patriotic poetry (*Roughing It in the Bush*, 287).

If the laureate's directive is to teach settlers to feel at home, then Moodie's strategic response is loyalty. "Canadians! Will You Join the Band. A Loyal Song" appeared in the first issue of the *Palladium of British America*, on 20 December 1837; John Moodie had brought the poem with him to Toronto, and his friend Charles Fothergill published it soon after in his journal.[50] Moodie's status as a laureate poet for British North America originates in the months following the outbreak of violence, limited and temporary as Mackenzie's rebellion eventually turned out to be. Mackenzie's challenge to British authority offered Moodie inspiration beyond the atmospheric materials to which she had more recently turned ("The Sleigh-Bells," for example, published in *The Albion, or British, Colonial, and Foreign Weekly Gazette*: "'Tis merry to hear, at evening time, / By the blazing hearth the sleigh-bells chime").[51] Her poems on the uprising, fiercely loyal and aggressive in their tone, were printed and reprinted throughout the colony, and they contributed to a moment historians now see as having consolidated British colonial power in both Upper and Lower Canada.[52]

Moodie's rhetorical moves throughout her patriotic poetry suggest a consistent strategy for swaying disgruntled colonialists back to the loyalist cause. "Canadians! Will You Join the Band" tempts readers with its title to respond in the affirmative. The band to which Moodie refers, however, is that of Mackenzie's rebels, and the poem teaches its readers to resist such a move:

> Canadians! will you join the band—
>   The factious band—who dare oppose
> The regal power of that bless'd land
>   From whence your boasted freedom flows?[53]

Moodie twists her reader's sentiments, manipulating their identification first as "Canadians" and then as British subjects. Canadians, according to Moodie, are children of a parental Britain—"The British sires who gave you birth"—and they owe allegiance and duty to Britain as a child would a parent. To do otherwise would be to "uplift[] the steel / To plunge it in a parent's heart." Moodie casts Mackenzie as a "despot" and a "tyrant," turning Mackenzie's own rhetoric against him (Mackenzie had called upon Upper Canadians to overcome the "tyrants" of "England's Aristocracy").[54] She concludes with a call to loyalty: "'God and Victoria!' be your cry, / And crush the traitors to the dust." The poem, according to Michael A. Peterman, was reprinted in seven other Canadian newspapers, reflecting its effectiveness as a call to arms.[55]

Mackenzie wasn't nearly as radical as the British thought. Carl Ballstadt notes that "the main tenets of the Proclamation were in accord with, now, well-recognized democratic principles: equal rights to all, civil and religious liberty, an administration responsible to the people through elections, vote by ballot, freedom of trade, access to education for every citizen."[56] Nonetheless, once Mackenzie framed his dissatisfaction in the language of rebellion, eventually marching on Toronto (in December 1837), the colonial government had little choice but to respond with force. The revolutionaries were overcome on 13 January 1838, and Mackenzie fled for refuge across the American border.[57]

The rebellion was dispatched with so quickly, some of Moodie's patriotic verses saw publication only after the threat had passed. In January 1838, the *Palladium* published Moodie's "On Reading the Proclamation Delivered by William Lyon Mackenzie, on Navy Island." The poem bristles with "honest indignation"—Moodie's words—at what she saw as Mackenzie's presumptuous call for liberty and freedom:

> 'Tis a strange mockery to hear them fall
> From felon's lips—to hear a wretch proclaim,
> (A self-elected demagogue), that he
> Can give to his misguided lawless band,
> The best,—the noblest,—highest gift of heaven![58]

Mackenzie, who could only be considered a felon in light of his rebellion, had in fact been elected multiple times to Upper Canada's legislative assembly, and in 1834 the people voted him mayor of Toronto.[59] Though "self-elected" to mount his rebellion, Mackenzie had many times won political office. More than that, his antimonarchical, pro-reform aspirations resonated among many Canadian settlers. Mackenzie was for these reasons a genuine threat to the colonial government, which explains why "On Reading the Proclamation" rhetorically frames the rebellion as equally criminal and absurd. Moodie calls on her readers to identify as both "Britons" and "Canadians" simultaneously, and to see resistance to Mackenzie as the "path of honour, rectitude, and peace."

Patriotic she may have been, but Moodie was never a true advocate for Canadian settlement; her work, both in poetry and prose, shows consistent ambivalence with respect to life in the colony.[60] She famously concludes her memoir with a double gesture, first reminding genteel readers of the challenges faced in the bush ("If these sketches should prove the means of deterring one family from . . . going to reside in the backwoods of Canada, I shall . . . feel that I have not toiled and suffered in the wilderness in vain"), and then celebrating in poetry, with a patriotic air, the beauty of the Canadian landscape:

> The Maple-Tree.
> *A Canadian Song.*
>
> Hail to the pride of the forest—hail
>   To the maple, tall and green;
> It yields a treasure which ne'er shall fail
>   While leaves on its boughs are seen.
> . . . .
>   May the nation's peace
>   With its growth increase,

And its worth be widely spread;
    For it lifts not in vain
    To the sun and rain
Its tall, majestic head.
    May it grace our soil,
    And reward our toil,
Till the nation's heart is dead. (331–32)

The disjunction between Moodie's prose and poetry, jarring as it appears on the page, makes sense generically. If realism was the domain of Moodie's prose memoir, *Roughing It in the Bush*, then poetry opened up for her more fanciful possibilities. The poems on Mackenzie's rebellion rhetorically allowed Moodie an emotional range, meant to inspire loyalist sentiment, that was largely absent from her prose writings. By invoking a community of readers aligned by political sentiment, Moodie's poems from 1837–38 fulfill a laureate function understood to be conservative and charged with the preservation of established culture.

Moodie's later poems on Canada, such as "The Maple-Tree," work in differently imaginative ways to facilitate a shared sense of belonging in the colonial landscape. These are poems looking to a future horizon, anticipating a better future for Canadian settler communities. In this latter register, Moodie moves beyond the limited domain of Horne's patriotic verse, and toward the work of more explicitly imaginative laureate writers like Fidelia Hill and Charles Sangster, the poets to whom we now turn.

Fidelia Hill, Imagining Adelaide

The South Australian city of Adelaide was mostly an encampment when Fidelia Hill arrived there in late 1836 (figure 11). Born in Yorkshire around 1790, Hill had spent five years in Jamaica with her husband, Robert Keate Hill, a captain in the East India Company.[61] Promised a better income in the colony that was to become Adelaide, the couple returned to England from Jamaica and then set out for Australia, Robert first, in May of 1836, and then Fidelia, in July. Four years later, with the publication of her 1840 volume *Poems*, Hill became the first woman to publish a volume of poetry in Australia.

Hill first set eyes on Adelaide in December 1836, at the beginning of the Australian summer. As the months passed, Hill's experience of the colony may have resembled that of the quasi-autobiographical heroine of Catherine

Figure 11. *View of the Proposed Site of Adelaide, about 1837.* Drawn by William Light and engraved by Robert Havell. State Library of South Australia, Adelaide.

Helen Spence's 1854 novel, *Clara Morison*. Clara notes on her arrival in Adelaide that "the grass was scanty, and so burnt up, that one wondered if it ever could have been green; there was not a flower to be seen; the sun was scorchingly hot; the wind, direct from the north, blew as if out of a furnace."[62] Official accounts of the new colony emphasized not the extreme heat of summer but the natural beauty of the region and its potential as a seat of power.

Also overlooked by historical account was the rudimentary state of Adelaide's buildings and infrastructure. In an 1837 *Athenaeum* report by the Royal Geographical Society, John Jeffcott imagined Port Adelaide "the future harbour of the *empire* of South Australia." Adelaide itself "is beautiful, on a rising ground commanding a fine view over a country much like an English park."[63] Jeffcott admired the beauty of Adelaide's landscape—and not its architecture—because the town had yet to be built. Seven years later, in 1844, a visitor still found the town "in a very primitive condition." Ambitious city planners had laid an outline, but Adelaide had yet to grow to inhabit it. "Many of the roads are not made, in some places they are in a deplorable condition. Within the bounds of the city are many vacant places."⁶⁴ Even after another decade, in the early 1850s, Spence's Clara notices that Adelaide's streets "were most irregularly built upon; houses of brick, wood, earth, and stone, seemed to be thrown together without any plan whatever, and looked too incongruous even to be picturesque."⁶⁵

"Adelaide," one of the first poems Hill composed in Australia, imagines the young colony in a very different state:

> I entered the wide spreading streets—methought
>   Of a vast city; all was bustle there:
> Crowds hurried on with eager looks befraught,
>   And hum of many voices filled the air.
> Then my eye rested upon buildings rare,
>   Circus and crescent to perfection brought,
> On splendid stores, where all things rich and rare
>   Exposed for sale, by young and old were bought,
> While many a rising spire, and spacious dome
>   Reminded me of London and of home!⁶⁶

The epigraph preceding this first stanza—"I dreamed a dream last night," from *Romeo and Juliet*—signals the fantastical nature of what follows, as does the dangling "methought" of the opening line. Read in isolation, "I entered the wide spreading streets—methought" suggests doubt and misgivings: just enough hesitation to warn the reader something may be amiss. Some of that doubt should accompany the reader as she finishes the phrase across the enjambment, "methought / Of a vast city"; this bustling, vibrant city does not yet exist for the dreamer of Hill's poem. Colonel William Light, responsible for envisioning Adelaide's layout, settled on the colony's specific location on 31 December 1836, a few days after Hill arrived at the encampment there.⁶⁷ Not only did the bustling streets not exist then, but their future location and layout had only just been determined.

Nonetheless, Hill dreams of Adelaide as a London-like metropolis, bustling with mercantile energy. The colony had been envisioned in such terms well before its founding. South Australia was an ambitious experiment, hatched by radical English thinkers in the heated atmosphere of the 1830s reform bills. The original framework for the colony was inspired by Edward Gibbon Wakefield's *Letter from Sydney* (1829), justifiably one of the "Ten Books That Shaped the British Empire" in Antoinette Burton and Isabel Hofmeyr's volume. Wakefield understood labor supply as key to developing colonial spaces: "in new countries," he argued, "capitalists often cannot obtain labourers," even when those capitalists were willing to pay out high salaries.[68] The challenge, as Wakefield saw it, was to build a free market economy without recourse to slavery or transportation. The solution, he believed, was to use funds from the sale of colonial land to pay for "the conveyance of British Labourers to the colony free of cost."[69] British investors could then depend on a ready source of labor, allowing for the colonial replication of both Britain's class structure and its economy. One significant result of Wakefield's plan, as Catherine Hall argues, was that in "breaking the link between Australia and convicts," he "[made] it a respectable place for the middle classes."[70] The London *Eclectic Review* in 1835 thus summarized the proposed South Australian colony as a place where "both the capitalist and the labourer [will] derive the greatest possible return from the employment of their industry and wealth."[71]

Hill's poem unfolds with new meaning when read with Wakefield in mind. The bustling streets of Adelaide's free market economy, "where all things rich and rare / Exposed for sale, by young and old were bought," were essential to the way the colony had been sold first to the British Parliament, which approved the South Australian Colonization Act in 1834, then to financial backers, and finally to the settlers arriving on its undeveloped shores.[72] Wakefield's genius—insidious to some, brilliant to others—was to orchestrate a new economic model, capitalist in nature, for emerging British colonies. Marx in fact dedicated a whole chapter of *Capital* (1867) to explaining Wakefield's strategy, showing how the 1834 Colonization Act established capitalism as foundational to colonial expansion. Specifically, Marx writes, poorer colonists who were brought over to Adelaide with money from the sale of land would then labor until they had earned "enough money to buy land" for themselves, at which point they could "turn [themselves] into . . . independent farmer[s]." By purchasing land, each new independent farmer would "provide a fund for bringing fresh labour to the colony," thereby perpetuating the capitalist cycle.[73]

Hill's dream-like vision for Adelaide, then, was exactly that set out by Wakefield and the British parliament. In the final stanza of the poem, Hill speculates on the city's future "grandeur" and "wealth," promising that the "settlers' toil" will be well repaid. The poem concludes with a rallying cheer to "commerce, health, and plenty," distinctly replicating for colonial readers the logic of South Australia's colonization. The poem also establishes an imaginary cityscape to which colonialists might attach their hopes and aspirations, a poetic version of what Paul Carter describes with respect to the art of mapping. Just as early colonial place names, in Carter's argument, brought an imaginative shape to the Australian landscape, poems such as Hill's imagined future scenes of a commercially thriving and architecturally inviting Adelaide.[74]

Such was not to be the case, however—at least, not during Hill's brief time in the colony. A second poem on Adelaide composed some three years later reveals significant shifts in Hill's thoughts about the young city. Titled "Recollections," the poem opens with a gesture to Wordsworth's "Tintern Abbey," pointing to a gap of time that inspired forms of self-reflection and a significant change of heart:

> Yes, South Australia! three years have elapsed
> Of dreary banishment, since I became
> In thee a sojourner; nor can I choose
> But sometimes think on thee; and tho' thou art
> A fertile source of unavailing woe,
> Thou dost awaken deepest interest still. (FH 64)

In Wordsworth's 1798 poem, the distance of five years allows the poet to think back on an earlier version of himself and to consider how he has matured: become less an innocent boy, more an adult aware of his place within the larger human community. Hill, too, has matured in her three years. No more the naïve optimist anticipating a new version of commercial London in the antipodes, Hill yet wants to imagine Adelaide a potential home for herself: "Thou dost awaken deepest interest still." Most surprising about "Recollections" may be that the poem as a whole remains optimistic, even following the opening gestures to "dreary banishment" and "unavailing woe." What has changed is not Hill's optimism, but her priorities; in place of a free market economy, Hill has come to privilege natural beauty and the domestic affections.

"Recollections" exchanges the commercial marketplace of "Adelaide" for the settlement's surrounding landscape: the mountains on which Hill gazes "with raptur'd sense" and which "mock'd the painter's art" because too lovely to capture on canvas (64). Hill describes the land that was to become Adelaide as "a wide waste, / But beauteous in its wildness" (65). She echoes John Jeffcott's report for the Royal Geographical Society in noting the "Park-like scenery" that "Burst on the astonish'd sight":

> For it did seem
> As tho' the hand of art, had nature aided,
> Where the broad level walks—and verdant lawns,
> And vistas graced that splendid wilderness! (FH 65)

The final verse paragraph of "Recollections" offers the most significant revision of "Adelaide" in its insistence that a loving home, no matter how simple, far surpasses any alternative:

> One tent was pitch'd upon the sloping bank
> Of the stream Torrens, in whose lucid wave
> Dipp'd flow'ring shrubs—the sweet mimosa there
> Wav'd its rich blossoms to the perfum'd breeze,
> High o'er our heads—amid the stately boughs.
> Of the tall gum tree—birds of brightest hues
> O'er built their nests, or tun'd 'their wood-notes wild,'
> Reposing on the rushes, fresh and cool,
> Which a lov'd hand had for my comfort strew'd:—
> This, this methought shall be my happy home!
> Here may I dwell, and by experience prove,
> That tents with love, yield more substantial bliss
> Than Palaces without it, can bestow. (FH 66)

Falling within the domain of a colonial laureate, "Recollections" works on multiple levels to establish a place in South Australia for Hill and her colonial readers. The verse paragraph above, laden with prepositions, points syntactically to the specific location of the encampment: upon, of, in, o'er, amid. Not the mere "fabric of a dream," as Hill described the future commercial Adelaide in her earlier poem, Hill locates the colony of "Recollections" in real time and space, among the actual settlers living there.

Hill seems to have been aware of her role as a laureate-like figure for the colony. In the opening pages of her volume, she presents herself in clear, bold terms as "the *first* [in Australia] who has ventured to lay claim to the title of Authoress."[75] Through her poetry, Hill teaches her fellow settlers how to "see" the colony before them. She also positions Adelaide in relation to Britain's literary heritage, first with the opening gesture to Wordsworth and then with "their wood-notes wild." Milton wrote in "L'Allegro" of Shakespeare's "warbl[ings]" as "native wood-notes wild," and Felicia Hemans borrowed the phrase to describe a pair of wandering lovers in her 1819 volume *Tales and Historic Scenes*:

> For he had roved a pilgrim there,
> And gazed on many a spot so fair
> It seem'd like some enchanted grove,
> Where only peace, and joy, and love,
> Those exiles of the world, might rove,
>   And breathe its heavenly air;
> And, all unmix'd with ruder tone,
> Their "wood-notes wild" be heard alone!
> Far from the frown of stern control,
> That vainly would subdue the soul,
> There shall their long-affianced hands
> Be join'd in consecrated bands.[76]

This second source seems more likely what Hill had in mind when composing "Recollections," allowing her to cast her arrival in South Australia as a romantic exile, a place where, as Hemans writes, a "home shall rise,/A shelter'd bower of paradise!" In effect a recollection of a recollection (Hill remembers Hemans remembering Milton, who was himself remembering the sounds of an earlier poet, Shakespeare), the South Australian poem formally suggests how poetry may work to replicate culture in uncharted, uncultured spaces. As the dreamscape of "Adelaide" recedes, and the specifics of "Recollections" come into focus, Hill offers her fellow settlers a framework for making sense of the new land in which they found themselves.

"Recollections" also shows the poet's shifting perspective: her move toward a more immediate point of view, privileging the domestic affections over the "splendid stores" of an imagined future city. In positioning Adelaide geographically (through both description and syntax) and culturally (in relation to English literary heritage), Hill's lyrics move well beyond the sentimental frameworks they seem to inhabit, suggesting a wider range of possibilities for laureate-like poetry in the colonies.

Charles Sangster, Romancing British North America

Elizabeth Barrett Browning's *Aurora Leigh* (1856) famously insists that poetry should involve itself in the rough and tumble of the present day:

> if there's room for poets in this world
> A little overgrown, (I think there is)
> Their sole work is to represent the age,

> Their age, not Charlemagne's,—this live, throbbing age,
> That brawls, cheats, maddens, calculates, aspires,
> And spends more passion, more heroic heat,
> Betwixt the mirrors of its drawing-rooms,
> Than Roland with his knights at Roncesvalles.[77]

Horne's struggles as a writer in Australia came about in part because he at first resisted engaging directly with the colonial world before him. Rather than taking as his materials the mining community around Blue Mountain or the emerging metropolis of Melbourne, he set his most ambitious Australian poem in the world of Greek mythology. In his explicitly laureate-like poems, such as the ode on the opening of the Intercolonial Exhibition, his writing turned didactic and largely unimaginative. This changed to a degree in the months leading up to his final departure from Australia, when Horne attempted a more significant work on the continent: "John Ferncliff: An Australian Narrative Poem." Though concentrated on the Australian continent, however, the unpublished and often illegible manuscript fails both stylistically and conceptually, capturing primarily Horne's belief that Australia was a place of gritty realism and little inspiration: "Here was reality, and no romance."[78] In believing reality and romance to be mutually exclusive, Horne saw the Australian colony as antithetical to the poetic impulse. The "live, throbbing age" of *Aurora Leigh* is nowhere to be found in Richard Hengist Horne's Australia.

Charles Sangster's *The St. Lawrence and the Saguenay* was published in the same year as *Aurora Leigh*, and the volume's title poem shares some of the aspirations of Barrett Browning's novel in verse: to capture the vitality of the present place and time. In the case of Sangster, that place was Upper Canada (now Ontario). Sangster (1822–93) was born in Kingston, Upper Canada (he was fifteen at the time of Mackenzie's 1837 rebellion), and in the middle decades of the nineteenth century he earned himself the title "poet-laureate of colonial Canada."[79] Edward Hartley Dewart, editor of the 1864 *Selections from Canadian Poets*, called Sangster one of "the pioneer bards of a past generation."[80] His work occupies a significant midpoint between that of earlier nineteenth-century colonial poets (Oliver Goldsmith, Susanna Moodie) and the later poems of Canadian Confederation (to be addressed in chapter 6). A "native" resident of Upper Canada, Sangster was proud of his land and comfortable with the colonial social structure; we find in his work neither McLachlan's nostalgia for a European home, Goldsmith's fear of the wooded Canadian landscape, nor Moodie's ambivalent relationship to colonial culture.

The St. Lawrence and the Saguenay relates a journey along the St. Lawrence river north from the Thousand Islands region of Sangster's birth, past Montreal and Quebec, and then west along the Saguenay to Trinity Rock, a trip taking the poet and his readers increasingly away from Canada's European settlements. Walt Whitman was to make this same trip in 1880, describing the land around the Saguenay as "a dash of the grimmest, wildest, savagest scenery on the planet, I guess."[81] In Spenserian stanzas that reminded his contemporaries of *Childe Harold's Pilgrimage*, Sangster imagines the Canadian landscape resonating—"pulsat[ing]"—with poetry and song:

> Hast thou not heard upon a summer's eve
> The musical pulsations of the air?
> The voices of the mountain pines, that weave
> Their low complainings with the atmosphere?
> Thus, throughout Nature, floating everywhere,
> Eternal symphonies, low, rich and deep,
> Pass from her Poet-lips. Her children hear
> And treasure up these lyrics, as they sweep
> With Zephyrus through the air, or visit them in sleep.[82]

The difference between this account of the Canadian forest and that of Goldsmith's *The Rising Village* is significant. Goldsmith found little positive in Nova Scotia's "deep solitudes" and "gloomy shades."[83] Sangster imagines instead a landscape notable as much for its beauty as for its musical sounds. "Mr. Sangster," wrote a reviewer for the *Athenaeum*, "who is a ready singer, rejoices in the magnitude and splendour of his own land."[84] Sangster also insists that Canada is a space both of and for poetry: a land where nature itself exudes symphonies and welcomes sympathetic poetic spirits.

Sangster succeeds as a laureate in part because he balances deep feeling with clear attention to the physical world around him; his poetry captures both sentiment and respect for the landscape. In addition to its celebration of the Canadian wilderness, *The St. Lawrence and the Saguenay* also dabbles in romance, and with it the language of the emotions. The addressee above—"Hast *thou* not heard?"—remains unnamed, but we know her to be female and the object of the speaker's love: "There is but one to whom my hopes are clinging," the poem opens, describing the poet's companion onboard their journey upriver (CS 44).

At various points in the poem, enthusiasm for the accompanying lover overlaps with and becomes indistinguishable from feeling for the Canadian landscape:

> A wild joy fills my overburdened brain.
> My ears drink music from each thunder peal.
> I glory in the lightnings and the rain.
> There is no joy like this! With thee to feel
> And share each impulse, makes my spirit kneel.
> Sing to me, love! my heart is pained with bliss!
> Thy voice alone can quicken and unseal
> The inner depths of feeling. Grant me this:
> Flood me with Song, and loose the founts of Happiness. (CS 49)

Both stylistically and thematically, Sangster channels a range of poetic impulses here, including the so-called Spasmodic movement of the early 1850s.[85] Though the Spasmodic poets were largely working class and distinctly outside the educated establishment, their brief popularity in both Britain and the United States had inspired more canonical poets, including Tennyson and Barrett Browning, to experiment with physiological and affective language.[86] Like the narrators of poems such as Alexander Smith's *A Life-Drama* (1853) and Sydney Dobell's *Balder* (1854), Sangster's speaker seems at times overwhelmed by feeling: "my overburdened brain," "pained with bliss." Like Smith and Dobell, Sangster turns to the physical body to articulate that experience.

Some of Sangster's flights of fancy resemble those of the Spasmodic phenomenon, but few would mistake *The St. Lawrence and the Saguenay* for a Spasmodic poem. The signal difference is Sangster's balancing of Spasmodic-like internalized sentiment with deictic pointing to specific features of the external world: "See, we have left the Islands far behind," "That is St. Pierre,/Where the tall poplars . . . /Lift their sharp outlines" (CS 48, 58). Balancing between exterior and interior, fact and fancy, Sangster's poetic inspiration may well have been Edmund Spenser, who believed poetry was meant "to fashion a gentleman or noble person" through the measuring of historical instruction against imaginative pleasure.[87] For this reason Sangster's own Spenserian stanzas more likely point back to *The Faerie Queene* rather than *Childe Harold's Pilgrimage*. Central to both Spenser's poetics and Sangster's poem is the idea that fact and fancy are not just compatible but mutually constitutive. Sangster refuses to be either a didactic poet of the Canadian frontier or an enthusiast of the human spirit: his poetry aims to capture both at once. Sangster moves energetically between interior and exterior as a strategy for bringing the glow of enthusiasm to the world through which he passes.

His status as "poet laureate" for Canada no doubt originates in this enthusiasm both for the landscape and for the human experience of Canada's vast spaces. The *Athenaeum* criticized Sangster for the ambiguity in some of his accounts: "*Definiteness* in descriptions of natural objects is the test of the true poet and master of his art,—and in a poem which professes to be a descriptive Panorama, a failure in the description cannot be compensated by any other quality."[88] But the *National Magazine* valued his writing for its movement between the real and the ideal, describing his occasional "incomprehensible sublimities" as a strength of the overall work: "He seeks not only to depict nature, but to soar above her, and not seldom rises into incomprehensible sublimities. But frequently, also, he is content to be regarded as nature's companion, and plays with her in her secluded places."[89] How different was Sangster's approach to the Canadian landscape than, say, Kendall's discomfort with the Australian bush or Horne's disgust with the "savage solitude" of Blue Mountain. In Sangster's account, Upper Canada stretches before the poet, and he glides through the landscape without effort, capturing his impressions of the world and positioning those impressions in relation to his own lived experiences. Sangster instructs his settler readers how to feel at home in the Canadian landscape.

Nothing like Sangster's enthusiasm finds its way into Susanna Moodie's poetry, or, in the Australian context, that of Richard Hengist Horne. Moodie and Horne rely too firmly on the didactic, and their conservative impulse keeps their work too moored in the framework of British history and literary tradition. For Horne and Moodie, the laureate function serves primarily to replicate culture from Britain to the colonies. Sangster takes up the opposite ideological view, imaginatively showcasing for readers the distinct features and experiences of North America. Like Fidelia Hill's poetry in Australia, Sangster's work challenges historical models of absolute cultural replication. Both Hill and Sangster understood poetry as more than the art of cloning British culture in the colonies: in their hands, adaptation and evolution become equally significant terms for the relationship between Anglo settler societies and their nineteenth-century settlements.

In later decades of the nineteenth century, adaptation and evolution turned increasingly toward nationalist frameworks for settler colonial culture. Canada Confederation was achieved in 1867, with Australia and New Zealand following, respectively, in 1901 and 1907. The final chapter of this study turns to the significant role poetry played in those moves from colony to nation.

CHAPTER 6

The Poetry of Greater Britain
Race and Nationhood at Century's End

> Greater Britain is not a mere empire, though we often call it so.
> Its union is of the more vital kind.
> —J. R. Seeley, *The Expansion of England* (1883)

Greater Britain, Imperial Federation, and the Anglo-Saxon World

In the later nineteenth-century, as forms of nationalism rose to prominence in Australia, New Zealand, and Canada, cultural coherence often took shape around ideas of race. The "shifting sands between cultural and racial accounts of 'Englishness,'" which John Plotz describes as characteristic of late-Victorian England, resulted in forms of instability throughout Britain's colonial spaces.[1] Poetry of the era reflected this instability, moving between pride in colonial identity and pride in an imagined Anglo-Saxon heritage that was thought to link all Britain's colonies.[2]

Late-Victorian colonialists in Australia, New Zealand, and Canada worried that nationalist pride would leave them alienated from Britain. The English historian John Robert Seeley (1834–95) did his best to mitigate these concerns in a series of lectures at Cambridge University, lectures eventually collected in his 1883 volume *The Expansion of England*. Urging his fellow Britons to understand Australia and Canada as part of the United Kingdom, held together by "community of race, community of religion, and community of interest," Seeley contributed to a broader and ongoing debate about "Greater Britain": an emerging catchphrase for the United Kingdom and its colonies.[3] The language of race and blood figures significantly in the rhetoric of Greater Britain, connecting the perceived triumph of Britain to a biological imperative toward expansion: "a population of English blood," "the English race."[4] Seeley and other theorists of Greater Britain imagined a global power unified by race and connected by the modern technologies of steamships and electric telegraph cables: for some, a white English core radiating out to its peripheral spaces; for others, a network of interconnected and equally significant parts.[5]

Sentiment ranged from those wanting the colonies to become independent nations to those endorsing an imperial federation. According to Robert Stout (1844–1930), a Scottish emigrant to New Zealand who served the colony as both premier and then chief justice, the years between 1870 and 1887 saw a shift of sentiment favoring "some form of union" between Britain and her colonies: "the hope is that separation will be prevented."[6] For Stout, the connections within Greater Britain would be upheld through both race—"the race feeling is strong"—and culture: "Is it unreasonable to expect that people speaking the same language, reading the same books, having the same creeds, and being reared from the same race, may learn to live in peace and mutually assist each other?"[7] One of the primary contributors to the debate, James Anthony Froude (1818–94), put forward the term *Oceana* in 1886 to describe the global amalgamation he imagined for Greater Britain: not an "empire," for "the English race do not like to be parts of an empire," but instead "a 'commonwealth' of Oceana held together by common blood, common interest, and a common pride in the great position which unity can secure."[8] Note that Froude's three commonalities—blood, interest, and pride—overlap almost completely with Seeley's, substituting just "pride" for "religion."

Ideas of Greater Britain and imperial federation found their way into and were to some extent shaped by British and colonial poetry, where the pomp of formal structure—rhythm, rhyme, meter—contributed to the patriotic, nation-building content. Meredith Martin has shown that the connection between poetic form and Anglo-Saxon identity had been firmly established in the early nineteenth century; by the turn of the twentieth century, Anglo-Saxon poetic forms had come to represent "stable English national culture."[9] That notion of stability was in turn projected out to the world at large and taken up in both colonial and imperial spaces to promote a global Anglo power.

Rudyard Kipling promoted the ideas of imperial federation in his poetry on the Second Boer War. After sailing from Britain to the Cape in April 1898, he pushed for a federated South Africa modeled on the confederation Canada had achieved in 1867.[10] Kipling saw the war as an opportunity for building camaraderie among British and colonial soldiers, camaraderie he anticipated would substantiate an imperial federation. Imagining men from Britain's colonies together in South Africa, he writes in "The Parting of the Columns": "Think o' the stories round the fire, the tales along the trek—/O' Calgary an' Wellin'ton, an' Sydney and Quebec."[11] The parade of colonial soldiers uniting to defend Britain's interests in South Africa warmed Kipling's heart. How "wonderful" it is, he writes in an 1899 letter, to witness "the spectacle of the three Free Nations"—Canada, Australia, and New Zealand—working together to "secure moderately decent Government for a sister people."[12] Even more, Kipling believed, those colonial soldiers sharing "stories round the fire" in South Africa would return to their homes in Canada, Australia, and New Zealand with a renewed commitment to Greater Britain and Imperial Federation.

Race is implicit Kipling's Boer War poems. In Benjamin George Ambler's *Ballads of Greater Britain and Songs of an Anglo-Saxon* (1900) it becomes explicit. The volume advocates for a worldwide Anglo community, a community understood to be white, using both rhythm and rhyme to emphasize global unity:

> Sons of the old world and heirs of the new,
>   Gather and listen—the earth hath her song.
> This is the saga she singeth to you:
>   Anglo-Saxons, arise and be strong,
> Be ye as brothers in arms and in art,
>   Clasping your kinsmen from over the sea;
> There is no war-cloud shall rend you apart,
>   If ye stand firm when the dark hour shall be.[13]

Ambler's volume links Anglo-Saxon identity to a global polity, a worldwide race of "Men and brothers" that will stand strong against the "savage horde."[14] Poetry from this angle explicitly rallies racialized communal sentiment to political ends, showcasing how verse, to borrow Martin's terms, was employed as "a disciplinary aspect of the imperial project."[15]

The language of race worked to unify a disparate Greater Britain, but it also competed in colonial spaces with the language of nation. Colonialists in Canada, Australia, and New Zealand were not always as sure that they shared a "community of interest" with the United Kingdom, though many of them wished for such connections. Paeans to imperial federation and Greater Britain competed with rallying cries for Canadian, Australian, and (to a somewhat lesser degree) New Zealand independence. New Brunswick native Martin Butler, for example, in an 1898 volume, *Patriotic and Personal Poems*, imagined a future Canada that was "great, glorious, FREE . . . a colony no more."[16] To the degree that individual colonies articulated their identity in racial terms, they were more likely to identify with their British roots. Advocates for colonial federation and various forms of new nationalisms, primarily in Canada and Australia, worked to articulate independence from Britain while still identifying racially as Anglo-Saxon. The tensions between nationalism and racial identification help explain why the 1901 Australian parliament, in Australia's first year as a federated nation, passed legislation that formally inaugurated the White Australia policy, restricting new Australian immigration primarily to whites.[17] Australia's parliament was in effect asserting that its Anglo-Saxon identification would persist even after achieving independence from Britain.

In what follows, I examine Australian and Canadian nationalism within the broader discourses of race and imperial federation. Becoming independent nations meant overcoming the sense of colonial dislocation articulated by poets like Henry Kendall and learning how to feel at home in lands first occupied by others. This explicitly communal endeavor drew strength from the era's patriotic verses: works by the Bulletin School in Australia and the Confederation Poets in Canada. As we have seen throughout nineteenth-century colonial spaces, examined in each of the preceding chapters, feeling and genre worked together as poems circulated through communities of readers. The sentimental tradition that enabled early settlers to feel at home developed at century's end into a variety of nationalist and racist traditions, encouraging readers to imagine themselves united as citizens of newly emerging nations.

We begin with a brief account of Anglo-Saxonism as a global Victorian phenomenon.

Anglo-Saxon Poetry

Race and national identity were nearly inseparable concepts in the nineteenth century, as the historian Nell Irvin Painter has shown. Common among Victorian theorists was the idea that the Anglo-Saxons, in Painter's words, were "respecters of freedom within their brotherhood and natural rulers of other races."[18] For example, Sharon Turner argued in *The History of the Anglo-Saxons* (1799) that Britain's "Saxon ancestors brought with them a superior domestic and moral character, and the rudiments of new political, juridical, and intellectual blessings."[19] Robert Knox went a step further in *The Races of Men: A Fragment* (1850): "Each race has its own ideas of liberty. There is but *one race* whose ideas on this point are sound; that race is the Saxon. He is the only real democrat on the earth, who combines obedience to the law with liberty."[20]

Anglo-Saxon origins were used to explain not just Britain's political successes but its culture as well. The "vague identification of culture with ancestry," writes John Higham in his classic study of American nativism, *Strangers in the Land* (1955), "served mainly to emphasize the antiquity, the uniqueness, and the permanence of a nationality."[21] We can see this extension of race to include culture, and specifically poetry, in Thomas Carlyle's *Chartism* (1840). Poetry, Carlyle understood, was an important component in the imagined reproduction of Anglo-Saxon culture. Writing in the voice of the faux German academic Herr Professor Sauerteig, Carlyle trumpets the achievements of the Anglo-Saxon peoples both at home and abroad: "Of a truth, whosoever had, with the bodily eye, seen Hengst and Horsa mooring on the mud-beach of Thanet, on that spring morning of the Year 449; and then, with the spiritual eye, looked forward to New York, Calcutta, Sidney [sic] Cove, across the ages and the oceans; and thought what Wellingtons, Washingtons, Shakespeares, Miltons, Watts, Arkwrights, William Pitts and David Crocketts had to issue from that business, and do their several taskworks so,—*he* would have said, those leather-boats of Hengst's had a kind of cargo in them!"[22] From the landing of Hengist and Horsa, the original Saxon invaders of England, Sauerteig traces lines of descent not only to British imperialism—the founding of colonies in North America, Asia, and Australia—but also to great military generals (Wellington, Washington), inventors (Arkwright), politicians, pioneers, and poets. That Saxon "cargo," carried from continental Europe to England in 449, now occupies the world over, from New York to Calcutta to Sydney Cove.

Carlyle's view was commonplace. Luke Owen Pike opens the first chapter of *The English and Their Origin* (1866) by asserting that "there are probably few educated Englishmen living who have not in their infancy been taught that the English nation is a nation of almost pure Teutonic blood, that its political constitution, its social customs, its internal prosperity, the success of its arms, and the number of its colonies have all followed necessarily upon the arrival, in three vessels, of certain German warriors under the command of Hengist and Horsa."[23] Like Carlyle, Pike conflates politics, culture, economics, military prowess, and colonial expansion under the umbrella of race; Britain's Saxon blood, we are led to believe, enabled its unprecedented success on the world stage. In 1849 the *Anglo-Saxon* proclaimed that the "whole Earth may be called the *Fatherland* of the Anglo-Saxon. He is a native of every clime—a messenger of heaven to every corner of this Planet."[24] Such optimism in the good Anglo-Saxons brought to the world at large was, according to Reginald Horsman, typical of the period.[25]

Anglo-Saxonism became an important idea not only for late-Victorian Britain and its colonies but for the United States as well. The rhetoric of Anglo-Saxon racial superiority that fueled the United States' territorial expansion under the banner of Manifest Destiny also inspired American poetic practice.[26] Sidney Lanier, one of the first professors of English at Johns Hopkins University, consistently regarded Great Britain as the origin of all that was great in American culture. Lanier's identification with British tradition firmly embraced the rhetoric of Manifest Destiny, specifically the fantasy whereby white Americans imagined their supposed Anglo-Saxon origins as proof of their being, in Horsman's words, "a chosen people with an impeccable ancestry."[27]

Writing from Baltimore, Maryland, in 1879, Lanier identified culturally as English. He suggests "the remarkable ease with which *our* English idioms run into the mould of the sonnet."[28] In a later essay on Anglo-Saxon poetry published posthumously in the *Atlantic Monthly*, he exhorts the "strong, bright, picture-making tongue *we* had in the beginning of the sixteenth century when the powerful old Anglo-Saxon had fairly conquered all the foreign elements into its own idiom."[29] Identifying here with that Anglo-Saxon tongue, a tongue that in the creation of its own distinct sounds and cadences had pushed out *the foreign*—and, later in the same paragraph, *the alien*—Lanier positioned both himself and his American readers as English linguistic subjects, the inheritors of an Anglo-Saxon cultural and literary heritage.[30]

Lanier's assumptions about poetry, race, and national identity help make sense of the rhetoric of Greater Britain, which proposed a global network of Anglo-Saxons, connected through race and shared political and aesthetic values. As the nineteenth century reached its close, colonialists loyal to Britain vied with those wishing for Canadian, Australian, and New Zealand political independence. "*The Past belongs to Europe,*" wrote the *Provincial*, a Halifax journal, in 1852, "but in Poetry, as in Art, Science, and all the great achievements of civilization, *the future belongs to [North] America.*"[31] Titled "The Poetry of Anglo-Saxon America," which would seem to link the Canadian provinces firmly with England, the essay nonetheless posits a future "national *literature*," which would "keep steadily in view the new and peculiar position" of the British North American colonies: "It was not by a servile imitation of the classic models . . . that Chaucer, Spen[s]er, and the other fathers of English song strung together their melodious and highly poetical verses."[32] This sort of double gesture, asserting a racial connection and a cultural distinction, captures the strain of racial and cultural thinking that divided colonialists at century's end.

The Bulletin School, Race, and Australian Federation

When Australia finally achieved federation on 1 January 1901, the celebrations in Sydney included the singing of "God Save the Queen" and "Rule Britannia."[33] Politically and financially, Australia would remain firmly tied to Britain until the period following the Second World War.[34] White Australia understood its connections to Britain additionally in terms of race; the Australian from this perspective was a version of the Anglo-Saxon, made stronger perhaps by the harsh realities of life in an often inhospitable climate.[35] "Racism," writes the labor historian Humphrey McQueen, "is the most important single component of Australian nationalism."[36] Racism at the turn of the twentieth century also linked Australia to Britain and the broader imperial federation. Alfred Deakin—the second Australian prime minister, an enthusiastic advocate for the White Australia policy and one of the leaders of the Federalist movement—called himself an "independent Australian Briton," showing the ease with which even those supporting Australian independence identified as both British and Australian.[37]

Douglas Sladen's 1888 anthology *Australian Ballads and Rhymes*, published on the centenary of British colonization, makes self-evident the paradox that racism simultaneously fueled both nationalism and attachment to Greater Britain. Sladen (1856–1947), an English-born writer who had lived in Melbourne and Sydney between 1880 and 1884, remained a lifelong advocate for Australian literary culture, and in particular the poems of Adam Lindsay Gordon. *Australian Ballads and Rhymes* was hailed by local Australian papers as the "first Australian Anthology."[38] Sladen dedicated the volume "to the English of Three Continents" (figure 12), marking his volume as part of the Greater Britain project. In an introductory poem he concludes:

> We are all English, born in one great union
> Of blood and language, history and song,
> All English, and to cherish our communion
> We will present a common front to wrong.[39]

Sladen emphasizes the Anglo-Saxon element in Australia and its poetry. "Separated by oceans from every considerable land," he writes, "and peopled

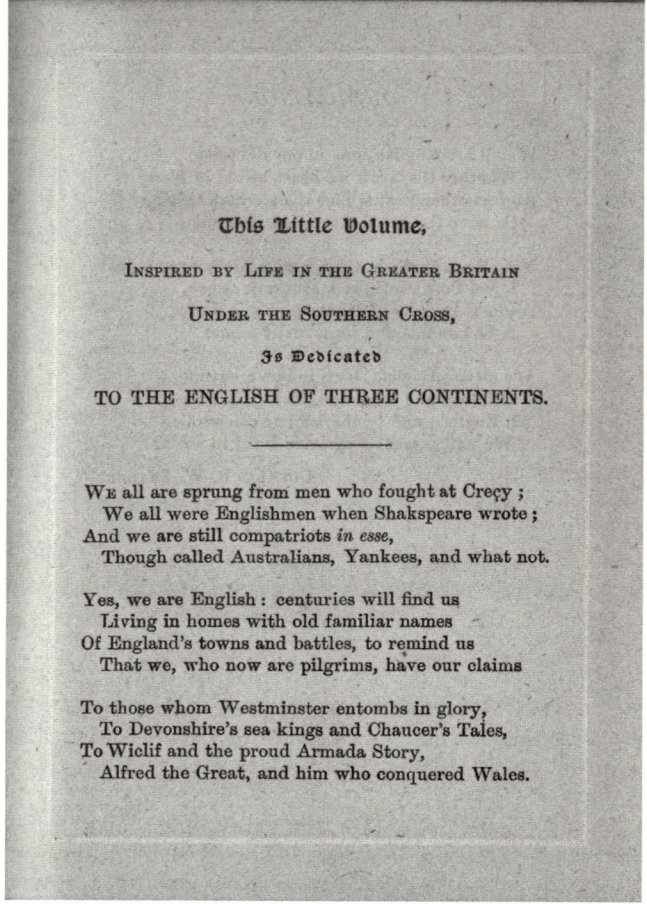

Figure 12. Dedication page to *Australian Ballads and Rhymes*, ed. Douglas Sladen (London: Walter Scott, 1888). Author's collection.

from the most adventurous of the colonising Anglo-Saxon stock," Australia demonstrates "a special love for all verse breathing the spirit of Anglo-Saxon manfulness" (ABR xiii, xviii). The emphasis here on white manliness is far from incidental, given the serious concern throughout the century that Australia's climate emasculated its white male immigrants.[40]

The suffering, wilting men of Henry Kendall's midcentury poetry (discussed in chapter 4) reflect this common anxiety about Australian manliness. Kendall's poems are absent from Sladen's volume (Sladen says he failed to receive permission to reprint them). But in an essay at the volume's end, Sladen explicitly identifies Kendall's style as distinct from the late-century Australian poetic mode he hopes to promote. Kendall, he writes,

> could paint loneliness admirably well. No one has drawn finer pictures of that aspect of Bush life which is peace or dreariness according as one pines for solitude or pines for society. He has written the most beautiful and the most terrible scenes we have of existence in the depths of the Bush—of the utter forsakenness of the explorer's fate.... But he had little sympathy with the roistering side of the bushman's nature. His own nature was too delicate, too poetic, too beautiful. This side of Bush life was reserved for men of rougher fibre, more robust and dashing in their genius. (ABR 279)

Kendall's melancholy does not align well with the boisterous, exuberant poems Sladen clearly wanted to celebrate. More to the point, Kendall's ambivalent relationship to the Australian landscape—his feeling of not quite belonging on the continent—was anathema to the late-century politics of both Greater Britain and Australian nationalism.

Sladen structured *Australian Ballads and Rhymes* to showcase what he took to be distinct features of Australian poetry. "This volume is essentially the work of people who have meditated in the open air, and not under the lamp," claims the introduction; "and if its contents often-times want the polish that comes only with much midnight oil, they are mostly a transcript from earth and sea and sky, and not from books" (ABR xiv). One of the volume's contributors, J. Steele Robertson, echoes and extends Sladen's claims in a review published in Melbourne's *Argus* entitled "The Australian Element in Australian Poetry":

> Here is a new land, vast in extent, separated from the older world by unfathomable seas, and containing within its borders every climate but that of the frozen north. Everyone has ample room for the full expression of physical and intellectual energies. Here we have no confinement; no cramping of the faculties in one narrow groove. Here are no effete feudal systems to grind the faces of men, but freedom and equality for all within the bounds of law and order. And this newness, this room, this freedom naturally affect the theme and method of the local poetry.[41]

The selections are meant to reflect openness and freedom both thematically and formally, often with the enthusiastically cannonading stanzas that Gordon had popularized and that came to be seen as quintessentially

Australian.⁴² The "freedom and equality" that Robertson perceives resonates with the language of Anglo-Saxonism we saw in Knox's *The Races of Men*, quoted above: "There is but *one race* whose ideas on this point are sound; that race is the Saxon. He is the only real democrat on the earth, who combines obedience to the law with liberty." Contrary to those who feared the white man would not survive the Antipodean climate, Sladen's anthology is at pains to show the freedom-loving, democratic Anglo-Saxon having found his natural habitat in the vast expanses of the Australian outback. He is "no effete" but is instead robustly "physical and intellectual." William Sharp's "The Stock Driver's Ride," reprinted in Sladen's anthology, captures this sentiment both formally and conceptually: "Thro' more ranges, thro' more gullies, down sun-scorched granite ways/We go crashing, slipping, thundering in our joyous morning race" (ABR 176).

In the decade following Sladen's anthology, two poets emerged as representative national voices: both born in Australia, both depicting the lives and experiences of working Australians with the galloping rhythms that Gordon had perfected, and both invested in the making of a white Australia. Henry Lawson (1867–1922) and Andrew Barton "Banjo" Paterson (1864–1941) published their early poems in Sydney's *Bulletin*, the journal credited as pushing nationalist sentiment from its founding in 1880 up through the early twentieth century. The *Bulletin* itself put forward Lawson and Paterson as representative Australian poets: "In these two writers," wrote A. G. Stephens in the February 1896 issue, "with all their imperfections, we see something like the beginnings of a national school of poetry. In them, for the first time, Australia has found audible voice and characteristic expression."⁴³ What that "voice" should have sounded like often appeared to be a mix of the progressive and the abhorrent. Christopher Lee notes that the *Bulletin* "was racist, misogynist, socialist, and republican."⁴⁴ The journal, with the motto "Australia for the White Man,"⁴⁵ framed its ideal readership, and by extension the ideal Australian, as "white men who come to these shores—with a clean record—and who leave behind them the memory of the class-distinctions and the religious differences of the old world; all men who place the happiness, the prosperity, the advancement of their adopted country before the interests of Imperialism."⁴⁶ These turn-of-the-century ideals broadly reflect what Russel Ward was to call the "Australian Legend."

Ward's famous study, *The Australian Legend* (1958), shows the "myth [of] the 'typical Australian' " to be a practical man, rough and ready in his manners and quick to decry any appearance of affectation in others.... He swears hard and consistently, gambles heavily and often, and drinks deeply on occasion.... He believes that Jack is not only as good as his master but, at least in principle, probably a good deal better, and so he is a great "knocker" of eminent people unless, as in the case of his sporting heroes, they are distinguished by physical prowess. He is a fiercely independent person who hates officiousness and authority.... Yet he is very hospitable and above all will stick to his mates through thick and thin, even if he thinks they may be in the wrong.[47]

One sees in these claims the staying power of Australia's 1890s egalitarianism. That "Jack" is white goes without saying, and Ward's legend has received apt criticism for leaving out the lives of women, nonpastoral working men, city dwellers, and nonwhites.[48] Nonetheless, Ward's legend essentially reflects the values apparent in the *Bulletin* of the 1890s, the ideological energy behind Australian federation. These are the values by and large apparent in the poetry of Lawson and Paterson.

Lawson's first full volume of poetry, *In the Days When the World Was Wide and Other Verses* (1896), falls roughly, though not entirely, within the parameters of the Australian legend. Lawson's mother, Louisa Lawson (1848–1920), was the publisher of the *Dawn* (the first Australian women's periodical) and one of the great women's rights advocates of the federation period. Henry Lawson followed suit in being supportive of women's rights, a view contrary to the *Bulletin*'s. But even if Lawson is sometimes thought to have "anticipated ... *critiques* of the Legend that focus on racial exclusivism, spurious appeals to solidarity, and a sexual division of labour," as Graham Huggan has suggested, in the 1890s his poems nonetheless were celebrated by those advocating for Australian white male, working-class solidarity.[49]

Moments of aggressive racism, directed primarily against Asian immigrants, sully poems otherwise focused on the lives of Australian workers.[50] William Lane's journal *The Worker* had race in mind when it characterized Lawson as having had "a more potent influence on the moulding of our national character and the shaping of our destiny than any politician." Lane was both a social reformer and a loudmouthed racist, having written an "Asian invasion" novel entitled *White or Yellow? The Race War of 1908 AD* (1888). The reviewer for his journal argues that Lawson "sympathise[s] truly with the Multitude, and hate[s] truly the brutalising conditions under which they are forced to live." Lawson "is not a sycophant, nor yet a lickspittle. The gifts he possesses are dedicated to the service of Truth and Justice."[51]

The "Truth and Justice" of Lawson's poetry was imagined by way of a white male community united through their spirit of comradeship. The racial homogeneity of his poetry is for the most part implicit, which has allowed it to be largely overlooked by contemporary readers. Take as an example two stanzas from "After All," part of the 1896 collection:

> The brooding ghosts of Australian night have gone from the bush and town;
> My spirit revives in the morning breeze, though it died when the sun went down;
> The river is high and the stream is strong, and the grass is green and tall,
> And I fain would think that this world of ours is a good world after all.
>
> The light of passion in dreamy eyes, and a page of truth well read,
> The glorious thrill in a heart grown cold of the spirit I thought was dead,
> A song that goes to a comrade's heart, and a tear of pride let fall—
> And my soul is strong! and the world to me is a grand world after all![52]

Lawson's dawn of optimism, waking up to "a grand world" with a grand future, reflects the aspirations, if not the realities, of the 1890s.[53] Christopher Lee suggests that both Lawson's poetry and Sladen's 1888 anthology were "well suited to the British market's desire for despatches on the fate of the Anglo-Saxon race at the colonial frontier."[54] A poem such as "After All" clears imaginative ground for white Australian readers, asserting an almost ontological relationship between Australia's distinct landscape and emerging nationalist sentiment. One might imagine the "brooding ghosts" of the first stanza to be Kendall's overheard haunting sounds; these are promptly banished and replaced by a communal "song that goes to a comrade's heart."

"For'ard," a poem about shearers sailing to New Zealand, similarly concludes with a vision of a future utopia of (white) class equality—and, in this case, equality between the sexes as well:

> the curse o' class distinctions from our shoulders shall be hurled,
> An' the influence of women revolutionize the world;
> There'll be higher education for the toilin' starvin' clown,
> An' the rich an' educated shall be educated down;
> An' we all will meet amidships on this stout old earthly craft,
> An' there won't be any friction 'twixt the classes fore-'n'-aft.
>   We'll be brothers, fore-'n'-aft!

Yes, an' sisters, fore-'n'-aft!
When the people work together, and there ain't no fore-'n'-aft.⁵⁵

In an 1896 review of Lawson's volume, Fred J. Broomfield suggested that Lawson was "only strongest when most pessimistic."⁵⁶ To read Lawson as pessimistic, however, is to overlook the deep social optimism that, more often than not, redeems Australia's harshness in Lawson's accounting of it. An 1896 reviewer for Melbourne's *Age* made roughly just this point:

> Mr Lawson in many of his verses gives a description of life as it is for men who have to earn their living in the desolate spaces which compose so much of the territory of eastern Australia. The pictures he draws are not cheerful. . . . But when he speaks of prospects at their lowest, and the future at its blackest, of the impotent rage of the social failure and the dull voiceless wrath of the hopeless bushman, he never loses the courage, half cynical, half humorous, which appears to lie at the basis of Australian character as it exists outside the town.⁵⁷

This strength of character stands out in both Lawson's poetry and his prose: for example, his short story "The Drover's Wife" (published first in the *Bulletin*, July 1892, and one of Australia's best-known literary works) features a woman left to care for herself and her children alone in the bush. "She is used to being alone," we are told: "Her husband is an Australian, and so is she."⁵⁸ Like "The Drover's Wife," *In the Days When the World Was Wide* offers less pessimism than dogged realism and the belief that strength in the face of adversity will lead to communal, and perhaps national, identity.

That whiteness is a necessary feature of Lawson's Australian nationalism is obvious even when unstated.⁵⁹ Just as we do not need to be told that the Drover's Wife is white, we understand that the various communities of Lawson's poetry are racially homogenous. More than that: those communities achieve coherent identity through their imagined relation to nonwhite populations, primarily Indigenous Australians and immigrants from Asia. Toni Morrison describes this phenomenon in the context of nineteenth-century America: "distancing Africanism became the operative mode" of those looking to articulate an "American coherence" that had its origins in Europe.⁶⁰ Like his American contemporaries, Lawson generally avoids noting the nonwhite presence against which he writes, but his work is shaped powerfully by that mostly unacknowledged presence.⁶¹ "In a wholly racialized society," writes Morrison, "there is no escape from racially inflected language," and this is surely as true in Australia as it is in the United States.[62] The ideals of community and genre that have been central to this study evolved into racial ideals across Britain's colonies at the turn of the twentieth century. Or, to put it another way, the implicit racial ideas that had undergirded colonial communities and genres from the beginning became somewhat more legible at this particular historical juncture, as the colonies moved toward forms of national identification. In wanting to believe in their own white racial coherence, Australians of European descent imagined versions of cultural coherence—aesthetic forms—that would reflect that coherence. This, in effect, is the poetic form we now call the "bush ballad."

Banjo Paterson's *The Man from Snowy River and Other Verses* (1895) offers a similar white fantasy of the Australian bush, in more heroic and optimistic terms than generally found in Lawson. The first edition of Paterson's volume sold out within a week of publication.[63] Featuring ballads on the riding feats of Australian bushmen, the "success of [the] book," according to the *Literary Year Book*, "was without parallel in Colonial Literary annals, nor could any living English or American poet boast so wide a public, always excepting Mr Rudyard Kipling."[64] Son of a lowland Scot who had emigrated to Australia in about 1850, Paterson's "bush ballads" resonate with both Scottish ballad tradition and Adam Lindsay Gordon's midcentury verses. Poems like "The Man from Snowy River" are explicitly about the making of Australian legend: "The man from Snowy River is a household word to-day, / And the stockmen tell the story of his ride."[65] Contemporaries saw in Paterson's work a "definite Australianness, if such a word may be coined"—this according to the Brisbane *Telegraph*: "a fine, healthy" spirit capturing "every day life, and the characteristic scenery of Australia."[66] Another review attests that "the volume smacks of the bush" and encourages "a greater appreciation of the charms of things purely Australian."[67]

Though the reviewers remain vague as to the qualities of Paterson's "Australianness," we might understand it first in relation to the terms Sladen set out in the introduction to his 1888 *Australian Ballads*: "This volume is essentially the work of people who have meditated in the open air, and not under the lamp." The poems of *The Man from Snowy River* capture both formally and thematically the expansiveness of this view, the notion of Australia as vast, open territory, with people there sharing in that vast, open spirit. "Clancy of the Overflow," for example, shows the drover Clancy moving across an idyllic, expansive outback behind his stock of cattle:

> And the bush hath friends to meet him, and their kindly voices greet him
> > In the murmur of the breezes and the river on its bars,
> And he sees the vision splendid of the sunlit plains extended,
> > And at night the wond'rous glory of the everlasting stars. (SR 21)

The next lines of the poem shift to urban Sydney, and Paterson marks that turn with both cramped rhythm and cannonading articulation:

> I am sitting in my dingy little office, where a stingy
> > Ray of sunlight struggles feebly down between the houses tall,
> And the fœtic air and gritty of the dusty, dirty city
> > Through the open window floating, spreads its foulness over all. (SR 21)

"Clancy of the Overflow" privileges the local, natural landscape as a site for colonial identity. The urban spaces of Sydney, by contrast, constrict and deaden, leaving the "I" of the poem envious of Clancy's freedom and fancying that he'd "like to change" places with him (SR 22). Paterson was himself a solicitor in Sydney, no doubt longing for the comparative liberty of his childhood in the country.[68] As John Pengwerne Matthews has suggested, Paterson's work reflects nostalgia for a rural mode of living that in Australia was undergoing radical change: "The old bushman saw the new railways pushing into the areas once only accessible on horseback or by bullock-wagon."[69]

Paterson also reflects "Australianness" and the values of the *Bulletin* with his folksy, egalitarian subjects, populated by individuals understood to be white. Like the Drover's Wife of Lawson's story, Paterson's figures come from humble origins and confront hardship, generally overcoming whatever stands in their way. In the federation period such pride in the working man was understood in nationalist terms. This is why the *Freeman's Journal*, which advocated for independence from Britain, aimed both to eliminate "all titular distinctions" and "to build up a Federated Australian Republic"; the two aspirations went hand in hand.[70] Paterson does not dismiss British tradition; the Anglo-Saxon connection was too important to white Australia. He instead celebrates the egalitarian qualities he saw as both distinctly Australian and foundational to a broader Australian identity.[71] In the federation period to be an "independent Australian Briton," as Alfred Deakin called himself, meant identifying as a white Australian of British descent who thrived outside the class structure of the United Kingdom: the connection to Britain was thus more biological than cultural. The "community of race," Seeley observed in *The Expansion of England*, was therefore an imagined racial community that inspired simultaneously Australian nationalism and nostalgic affiliation with Greater Britain.

Making a Canadian Homeland

As in Australia, national identification in late-Victorian Canada was a complicated sentiment. Popular Canadian poetry from the period clearly supports the argument that Canadian nationalism grew between the 1867 confederation and the First World War. That same body of poetry also shows that Canada through those decades remained enthusiastically loyal to the British Empire. Racial identification makes partial sense of this apparent contradiction. At least some white Canadians identified with Britain through the logic of blood, as suggested by James D. Edgar's "This Canada of Ours. A National Song" (1867), composed in the year of confederation:

> We love those far-off ocean Isles,
>   Where Britain's monarch reigns;
> We'll ne'er forget the good old blood
>   That courses through our veins;
> Proud Scotia's fame, old Erin's name,
>   And haughty Albion's powers,
> Reflect their matchless lustre on
> This Canada of ours.
>   Fair Canada,
>   Dear Canada,
> This Canada of ours!
>
> May our Dominion flourish then,
>   A goodly land and free,
> Where Celt and Saxon, hand in hand,
>   Hold sway from sea to sea;
> Strong arms shall guard our cherished homes,
>   When darkest danger lowers,
> And with our life-blood we'll defend
> This Canada of ours.
>   Fair Canada,
>   Dear Canada,
> This Canada of ours![72]

Edgar (1841–99) was a Canadian-born descendant of Scots immigrants, best known as a member of parliament for the Liberal Party. His poem locates the source of Canada's strength in its British origins, specifically the Scottish, Irish, and English blood flowing through Canadian veins (Wales was understood in the period as racially distinct from the rest of Britain).[73] Canada's strength comes from both that lineage and its more egalitarian politics: one finds in Canada "no baronial halls" (this from an earlier stanza) but instead Celt and Saxon linked "hand and hand." The historian Phillip Buckner argues that "the notion that Imperial enthusiasm waned as Canadian nationalism waxed is simply not borne out by the evidence."[74] Edgar's poem suggests that racial thinking was an important component of that continued British loyalty.

By the turn of the century, more complicated perspectives on race had surfaced in Canadian poetry. In a volume entitled *Canadian Born* (1903), E. Pauline Johnson (1861–1913) offered geography, not biology, as an alternate source of Canadian belonging. Johnson, who also published under the name *Tekahionwake*, was born to an English mother and a Mohawk father on the Six Nations Reserve in what was then Upper Canada. She writes:

> We are the pulse of Canada, its marrow and its blood;
> And we, the men of Canada, can face the world and brag
> That we were born in Canada beneath the British flag.[75]

Marrow and blood, which might have been used to distinguish Canadians in racial terms, are here instead metaphors embracing all Canadians born in British North America ("White Race and Red are one if they are but Canadian born," she writes in her prefatory "Inscription").[76] Johnson's universalizing of "marrow and ... blood" suggests a self-conscious challenge to the rhetoric of Anglo-Saxonism. Charles Mair (1838–1927) makes a related point in the introduction to his 1901 edition of *Tecumseh: A Drama*, referring to "those primitive inter-racial and formative influences which, together with a time-honoured polity, are the source of the Canadian tradition."[77] Both Johnson and Mair were prominent figures in the turn-of-the-century literary scene. Johnson especially was renowned for her poetic recitals in Canada, the United States, and England, which she performed in varieties of native dress and "elegant evening wear," navigating between her Native American and English backgrounds.[78]

Johnson and Mair were also each included in William Douw Lighthall's anthology *Songs of the Great Dominion* (1889), the Canadian equivalent of

Sladen's 1888 *Australian Ballads and Rhymes* (the two were published by the same London press). Lighthall's volume encompasses a range of sentiment: Canadian nationalism, affection for the British Empire, and nostalgic recognition of Canada's Indigenous peoples. In addition to Johnson and Mair, Lighthall included translations of Wabanaki and Caughnawaga songs, along with other poems addressing Native American culture. Lighthall was a collector of Iroquois masks, and according to Robert Lecker, he thought of Native American culture as a model for "militarist" masculinity and an "imperialist ideal."[79] By 1889 Native American resistance in Canada seemed largely quashed. Louis Riel, leader of two Métis uprisings in Saskatchewan, had been hanged in 1885; multiple treaties governing land use across the Canadian prairies had been signed.[80] Lighthall's anthology thus reflects both his own affection for Native American culture and a broader sense among white Canadians that the continent's Indigenous peoples had been mostly incapacitated. No longer seen as a threat, *Songs of the Great Dominion* absorbs and even celebrates elements of Native American culture.

Even more passionately, *Songs of the Great Dominion* connects the Canadian national project to the British Empire. Lighthall introduces Canada as the "Eldest Daughter of the Empire."[81] "The Imperial Spirit," the first section of the anthology, features poems such as Mary Barry Smith's "Advance of the Empire" and the anonymous "Canada to England," in which Canadians with "loving hearts and outstretched hands" reach toward the mother country, Great Britain (SGD 7). The anthology's second section, "The New Nationality," opens with "Dominion Day," by Agnes Maule Machar (1837–1927), describing Canada as "the Britain of the West":

> The English honour, nerve, and pluck,—the Scotsman's love of right,—
> The grace and courtesy of France,—the Irish fancy bright,—
> The Saxon's faithful love of home, and home's affections blest;
> And, chief of all, our holy faith,—of all our treasures best. (SGD 16)

Here again the rhetoric of Anglo-Saxonism bolsters the continued British-Canadian transatlantic relationship, even as the Young Canada movement of the 1880s aspired to inaugurate a specifically Canadian poetic tradition.

"Young Canada" drew on Romantic notions of nationality to argue, in D. M. R. Bentley's words, "that literature, especially poetry, is an essential ingredient of national consciousness and cohesion."[82] Dewart's 1864 *Selections from Canadian Poets* had aimed to establish a national literature, to offer what Robert Lecker calls "a concrete symbol of Canada's rising currency."[83]

In his "Introductory Essay," Dewart urged readers to believe "that a Canadian lyric might have as deep and true feeling as those they have most admired . . . that a Canadian Poet might be as highly gifted as some of the favourite names who are crowned with the wreaths of unfading fame."[84] The poets of the Young Canada movement, including Charles G. D. Roberts (1860–1943), Archibald Lampman (1861–99), and Bliss Carmen (1861–1929), were born in the decade of confederation, and they saw themselves as part of an emerging nationalist project. Their explicit intent was to build a national school of Canadian poetry. The terms of this nationalist project, especially as articulated by Charles G. D. Roberts, were more inclusive than the terms of Australian nationalism, but race nonetheless remained a crucial, implicit frame.

Born in the town of Douglas, about seventy-five miles northwest of Saint John, New Brunswick, Roberts was a professor of English and French literature, and then economics, at King's College, in Windsor, Nova Scotia.[85] He published his first book of poetry, *Orion and Other Poems* (1880), at the age of twenty, followed by *In Divers Tones* (1886). Roberts has consistently garnered positive scholarly attention, especially for his role as ringleader of the "Confederation" poets. Bentley calls Roberts a "cosmopolitan nationalist," by which he means someone "positioned [both] in and above his provincial environment."[86] Canadian literature, Roberts believed, existed in necessary relationship to both British and American literature. He argued in an 1883 lecture, "The Beginnings of Canadian Literature," that "the domain of English letters" "knows no boundaries of Canadian Dominion, of American Commonwealth, nor yet of British Empire."[87] Like Lighthall, Roberts aspired toward a Canadian national poetry that yet maintained a multivalent perspective.

Two poems demonstratively patriotic in tone exemplify Roberts's double gesture with respect to race and Canadian nationalism. In "Canada," published in the Toronto *Globe* (4 January 1886), Roberts writes of "The Saxon force, the Celtic fire, / These are thy manhood's heritage!"[88] A different view of Canadian sentiment appears in "Collect for Dominion Day," also from 1886, which implores instead "Father of unity, make this people one! / Weld, interfuse them in the patriot's flame" (DT 1). Bentley suggests that Roberts's plea for unity came specifically in response to Louis Riel's 1885 uprising;[89] the year 1885 also marked the completion of the transcontinental railway, which likely inspired thoughts of interconnectedness. The perspective may well be that of the victor calling for consensus after a contentious election.

In the aftermath of Riel's defeat and at a moment of high nation-building sentiment, Roberts implores all peoples to rally behind nationalist sentiment, "the patriot's flame." A less explicit but ultimately more powerful version of this triumphalism governs Roberts's best-known poem, "Tantramar Revisited," a meditative, loco-descriptive poem originally published in 1883.

Whiteness is as much a feature of "Tantramar Revisited" as it was in the poems of Lawson and Paterson. Just as no one need tell us that Clancy of the Overflow is white, so too the voice of Roberts's most admired poem emanates from a position of implicit whiteness. London's *Westminster Review* noted in 1888 that, while "as a rule, minute descriptions of unfamiliar scenery, interspersed with barbarous names, fail to awaken the interest of untravelled readers, but in the lines headed.... 'Tantramar Revisited,' we have something very like a poet telling us about a new land."[90] The poem, in other words, is implicitly colonial in its gaze. From a position of elevation, "Tantramar Revisited" observes a panoramic scene, allowing readers the illusion of an all-encompassing view. In this way, the poem functions very much like London's visual panoramas, those painted "portal[s] to the rest of the world," which, Tanya Agathocleous shows, "situated [particular] landscapes within a global whole."[91]

Roberts also situates his readers in a broader poetic landscape, with references to a range of poetic precursors. Like Fidelia Hill's "Adelaide," "Tantramar Revisited" opens with a gesture to "Tintern Abbey": "Summers and summers have come, and gone with the flight of the swallow." In setting up a retrospective dynamic, the passing of summers between a youthful version of the poet and the present of the poem's voice, Roberts distinctly invokes the temporality of "Tintern Abbey": "Five years have passed; five summers, with the length / Of five long winters!" Metrically, however, Roberts takes readers in a different direction, adapting a form of the hexameter line that in the 1880s would have signaled Longfellow's *Evangeline* (1847). William Strong notes that "Tantramar Revisited" alludes to *Evangeline* not only in its meter but also in its Westmoreland setting, a region between New Brunswick and Nova Scotia near the forest primeval of Longfellow's poem.[92] Formally, then, "Tantramar Revisited" enacts the broad internationalism of Roberts's lecture on "The Beginnings of Canadian Literature"; it "knows no boundaries," looking both across the Atlantic to Wordsworth's England and south to Longfellow's America.

"Tantramar Revisited" concerns itself with both time and location: specifically, the present moment and place of the speaking poet, or whoever we are meant to imagine articulating the poem. I offer the opening fourteen lines (a sonnet of sorts, as readers have often noticed):

> Summers and summers have come, and gone with the flight of the swallow;
> Sunshine and thunder have been, storm, and winter, and frost;
> Many and many a sorrow has all but died from remembrance,
> Many a dream of joy fall'n in the shadow of pain.
> Hands of chance and change have marred, or moulded, or broken,
> Busy with spirit or flesh, all I most have adored;
> Even the bosom of Earth is strewn with heavier shadows,—
> Only in these green hills, aslant to the sea, no change!
> Here where the road that has climbed from the inland valleys and woodlands,
> Dips from the hill-tops down, straight to the base of the hills,—
> Here, from my vantage-ground, I can see the scattering houses,
> Stained with time, set warm in orchards, meadows, and wheat,
> Dotting the broad bright slopes outspread to southward and eastward,
> Wind-swept all day long, blown by the south-east wind. (DT 53–54)

Roberts describes the passing of time and the changing world before him. More immediately, however, the landscape remains static: "Only in these green hills, aslant to the sea, no change!" With deictic pointing ("Here.... Here"), the poem conjures a hilltop on which the poet rests, looking out on the familiar, unchanging scene below: the "scattering houses," the "orchards, meadows, and wheat." Roberts's medial caesurae and balanced alliterations invoke not just Longfellow's *Evangeline* but the poetics of Anglo-Saxon England, as well. Readers have also tended to overhear throughout Roberts's poem Swinburne's style of sonic and rhythmic playfulness.[93] The "vantage-ground" from which "Tantramar Revisited" looks out, then, takes into account both the immediacy of the Canadian Maritime landscape and, in its formal echoing, far distant scenes of Britain and America.

As "Tantramar Revisited" proceeds, Roberts continues to emphasize the play of memory in relation to the Canadian landscape: "How well I remember those wide red flats, above tide-mark / Pale with scurf of the salt"; "Well I remember the piles of blocks and ropes, and the net-reels / Wound with the beaded nets, dripping and dark from the sea!" (DT 55). At the poem's conclusion, Roberts even privileges memory in favor of immediate experience: "Muse and recall far off, rather remember than see,— / Lest on too close sight I miss the darling illusion" (DT 58). These lines mark an important shift from what we've seen through most of this study. Though structurally the poem recalls works from abroad, Roberts's subject remains firmly Canadian: memory grounded in the landscape and dwellings of the Tantramar marshes. In this way he distinguishes himself from the Australian-born Henry Kendall, whose nostalgia was for a far-off England he had never visited, and from both Alexander McLachlan and Thomas Pringle, whose views respectively of Canada and South Africa were tinted always by memories of their native Scotland. Though Britain plays a part in Roberts's thinking, the nostalgia of his poetry is for Canada, not lands abroad.

Roberts thus paints the lands around Tantramar eminently as a Canadian homeland. Goldsmith's *Rising Village* (1825) described the "lonely settler" facing ambivalence "amid a wilderness of trees" and "deep solitudes." Roberts, by contrast, has the privilege of an unobstructed view. "Here, from my vantage-ground," he writes, "I can see the scattering houses" and the windswept "broad bright slopes outspread" (DT 54). The poem's formal and geographical references to *Evangeline* further encourage readers to connect that unobstructed, panoramic view to the clearing of peoples who lived there before: not only the French-speaking Acadians, whose expulsion Longfellow narrates, but the original Mi'kmaq as well. This is a landscape forcefully claimed and now comfortably inhabited, a landscape made white and English-speaking. The voice of Romantic nostalgia that has made "Tantramar Revisited" among the more canonical of nineteenth-century Canadian poems emerges from a position of privilege and unquestioned belonging. To the extent that this landscape is a homeland, it has been made so by force.

Also afforded from Roberts's confident vantage ground is a version of Canadian nationalism unthreatened by the outside world. The title of Roberts's 1886 volume, *In Divers Tones*, points to the range of themes and feelings explored between its covers. References include not only poets from the English tradition—Shakespeare, Shelley, Keats—but from classical mythology as well. Together they form a Western cultural heritage that Roberts understands Canada to share with Greater Britain. If we expand the internationalist scope further, we see Roberts attending consistently to influences both French—poems entitled "Tout or Rien," "Liberty (*From the French of Fréchette*)," and "Rondeau"—and American: an epigraph by Whitman for "The Marvellous Work" and two poems on Sidney Lanier. All these coexist with poems on Canadian subjects: for example, "Birch and Paddle," "The Quelling of the Moose. A Melicete Legend," and "Tantramar Revisited."

Roberts's identification with a broader Anglo culture, and his sense that Canadian culture would develop in necessary relation to both Britain and America, helps explain his affinities for Sidney Lanier. Like Lanier, who believed in America's Manifest Destiny and its dependence on an Anglo-Saxon cultural heritage, Roberts demonstrates throughout his poetic career his confident inheritance of an Anglo poetic tradition. In his poem "To the Memory of Sidney Lanier," Roberts writes:

> My spirit made swift with love
> > Went forth to you in your place
> Far off and above.
> > Tho' we met not face to face,
> My Elder Brother, yet love
> > Had pierced through space! (DT 96)

Roberts identifies Lanier as an "Elder Brother" because he sees both himself and his American counterpart as pioneering national poets writing from within a global Anglo culture. In his 1883 lecture "The Beginnings of a Canadian Literature," Roberts explicitly cautioned his audience against limiting their poetic imagination to Canadian themes. "Now it must be remembered," implored Roberts, "that the whole heritage of English Song is ours"—that is, Canada's—"and that it is *not* ours to found a *new* literature. The Americans have not done so nor will they. They have simply joined in raising the splendid structure, English literature, to the building of which may come workmen from every region on earth where speaks the English tongue."[94] In this way Roberts set out a future for Canadian poetry grounded, in the spirit of "Tantramar Revisited," both in a particular, occupied North American landscape and a broad Anglo-Saxon tradition of "English Song."

Lighthall's *Songs of the Great Dominion* (1889), discussed above, followed suit in showcasing nationalist panegyrics alongside poems by E. Pauline Johnson, the Native American poet, and French Canadian authors. Lighthall addresses his reader with the confidence of a panoramic, imperial view: "You shall come out with us . . . paddling over bright lakes and down savage rivers; singing French *chansons* to the swing of our paddles, till we come . . . to moor at historic cities whose streets and harbours are thronged with the commerce of all Europe and the world. You shall hear there the chants of a new nationality, weaving in the songs of the Empire, of its heroes, of its Queen" (SGD xxiv). Like Banjo Paterson riding across the Australian outback, Lighthall traverses vast colonial spaces, encouraging his readers to join him in his seeming mastery over the land: a self-possessed Canadian homeland situated in relation to the global whole—all of Europe and the world as well.

Poetry and Imperial Federation at the Battle Front

The Second Boer War in South Africa, 1899–1902, offered a concrete test of imperial federation just as Australia was transitioning into its new, federated status. After Britain went to war against the South African Republic and the Orange Free State, soldiers from Canada, Australia, and New Zealand, among other British colonial spaces, leant their support to the British cause. More than that: those British colonial spaces saw the British cause as *their* cause, one and the same. The Australian colonies sent troops and also raised the funds to pay for them: about one million pounds, according to England's *National Review*.[95] Banjo Paterson himself went out to South Africa as a special war correspondent for the *Sydney Morning Herald*.

The war in South Africa allowed for the interaction of colonialists from all Britain's territories. Among the most significant was the meeting between Paterson, the poet most associated with Australian federation, and Rudyard Kipling, the poet most associated with the British Empire. The former wrote about the encounter in the *Sydney Morning Herald*:

> I asked [Kipling] what sort of Government he purposed to put in place of the Boers'.
>
> "Military rule for three years, and by that time they will have enough population here to govern themselves. We want you Australians to stay over here and help fetch this place along."
>
> I said that our men did not think the country worth fighting over, and that all we had seen would not pay to farm, unless one were sure of water.
>
> "Water! You can get artesian water at 40ft. anywhere! What more do they want?"
>
> I pointed out that there is a vast difference between artesian water which rises to the surface, and well-water which has to be lifted 40ft. When it comes to watering 100,000 sheep one finds the difference.
>
> "Oh, well," he said, "I don't know about that; but, anyhow, you haven't seen the best of the country. You've only seen 500 miles of Karoo desert yet. Wait till you get to the Transvaal!"[96]

Paterson delicately suggests to his Australian readers that Kipling may not know anything of farming in a dry land and therefore may not be the best judge of Britain's colonial ambitions in South Africa. Those raised to eke out a living from the Australian outback, as Paterson well knew, would have looked with a skeptical eye on the South African desert. Kipling likewise seemed largely ignorant of Australian politics, questioning the colony's drive toward federation:

> "I can't understand there being so many radicals in Australia. What do they want? If they were to become independent, what do they expect to do? Will they fork out the money for a fleet and a standing army? They'd be a dead gift to Germany if they didn't. What more do they want than what they've got."
>
> I didn't feel equal to enlightening him on Australian politics, so I said, "What are you going to do with the Boers if you take their country?"

Paterson knew that Kipling would be averse to pro-federation arguments. Paterson's reference to South African land as "their country"—the country of the Boers—may also have been a subtle critique of Britain's possessive tendencies abroad, including their approach to Australia.

Nonetheless, Kipling and Paterson struck up a friendship of sorts, and Paterson's poems from the Boer front, later published in *Rio Grande and Other Verses* (1902), share sympathies with Kipling's Boer War poems. Like Kipling's "The Parting of the Columns" (discussed at the opening of this chapter), Paterson's "With French to Kimberley" highlights the united efforts of colonial soldiers, in this case under the leadership of British Major-General John French, whose forces overcame the Boers in a protracted siege of Kimberley:

> His column was five thousand strong—all mounted men—and guns,
> There met, beneath the world-wide flag, the world-wide Empire's sons;
> They came to prove to all the earth that kinship conquers space,
> And those who fight the British Isles must fight the British race!
> From far New Zealand's flax and fern, from cold Canadian snows,
> From Queensland plains, where hot as fire the summer sunshine glows—
> And in the front the Lancers rode that New South Wales had sent.
> With easy stride across the plain their long, lean Walers went.
> Unknown, untried, those squadrons were, but proudly out they drew
> Beside the English regiments that fought at Waterloo.
> From every coast, from every clime, they met in proud array,
> To go with French to Kimberley to drive the Boers away.[97]

Paterson was demonstrably proud to see his fellow Australians fighting alongside both colonialists from New Zealand and Canada and the "English regiments," whose forefathers might have fought Napoleon at Waterloo. Like James Anthony Froude, who saw a global Anglo community united by "common blood, common interest, and a common pride," and like John Seeley, who wrote of "community of race, community of religion, and community of interest," Paterson here understands the army at Kimberly to be of a singular "British race." The "kinship" afforded by that connection overcame the differences arising from geography and experience. Similar rhetoric marks the Boer War poetry of Frederick George Scott (1861–1944), one of Canada's Confederation poets who fought with the British in South Africa.[98] In "A Hymn of Empire," Scott suggests the war effort will "bind our realms in brotherhood" and, ultimately, "make illustrious and divine / The sceptre of our race."[99]

What emerges in the context of the South African war is a collective political and aesthetic tradition understood foremost through the terms of race. From the perspective of poets like Roberts, Paterson, and Scott, Canadian, Australian, and New Zealand history would always also be the history of the United Kingdom; all of Britain's postcolonial spaces share a collective history. *Nation* and *nationalism* therefore seem insufficient terms in the context of late-Victorian imperial federation, unable to account for the profound solidarity felt across colonial and postcolonial lines.[100]

Nationalism in Canada and Australia appeared largely indistinguishable in aesthetic terms, and each bore a striking resemblance to Kipling's imperial poetics. These similarities would have been understood primarily according to the essentializing logic of late-Victorian racial theory, whereby Anglo-Saxon blood inspired modes of aesthetic production throughout the British Empire: a global Anglo-Saxon poetics. From this point of view, the rhythms and rhymes of writers like Roberts and Paterson represented both distinct emerging national sentiments in Canada and Australia and an Anglo-Saxon aesthetic practice whose roots would always be traced back to Britain itself. The collectivity enabled by late-century colonial poetry therefore took its strength from the intertwining logics of genre and race: a set of circulating aesthetic practices and cultural constructs that, across the vast distances of empire, encouraged in colonial readers and auditors the illusion of feeling together as one.

CONCLUSION

Genres of Belonging

I have argued throughout this book that poetry in British colonial spaces allowed emigrants to imagine new forms of belonging: new affinities, new relations to the landscape, new alliances with one another. The affective reality of these feelings was crucial, as was the communal nature of the experience. Beginning with the long journey, and through various forms of dislocation and settlement, these chapters have shown emigrant experience, alternately aspirational, confounding, and injurious, to be a communal endeavor. They have shown that poetic genre was central both to the circulation of feeling in British colonial spaces and to the sense of community that developed as a result of that circulation. Parodic shipboard publications, sentimental lyrics, dialect poetry, meditations on home and belonging, and patriotic songs—through each of these poetic forms, emigrants imagined the shared experiences of migration.

A comparable phenomenon is apparent in poetry of our present moment, distinct as the circumstances may be in cultural and political registers. Consider, for example, an immigrant rights rally in Amherst, Massachusetts, in May 2006, at which the poet Martín Espada (born in Brooklyn, New York, in 1957) read aloud a work honoring the deaths of immigrants both documented and undocumented in the attacks of 9/11. Espada dedicates his poem "Alabanza" (Spanish for *praise*) to the lost employees of Windows on the World, the restaurant that looked out over Manhattan from the top floor of the World Trade Center:

> Praise the great windows where immigrants from the kitchen
> Could squint and almost see their world, hear the chant of nations:
> *Ecuador, México, República Dominicana,*
> *Haiti, Yemen, Ghana, Bangladesh.*
> *Alabanza*.[1]

Online videos from the Amherst rally show Espada reading his poem passionately, and the crowd responding in chorus to the repeated call "Alabanza!" In the poem, Espada imagines a broad synthesis of immigrant experience, varied according to the different nations from which individuals came, but united by the particulars of immigrant kitchen labor, by the ideals that accompanied immigration, and ultimately by the tragedy of 9/11 itself. The crowd's responses to Espada—their choruses of the Spanish "Alabanza!" in a predominantly English poem—suggest another level of shared identity and shared experience, an emotional and linguistic connection among both immigrants and those, like Espada, who are sympathetic to immigrant rights. "Alabanza" marks less a specifically Spanish-speaking identity and more one located adjacent to English. Spanish-speaking immigrants from Ecuador, Mexico, and the Dominican Republic join in chorus with immigrants from Haiti, Yemen, Ghana, and Bangladesh to offer a communal form of praise: multilingual, multicultural, and united in the shared experiences of both dislocation and mourning.

We have seen that poetry enabled similar moments of communal identification throughout nineteenth-century British colonial spaces. In 1859 Alexander McLachlan addressed a "Scottish Gathering" in Toronto with poetry modeled on that of Robert Burns, and in 1869 the Scottish immigrant John Barr recited poems to a New Zealand crowd celebrating the birthday of the Scottish bard. Richard Hengist Horne's poem on the settlement of Australia, *The South-Sea Sisters*, was performed with music for large audiences at the 1866 Intercolonial Exhibition in Melbourne. The many newspaper poems published on emigrant ships and circulating in early colonial cities offered yet more ways for settlers to identify as part of affective communities. In schoolrooms, churches, public squares, theaters, and elsewhere throughout the British Empire, Victorian emigrants turned to poetry as a vehicle for affective identification: a way of feeling together, if only imaginatively, the shared experiences of migration and resettlement.

In addition to shared feeling, the wary reader no doubt will also find in these communal experiences the mechanisms of empire that enabled the murder and displacement of Indigenous peoples throughout British colonial spaces. I find them there, too, and my work in the preceding chapters has in no way meant to cast settler poetry as naively reparative or redemptive. Instead, I have acknowledged the broad suffering entailed by settler colonialism while offering strategies for making better sense of colonial literary culture: strategies that take us beyond the copy-and-paste model of replication that has too often shaped our view of the nineteenth-century colonial world. What emerges is both familiar and alien: mundane, everyday life under pressure from contexts outside the norm; emotions and life events transpiring much as they would have in Great Britain, but under the strains of profound dislocation; and emigrants, tremendously mistreated by the British class system, becoming themselves agents of an iniquitous colonial machinery.

British colonial poetry reflects these broader dynamics of the familiar and the strange. Part of the familiarity comes from a characteristic that largely defined nineteenth-century poetry: its investment in the communal and affective potential of poetic form, a subject I examined in my first book, *Electric Meters: Victorian Physiological Poetics* (2009). The present volume suggests why this communal mode of poetic experience had especial force, and especial significance, in British colonial spaces. The desire to belong, to be at home, is fundamental to human experience, and the affective registers of Victorian poetry meant that verse forms would play an outsized role in establishing for nineteenth-century emigrants the feelings of home. At the very least, poetry offered emigrants hints of familiarity amidst the dislocations of settler experience.

Consider as a final example one last colonial poem, a reprinting of Matthew Arnold's "Dover Beach" published in the *Wallaroo Times and Mining Journal* in 1870. Wallaroo grew as a settlement through the 1860s, an important port to the northwest of Adelaide. Arnold's South Australian readers, looking out at their continent's rugged southern coastline, would have heard as well as anyone on an English shore "the g[ra]ting roar / Of pebbles which the waves suck back, and fling." The universality of that sound, of course, is central to Arnold's poem:

> Sophocles long ago
> Heard it on the Ægean, and it brought
> Into his mind the turbid ebb and flow
> Of human misery; we
> Find also in the sound a thought,
> Hearing it by this distant northern sea.[2]

Colonial readers may have felt a certain comfort in the timelessness—and, ultimately, the placelessness—of Arnold's sea, the recurring ebb and flow against the world's shores: as in ancient Greece, and as in Arnold's England, so too in South Australia. One column over in the *Wallaroo Times*, an article on "Postal Communication with England" enthused that new ocean steamers were to result in cheaper and more rapid postal service between Britain and Australia. Just above that, a string of "Intercolonial Telegrams" related news from Great Britain, Italy, Spain, France, and the adjacent colony of Victoria. The South Australian newspaper thus clearly situates Arnold's global ebb and flow in relation to worldwide communication and connectivity.[3]

The circulation of Arnold's lyric allows us to imagine on a global scale the communities of feeling that sustained nineteenth-century emigrant cultures. In the processes of feeling together, literally and fancifully, British emigrants found ways of imagining new homelands for themselves on alien shores. I have argued that the tools of this imaginative work were fundamentally generic, and that emigrant readers found comfort in that generic familiarity. Standing on the southern coast of the Australian continent, an emigrant reader in 1870 may well have heard in the ocean waters "the turbid ebb and flow / Of human misery," and she may have imagined through those sounds, and through Arnold's poem, a deeply consoling global collectivity.

APPENDIX A

Colonial Ship Journals

BL   British Library, London
ML   Mitchell Library, State Library of New South Wales, Sydney
NLA   National Library of Australia, Canberra
NMM National Maritime Museum, Greenwich, England
SLV   State Library of Victoria, Melbourne
UCT   University of Cape Town Library

I list here only those journals used in the book, by date of the voyage's end. Most journals were subsequently republished, after arriving at their destinations.

1841	*Wanderer's Gazette*, London to Melbourne (ML)
1849	*Nautical Magazine*, England to India (NMM)
1855	*Lightning Gazette*, Liverpool to Melbourne (NLA)
	White Star Journal, Liverpool to Melbourne (SLV)
1856	*James Baines Times*, Melbourne to Liverpool (ML)
1857	*Argo*, Portsmouth to Madras (BL)
	Lightning Gazette, England to Melbourne (ML)
1860	*Vain Effort*, Melbourne to Liverpool (NLA)
1861	*Marco Polo Observer*, Melbourne to England (NLA)
	(Printed in Valparaiso, Chile, after the ship hit an iceberg on 7 March 1861.)
1862	*Colonial Empire Argus*, [London to Melbourne?] (ML)
1863	*Fiery Star Gazette*, London to Queensland (NLA)
	Salmagundi, London to Brisbane (ML)
1864	*British Empire Gazette*, London to Canterbury (ML)
1866	*Illustrated Celtic Record*, England to Cape Town (UCT)
1868	*Maori Times*, London to Auckland (ML)
1869	*Lady Jocelyn Weekly Mail*, Melbourne to London (NLA)
	Somersetshire News, Plymouth to Melbourne (SLV)
1870	*Commissary Review*, London to Sydney (ML)
1871	*Pioneer*, Plymouth to Melbourne (NLA)
1872	*John o'Gaunt News*, Liverpool to Melbourne (ML)

1875   *Sobraon Occasional*, Plymouth to Melbourne (NLA)
1877   *Caldera Clippings*, London to Cape Town (BL)
        Nemesis Times, [London?] to Melbourne (ML)
1879   *Aconcagua Times*, Adelaide to Plymouth (NLA)
1882   *Superb Gazette*, [London?] to Melbourne (NLA)
1885   *Rodney World*, London to Melbourne (ML)

APPENDIX B

Timeline of British Colonial Poetry

A selection of key colonial works discussed in this book, with place of original publication noted.

1810	Michael Massey Robinson, "Ode: for His Majesty's Birth Day" (Sydney)
1819	Barron Field, *First Fruits of Australian Poetry* (Sydney)
1824	Thomas Pringle, "Afar in the Desert," "An Emigrant's Song" (Cape Town)
1825	Oliver Goldsmith, *The Rising Village* (Halifax)
1826	Charles Tompson, *Wild Notes, from the Lyre of a Native Minstrel* (Sydney)
1828	Thomas Pringle, *Ephemerides; or, Occasional Poems, written in Scotland and South Africa* (London)
1828	R. J. Stapleton, ed., *Poetry of the Cape of Good Hope* (Cape Town)
1831	Andrew Shiels, *The Witch of Westcot; A Tale of Nova-Scotia* (Halifax)
1837	Susanna Moodie, "Canadians! Will You Join the Band. A Loyal Song" (Toronto)
1838	Eliza Hamilton Dunlop, "The Aboriginal Mother (From Myall's Creek)" (Sydney)
1840	Fidelia Hill, *Poems and Recollections of the Past* (Sydney)
1845	Catherine Helen Spence, "South Australian Lyrics" (Adelaide)
1852	William Golder, *New Zealand Minstrelsy* (Wellington)
1852	Susanna Moodie, *Roughing It in the Bush* (London)
1853	Caroline Leakey, *Lyra Australia; or, Attempts to Sing in a Strange Land* (London)
1854	Richard Henry Horne, *Orion, an Epic Poem*. Australian edition (Melbourne)
1856	Charles Sangster, *The St. Lawrence and the Saguenay* (Kingston)
1858	Alexander McLachlin, *Lyrics* (Toronto)
1860	William Murdoch, *Poems and Songs* (Saint John, NB)
1861	John Barr, *Poems and Songs, Descriptive and Satirical* (Edinburgh)
1861	Alexander McLachlin, *The Emigrant, and Other Poems* (Toronto)
1862	Henry Kendall, *Poems and Songs* (Sydney)

1864	Edward Hartley Dewart, *Selections from Canadian Poets* (Montreal)
1864	Richard Henry Horne, *Prometheus the Fire-Bringer* (Edinburgh)
1866	Richard Henry Horne, *The South-Sea Sisters, A Lyric Masque* (Melbourne)
1867	John Le Page, *The Island Minstrel* (Charlottetown, PEI)
1868	William Roger Thomson, *Poems, Essays, and Sketches, with a Memoir* (Cape Town)
1869	Henry Kendall, *Leaves from Australian Forests* (Melbourne)
1869	Letitia F. Simson, *Flowers of the Year and Other Poems* (Saint John, NB)
1870	Adam Lindsay Gordon, *Bush Ballads and Galloping Rhymes* (Melbourne)
1880	Henry Kendall, *Songs of the Mountains* (Sydney)
1884	Isabella Valancy Crawford, *Old Spookses's Pass, Malcolm's Katie, and Other Poems* (Toronto)
1886	Charles D. G. Roberts, *In Divers Tones* (Boston)
1888	Douglas B. W. Sladen, ed., *Australian Ballads and Rhymes: Poems Inspired by Life and Scenery in Australia and New Zealand* (London)
1889	William Douw Lighthall, ed., *Songs of the Great Dominion: Voices from the Forests and Waters, the Settlements and Cities of Canada* (London)
1893	James D. Edgar, *This Canada of Ours, and Other Poems* (Toronto)
1893	Elizabeth MacLeod, *Carols of Canada* (Charlottetown, PEI)
1895	Andrew Barton Paterson, *The Man from Snowy River and Other Verses* (Sydney)
1896	Henry Lawson, *In the Days When the World Was Wide and Other Verses* (Sydney)
1901	Charles Mair, *Tecumseh: A Drama*, 2nd ed. (Toronto)
1902	Agnes Maule Macher, *Lays of the "True North," and Other Canadian Poems*, 2nd ed. (London)
1902	Andrew Barton Paterson, *Rio Grande and Other Verses* (Sydney)
1903	E. Pauline Johnson, *Canadian Born* (Toronto)
1903	Rudyard Kipling, *The Five Nations* (London)
1905	Dora Wilcox, *Verses from Maoriland* (London)
1906	Frederick George Scott, *A Hymn of Empire, and Other Poems* (Toronto)

NOTES

The colonial periodicals referenced in the notes have been drawn primarily from the following digital archives: *Papers Past* (National Library of New Zealand) and *Trove* (National Library of Australia).

Introduction • Unsettling Colonial Poetry

1. Quoted in R. Hughes, *The Fatal Shore*, 87.
2. Karskens, *The Colony*, 34.
3. Syron, "Invasion Day."
4. P. Carter, *The Road to Botany Bay*, xvii.
5. Other historians have followed Carter's innovative lead, including Grace Karskens. Her important study of early Sydney, *The Colony*, makes use of "topography, geologies, soils, climate, ecologies" to "excavate the meanings [that places] held for past as well as present generations, to foster an historical consciousness of place" (4, 18).
6. Marjory Harper and Stephen Constantine explain that numbers for British emigration are inexact. Prior to 1852, roughly 91,000 left the United Kingdom annually. Between 1853 and 1869, that number rose to an average of 158,000 per year and settled down to 141,000 annually between 1870 and 1913 (*Migration and Empire*, 1–2). For the sake of convenience, I use the terms *Australia*, *New Zealand*, *Canada*, and *South Africa* throughout this book, even though the spaces described were at first called by other names.
7. "Miss Aitken's Entertainment," *Bendigo Advertiser* (16 May 1863): 2 (*Trove*).
8. "Miss Aitken's Readings," *Sydney Morning Herald* (11 Sept. 1866): 4 (*Trove*).
9. "Miss Aitken at St. George's Hall," *The Age* (28 Sept. 1866): 5 (*Trove*).
10. Veracini, *Settler Colonialism*, 54.
11. Mill, "What Is Poetry?," 64.
12. V. Jackson, *Dickinson's Misery*, 7.
13. On the political work of nineteenth-century British poetry, see, e.g., I. Armstrong, *Victorian Poetry*; Kuduk Weiner, *Republican Politics and English Poetry*; Sanders, *Poetry of Chartism*; and my own *Electric Meters*.
14. B. Bell, "Bound for Australia," 121–22.
15. Martin, "Imperfectly Civilized," 350.

16. Stedman, *A Victorian Anthology*, xiv.
17. Belich, *Replenishing the Earth*, 168.
18. Cannadine, *Ornamentalism*, 29.
19. Moretti, *Distant Reading*, 48.
20. Rushdie, *Imaginary Homelands*, 10.
21. I distinguish throughout this work between the colonialism of occupation (India, Hong Kong) and the colonialism of settlement (Australia, New Zealand, Canada). Both forms of colonialism entailed the violent suppression of Indigenous peoples. The former, however, was more often driven by privilege (administrators of the Imperial project), the latter by misfortune: for example, convicts sent to penal colonies; working-class Scots displaced from traditional rural economies; Irish paupers fleeing the Great Hunger; and struggling middle-class families in search of cheaper land. As Anna Johnston and Alan Lawson argue, these settlers were most often looked down upon by the British at home, and they "tended to retain a more limited allegiance to the home country than those sent to rule in colonies of occupation" ("Settler Colonies," 363).
22. "My Persian Tent," 249.
23. I have in mind scholarship by members of the Nineteenth-Century Historical Poetics reading group, of which I am a part. See especially Cavitch, *American Elegy*; Michael Cohen, *The Social Lives of Poems*; Gibson, *Indian Angles*; Virginia Jackson, *Dickinson's Misery*; Lootens, *The Political Poetess*; Martin, *The Rise and Fall of Meter*; McGill, *The Traffic in Poems*; Prins, *Ladies' Greek*; Richards, "Correspondent Lines"; Socarides, *Dickinson Unbound*; and Williams, "Poetry and Poetic Tradition" and "Parodies of the Pre-Raphaelite Ballad Refrain."
24. Prins, "What Is Historical Poetics?," 14.
25. Burton and Hofmeyr, *Ten Books That Shaped the British Empire*, 5.
26. Simson, *Flowers of the Year*, 22.
27. Ibid., 20.
28. Hemans, "The Homes of England," 392.
29. J. E. Muddock, "What and Where Is Poetry?," *Somersetshire News* 5 (21 Aug. 1869): 14. Published aboard the S. S. *Somersetshire* on her passage from Plymouth to Melbourne (repr., Melbourne: Sands & McDougall, 1869).
30. McLachlin, *The Emigrant*, 13.
31. Charles Harpur, "The Voice of the Native Oak," *Empire* (Sydney) (13 Sept. 1851): 3 (*Trove*).
32. Wright, *Preoccupations in Australian Poetry*, 9.
33. J. Campbell, *Travels in South Africa*, 225.
34. Gibson, *Indian Angles*, 4.
35. Chapman, *Networking the Nation*, xxix.
36. James Belich, *Replenishing the Earth*, offers the most comprehensive view of British settler culture in the nineteenth century. Important recent work on British imperialism includes Duncan Bell, *The Idea of Greater Britain*, and John Darwin, *The Empire Project*. The Oxford History of the British Empire companion series includes several useful volumes: Deryck M. Schreuder and Stuart Ward, *Australia's Empire*; Marjory Harper and Stephen Constantine, *Migration and Empire*; Philippa Levine, *Gender and Empire*; Phillip Buckner, *Canada and the British Empire*; and Robert Bickers, *Settlers and Expatriates*.

37. For the Australian poetic tradition, see Judith Wright, *Preoccupations in Australian Poetry*; Michael Ackland, *That Shining Band*; and Paul Kane, *Australian Poetry*. For the Canadian tradition, see Northrop Frye, *The Bush Garden*; and D. M. R. Bentley, *The Confederation Group* and *Mimic Fires*. For New Zealand, see Jane Stafford, "No Cloud to Hide"; and Jane Stafford and Mark Williams, *Maoriland*. With the exception of Thomas Pringle, the early British poetic tradition in nineteenth-century South Africa remains largely unstudied. On the literature of the Boer wars, see Paula Krebs, *Gender, Race, and the Writing of Empire*.

38. John Pengwerne Matthews, *Tradition in Exile*, is one of few works to consider connections between two bodies of British colonial poetry.

39. I discuss E. Pauline Johnson, a Canadian poet of Mohawk and English descent, in chapter 6.

40. With few exceptions, the poets of British colonialism would not register among the subjects of Leela Gandhi's *Affective Communities*, which considers anticolonial thought at the turn of the twentieth century; they rarely reflect "the disparate energies of Marxism, utopian experimentation, and continental anarchism" that inspired the revolutionaries Gandhi examines (9).

41. Said, *Culture and Imperialism*, xii. Recent work in nineteenth-century maritime and colonial studies continues Said's investment in narrative. See Hester Blum, *The View from the Masthead*; Margaret Cohen, *The Novel and the Sea*; and Tamara Wagner, ed., *Domestic Fiction in Colonial Australia and New Zealand*. Jude Piesse, *British Settler Emigration in Print*, looks beyond novels to consider periodical culture, but her attention remains on English representations of emigration, rather than literature by emigrants themselves. Samuel Baker, *Written on the Water*, elegantly addresses poetry's engagement with the sea from the perspective of Britain's canonical writers: Wordsworth, Coleridge, Byron, and Arnold.

42. "Globe-traversing influences, energies, and resistances," writes Jahan Ramazani, "have arguably styled and shaped poetry in English, from the modernist era to the present" (*A Transnational Poetics*, 23). Important work on nineteenth-century Anglophone poetry in India begins to resituate the British canon; in addition to Mary Ellis Gibson, *Indian Angles*, see Tricia Lootens, "Alien Homelands." Few similar efforts have been made for emigrant poetry elsewhere in the British Empire.

43. On the Victorian memorization of poetry, see Catherine Robson, *Heart Beats*. On the use of poetry to propagate notions of English national culture, see Meredith Martin, *The Rise and Fall of Meter*.

44. *Wanderer's Gazette* 8 (6 Nov. 1841), n.p. (State Library of New South Wales (Q84/156)).

45. Boehmer, *Colonial and Postcolonial*, 112.

46. See Ashcroft, Griffiths, and Tiffin, *The Empire Writes Back*: "White European settlers in the Americas, Australia, and New Zealand faced the problem of establishing their 'indigeneity' and distinguishing it from their continuing sense of their European inheritance.... The colonial settlers had to create the indigenous, to discover what they perceived to be, in Emerson's phrase, their 'original relation with the universe'" (134).

47. Gikandi, *Maps of Englishness*, 37.

48. Kendall, "*Verses. By Henry Kendall*," 394.

49. Horne, *Orion* (Australian edition), iii.

50. Blainey, *The Farthing Poet*, 233, 231. Horne changed his middle name from *Henry* to *Hengist* while in Australia.

51. I. Armstrong, *Victorian Poetry*, 7

Chapter 1 • Floating Worlds: Poetry and the Voyage Out

1. McCreery and McKenzie, "The Australian Colonies in a Maritime World," 570.
2. Trollope, *John Caldigate*, 1:46.
3. Spence, *Clara Morison*, 17; Spence, *An Autobiography*, 17.
4. "The Press at Sea," 488.
5. I draw these observations from more than sixty ship journals currently housed at the State Library of New South Wales (Sydney), the National Library of Australia (Canberra), the State Library of Victoria (Melbourne), the National Library of New Zealand (Wellington), the National Maritime Library (Greenwich, England), the British Library (London), and the library at the University of Cape Town (South Africa).
6. See, e.g., the *Nautical Magazine*, written aboard the ship *Equestrian* on its journey from England to India in 1849. Manuscript held at the National Maritime Museum, Greenwich (MS NWT/6). Shaikh describes two Australia-bound handwritten journals in "The Alfred and the Open Sea." See also de Schmidt, "This Strange Little Floating World of Ours."
7. These bound keepsake editions are by and large the only journals that have survived.
8. Unless otherwise noted, all shipboard publications are anonymous; some articles and poems are untitled. For details on library holdings, see appendix A. "What Is Going On?," *Pioneer* 3 (10 Dec. 1870) (repr., Melbourne, 1871): 27; *Vain Effort* 3 (12 Mar. 1860) (repr., Bristol, 1860): 7; "Our First Number," *Lightning Gazette* 1 (16 May 1857; Melbourne, 1857): n.p.
9. *Sobraon Occasional* 1 (23 Oct. 1875) (repr., Melbourne, 1876): 1.
10. Boehmer, *Colonial and Postcolonial Literature*, 111.
11. Ashcroft, Griffiths, and Tiffin, *The Empire Writes Back*, 135.
12. "The Coming Fortunes of Our Colonies in the Pacific," 270.
13. For data on British emigration to Australia and New Zealand, see A. N. Porter, *Atlas of British Overseas Expansion*, 85. For the end of the transportation system, see R. Hughes, *The Fatal Shore*, 162.
14. *White Star Journal* 2 (5 May 1855): 3 (State Library of Victoria, MS Box 989/2(d)).
15. Jameson, *New Zealand, South Australia, and New South Wales*, 3.
16. B. Anderson, *Imagined Communities*, 44.
17. Digby T. Brett, ed., *Maori Times* 10 (Sat., 4 Jan. 1868): 29.
18. On the conditions for emigrants at sea, see Charlwood, *The Long Farewell*, 105–31.
19. "What to Take to Australia," 365.
20. "Aboard an Emigrant Ship," 113.
21. Mereweather, *Life on Board an Emigrant Ship*, 1, 56, 64, 33.
22. See, respectively, "Florence Nightingale," *James Baines Times* 6 (14 Jan. 1856) (repr., Birmingham, 1856): 2; "The Sea-Sick Man," *Colonial Empire Argus* 1 (21 Mar. 1862) (repr., Sydney, 1862): 11; *Salmagundi* 1 (14 Feb. 1863) (repr., London, 1863): 2; "Lament of the Single Ladies," *Lightning Gazette* 3 (22 Sept. 1855): n.p.

23. For Coleridge, see, e.g., the *Lightning Gazette* 7 (20 Oct. 1855): n.p.
24. "Poetical Log of 'The Queen of the Thames,'" *Pioneer* (26 Nov. 1870): 2.
25. L. Hughes, "What the Wellesley Index Left Out," 94, 99.
26. M. Rose, *Parody*, 45–46. Rose notes that the ambiguity of *para*, the root of *parody*, has meant the term to mean "both a song sung 'against' or 'in opposition' to another and a song sung 'beside' or 'near to' another" (46). On the importance of poetic parodies within Victorian periodical publications, see Houston, "Newspaper Poems," 233–42.
27. Williams, *Gilbert and Sullivan*, 9.
28. Boym, *The Future of Nostalgia*, xiii.
29. Harper, "British Migration and the Peopling of the Empire," 75, 86. Poetry's role in Australian colonial nationalism is well documented in the Spring 2002 special issue of *Victorian Poetry* on *Nineteenth-Century Australian Poetry*, ed. Meg Tasker. See esp. Garlick, "Colonial Canons," and Lee, "An Uncultured Rhymer and His Cultural Critics."
30. "The Homes of the South," 302; "A Voice on Emigration to Australia," 210.
31. R. H. Horne, "Public Works before Fine Arts," *Argus* (Melbourne, 31 Jan. 1853): 5 (*Trove*).
32. "Come into the Boat, My Lads," *Rodney World* (25 July 1885) (repr., Melbourne, 1885): 11.
33. Ibid., 11.
34. Hamilton, *Parodies of the Works of English and American Authors*.
35. Tennyson, *Maud*. In *The Poems of Tennyson*, 2:562–63.
36. Ibid., 2:564.
37. "Come into the Boat, My Lads," 11.
38. Hood, *The Complete Poetical Works*, 625.
39. "The Song of the Ship," *Nemesis Times* 3 (26 Dec. 1876) (repr., Melbourne: Mason, Frith & M'Cutcheon, 1877): 3.
40. Carter, *The Road to Botany Bay*, 67.
41. "The Song of the Ship," 3.
42. My reading of meter works counter to arguments found in Gaston Bachelard's *Poetics of Space*, which suggests a more generalized phenomenology of poetic reading, as well as those of Martin Heidegger, who proposes poetry as that which "really lets us dwell." Both philosophers understand reading poetry as an inhabiting of an abstract domestic space: primal, interior, subjective. Heidegger, "Poetically Man Dwells," 111.
43. "Lines after the Style of Hiawatha," *Fiery Star Gazette* (26 Sept. 1863) (repr., Queensland, 1863): n.p.
44. Review of *The Song of Hiawatha*, *Chambers's Journal*, 7.
45. Review of *The Song of Hiawatha*, *Athenaeum*, 1295.
46. "Hiawatha Again," *South Australian Register* (25 Sept. 1856): 3 (*Trove*).
47. Hiawatha's last words to his people are to heed the "words of wisdom" spoken by the "guests [he] leave[s] behind." Henry Wadsworth Longfellow, *Poems and Other Writings*, 278. On the ways Longfellow's poem became a means for "subsuming the [Native American] aboriginal into . . . Anglo-Saxon nationality," see Trachtenberg, *Shades of Hiawatha*, 74.

48. Longfellow, *Poems and Other Writings*, 278.
49. Flint, *The Transatlantic Indian*, 132.
50. "Lines after the Style of Hiawatha," n.p.
51. Hogan, *The Irish in Australia*, 163. Hogan notes that Dunne was responsible for transporting roughly six thousand Irish to Australia between 1861 and 1864: "All of them who permanently settled in the colony, and avoided the curse of their race, strong drink, have prospered to a remarkable degree, and enjoyed the esteem and good-will of their fellow-colonists of other nationalities" (163).
52. "Erin Machree," *Fiery Star Gazette* (17 Oct. 1863): n.p.
53. "Our Adopted Land," *Fiery Star Gazette* (24 Oct. 1863): n.p.
54. "Poetry under a Cloud," 13.
55. Trumpener, *Bardic Nationalism*, 254.
56. "Our Adopted Land," n.p. David Fitzpatrick argues in *Oceans of Consolation* that "perceptions of Irish politics . . . had doubtless been modified by departure from Ireland" (559); he suggests that, overall, working-class Irish emigrants demonstrated a "reticence concerning politics," tending not to mention political goings on in letters home (607).
57. "Killing Time," *Caldera Clippings* (9 Apr. 1877) (repr., Pietermaritzburg, 1877): 12.
58. *Sobraon Occasional* 1 (23 Oct. 1875): 1.
59. *Aconcagua Times* (2 Aug. 1879) (repr., London, 1879): 3. Ships returning to England from the colonies also printed journals on board, but their content was notably different from that of those on outbound journeys. As a contributor to the *Marco Polo Observer*, en route from Melbourne to England in 1861, observed: "Careening on towards the goal where his golden dreams are to be realized, the emigrant is apt to clothe all he encounters with the bright hue of his own imaginings, and the attempt to amuse him would indeed be rude and ill-conceived that failed in its object. . . . How different are the feelings of the generality of passengers in the 'homeward-bound'" (Sat., 2 Mar. 1861) (repr., Valparaiso, 1861): n.p. The *Marco Polo Observer* was printed in Valparaiso, Chile, after the ship hit an iceberg on 7 March 1861.
60. *Argo* (28 Dec. 1857): n.p. (British Library Oriental Collections (MS ORB.40/714)).
61. Williams, *Gilbert and Sullivan*, 7.
62. Dames, *Amnesiac Selves*, 236.
63. "Home," *"Commissary" Review* (19 May 1870) (repr., Sydney, 1870): 21.
64. "The Sailor to His Love," *Illustrated Celtic Record* (Oct. 1866) (repr., Cape Town, 1866): 6 (University of Cape Town Library (BC 686)).
65. Meredith Martin demonstrates that the "stable ballad stanza form is an abstraction of actual verse history"; the apparent "purity" of its structure is in fact "a fantasy" ("Imperfectly Civilized," 361). See also Meredith McGill's questioning of the ballad form: "What Is a Ballad?" On the "enormous weight of social and cultural resonance" implicit in poetic forms such as the ballad, see Susan Stewart, *Poetry and the Fate of the Senses* (119).
66. On the culture of Victorian popular ballad poetry, see J. S. Bratton, *The Victorian Popular Ballad*. On the association of Victorian ballad poetry with national sentiment, see my "On Cultural Neoformalism, Spasmodic Poetry, and the Victorian Ballad."

67. Xaverius Thomas McNiven, "A Dream," *John o'Gaunt News* (6 Apr. 1872) (repr., Geelong, 1872): 37.

68. William Inglis, *John o'Gaunt News* (4 May 1872): 53.

69. "A Dream," *Sobraon Occasional* (11 Dec. 1875): 40.

70. Mackail, *Latin Literature*, 123–24. Formally speaking, the pentameter line of an elegiac couplet is not a strict pentameter, but rather—as James Wilson Bright notes in his 1910 *Elements of English Versification*—a "so-called dactylic pentameter, which is . . . a special form of hexameter, lacking the thesis after the caesura and at the end of the line" (38).

71. Ovid, *The Poems of Exile*, 95. I owe Yopie Prins a debt of gratitude for pointing me to Ovid's elegiac couplets; Meredith Martin helped me untangle the peculiarities of the Victorian elegiac couplet.

72. Peter Green, "Introduction," *Ovid: The Poems of Exile*, xxv.

73. Ovid, *The Poems of Exile*, 23.

74. B. Anderson, "Exodus," 319.

75. In *Nostalgia in Transition*, Linda Austin frames Emily Brontë's poetry in similar terms: "the poems ease homesickness by relaxing personal obsession and rerouting it through aesthetic categories of landscape" (30).

76. "A Dream," *Sobraon Occasional* (11 Dec. 1875): 40.

77. "Home," *Commissary Review*, 23.

78. *Colonial Empire Argus* 4 (11 Apr. 1862): 19.

79. Adams, "Two Australian Writers," 352–53.

80. A. Martin, "An Australian Poet," 209.

81. Smeaton, "A Gallery of Australasian Singers," 479.

82. R. H. Horne, *John Ferncliff*, 15.

83. The point is roughly two thousand miles to the west-southwest of Perth.

84. "Lines: Composed on the death of a chaffinch, which flew on board while going down Channel, and died in lat. 42° S., long. 82° E." *Superb Gazette* (2 June 1882) (repr., Melbourne, 1882): 21.

85. Percy Shelley, *Poetry and Prose*, 226.

86. "Lines: Composed on the death of a chaffinch," 21–22.

87. "Visitants of Ships at Sea," 410. The chaffinch as a species is native to Western Europe but was introduced to the British colonies through the eighteenth and nineteenth centuries. A *Penny Magazine* article from 1838 touts "those little songsters," which are "prized as an object of the greatest value" throughout Europe ("The Song of the Chaffinch on the Continent," 260). A *Saturday Review* essay from 1907, however, explains that the introduction of European birds to New Zealand, including the chaffinch—brought over in large part to combat insects that were destroying crops there—completely backfired: "There is a hue and cry against them, and most farmers in the colony would now willingly banish them from the land if they could" ("English Birds in New Zealand," 168). The birds, apparently, ate more of the crops than the insects had.

88. Virginia Jackson shows that we might take for granted the nineteenth-century reading of birdsong, whereby "a bluebird's . . . or a nightingale's or a sky-lark's or a bobolink's or a darkling thrush's . . . tune would always already have been . . . a lyric poem" (*Dickinson's Misery*, 27). Jackson writes specifically of Emily Dickinson, but the same would have been true for most educated readers in the nineteenth century.

Chapter 2 • Colonial Authenticity: Circulation, Sentiment, Adaptation

1. Hazlitt, "Introduction," lxiii–lxiv. Authorities apparently charged Wainewright for forgery, a capital offense at the time, because murder would have been harder to prove.
2. Wilde, "Pen, Pencil and Poison," 993.
3. Ibid., 1007.
4. R. Hughes, *The Fatal Shore*, 297.
5. Jupp, *The English in Australia*, 46.
6. R. Hughes, *The Fatal Shore*, 72.
7. "From a Correspondent," *Sydney Gazette* (2 Jan. 1830): 2 (*Trove*).
8. L. Cohen, *The Fabrication of American Literature*, 2.
9. Stewart, *Crimes of Writing*, 5.
10. Smeaton, "A Gallery of Australasian Singers," 478–79. Belich, *Replenishing the Earth*, 168.
11. "The New British Province of South Australia," 187.
12. Horne, "Canvass Town," 361.
13. "Emigrant Voices from New Zealand," 355.
14. Spence, *An Autobiography*, 26.
15. Serle, *The Golden Age*, 381.
16. MacD. P. Jackson, "Poetry: Beginnings to 1945," 348.
17. Paz, *Popular Anti-Catholicism in Mid-Victorian England*, 65.
18. McGill, *American Literature and the Culture of Reprinting*, 1.
19. Stapleton, *Poetry of the Cape of Good Hope*, n.p.
20. *South African Chronicle, and Mercantile Advertiser* 1.12 (3 Nov. 1824), n.p.
21. Review of *Poems*, by William Cullen Bryant. *United States Literary Gazette* 1 (1 Apr. 1824). In *The United States Literary Gazette*, vol. 1, ed. Theophilus Parsons (Boston: Cummings, Hilliard, 1825), 8 (*Hathi Trust*).
22. "News from Parnassus. No. XVII. Specimens of the American Poets," 314.
23. "Waterfowl," *Oxford English Dictionary*.
24. Stapleton, *Poetry of the Cape of Good Hope*, 1.
25. In the *Sydney Herald* version, *waterfowl* is printed as one word. The newspaper presents the poem, along with "A Song of Pitcairn's Island," under the title "American Poetry" and notes that the poems have been reprinted from *Blackwood's Magazine*.
26. *South African Chronicle, and Mercantile Advertiser* 1.2 (25 Aug. 1824), n.p. The editor of the *South African Chronicle* may have read Holford's poem in a review of Baillie's volume published in the *Eclectic Review* (Sept. 1823): 268–69.
27. Baillie, *Collection of Poems, Chiefly Manuscript*, 246.
28. McGill, *American Literature and the Culture of Reprinting, 1834–1853*, 20.
29. L. Price, *The Anthology and the Rise of the Novel*, 68.
30. Peires, "The British and the Cape, 1814–1834," 478.
31. For example, Somerset was responsible for shutting down the *South African Journal* (1824), the literary journal started by Scottish émigrés Thomas Pringle and John Fairbairn (about whom more in chapter 3). Pringle and Fairbairn had provoked Somerset's ire by writing, among other things, that the "industry" of British settlers on the colonial frontier "has failed; their independence is destroyed; their hopes are disappointed; their spirits are flagging; and they are fast sinking into a state of deg-

radation, indolence, destitution, and despair" (*South African Journal* 2 [Mar.–Apr. 1824]: 152).

32. Lester, *Imperial Networks*, 23.
33. L. Thompson, *A History of South Africa*, 60.
34. Peires, "The British and the Cape, 1814–1834," 479.
35. Pitts, *A Turn to Empire*, 15.
36. R. Price, *Making Empire*, 9.
37. Macaulay, "Minute on Indian Education," 107.
38. Mill, *Autobiography*, 121.
39. Mill, "What Is Poetry?," 60.
40. Stapleton, *Poetry of the Cape of Good Hope*, n.p.
41. Chakrabarty, *Provincializing Europe*, 7.
42. See Stapleton, *Poetry of the Cape of Good Hope*: Henry Scott Riddell, "Lines to a Daisy" (62–63); James Montgomery, "Song" (93); Edward Daniel Clarke, "Ode to Enterprise" (40–42).
43. *South African Journal* 2 (Mar.–Apr. 1824): 105–7.
44. Stapleton, *Poetry of the Cape of Good Hope*, 97.
45. Shum, "Improvisations of Empire," 128.
46. Coetzee, *White Writing*, 9.
47. Pringle's poem benefited from Samuel Taylor Coleridge's editing. The proofs of "Afar in the Desert," housed at the State Library of South Africa in Cape Town, show that Coleridge suggested the third and fourth lines of this verse paragraph (Pringle's original two lines read "And feel the unprisoned soul expand / To freedom in the Eternal's hand"). (National Library of South Africa, Cape Town. MSB 393.1 (8)).
48. Trollope, *South Africa*, 1:70.
49. Coetzee, "The Poems of Thomas Pringle," 206.
50. Bird, *The Englishwoman in America*, 218.
51. Ibid., 218. Hemans's poem "The Traveller at the Source of the Nile" was first published in the *Monthly Magazine* (July 1826): 11–12 (*British Periodicals*).
52. Quoted in footnote to Hemans, "The Traveller at the Source of the Nile," 12.
53. Bird, *The Englishwoman in America*, 218, 219.
54. Later versions of Hemans's poem substituted "thousand" for "sounding."
55. Robson, *Heart Beats*, 47.
56. V. Jackson, *Dickinson's Misery*, 7, 55.
57. Bird, *The Englishwoman in America*, 218. Italics added.
58. Isobel Armstrong pioneered this line of inquiry, and many have followed. See Armstrong, "The Gush of the Feminine." On Hemans specifically, Emma Mason writes that, "like Wordsworth, Hemans recognized poetry as an overflow of feeling, but she believed the dissemination of such feeling through lyric would soften society, easing political strife, diminishing support for war and encouraging a shared sense of respect between the sexes. Thus, for her, the arousal of emotion in her readers was a political move." *Women Poets of the Nineteenth Century*, 24.
59. Review of *The Sceptic; a Poem*, by Felicia Hemans, *Edinburgh Monthly Review* 3 (Apr. 1820), 373–83: 374. I discuss Hemans's balance between passionate feeling and thoughtful form in "Hemans' Passion."

60. Berlant, *The Female Complaint*, 4.

61. *Sydney Gazette and New South Wales Advertiser*, 17 Oct. 1829; 10 Nov. 1829; 9 Mar. 1830; 10 Apr. 1830; 15 May 1830; 8 July 1830; 16 Sept. 1830; 12 Oct. 1830; 2 Dec. 1830 (*Trove*).

62. *Australian*, 2 July 1830; 24 Dec. 1830 (*Trove*).

63. See appendix B of Webby, "Literature and the Reading Public in Australia, 1800–1850."

64. *Sydney Monitor* (1 Oct. 1838): 3 (*Trove*).

65. "Soiree," *Taranaki Herald* (28 Aug. 1858): 3 (*Papers Past*).

66. *Sydney Gazette and New South Wales Advertiser* (9 Mar. 1841): 4; *Colonial Times* (Hobart, 23 Mar. 1841): 4; *Morning Chronicle* (Sydney, 8 Feb. 1845): 4 (*Trove*).

67. Lootens, "Hemans and Home," 248.

68. Felicia Hemans, "The Homes of England," *Blackwood's* 21 (Apr. 1827): 392 (*British Periodicals*). This was the first publication of Hemans's poem.

69. "The Happy Homes of England: A Radical Ditty," *South Australian* (Adelaide, 25 Apr. 1845): 1 (*Trove*).

70. Whitelock, *Adelaide*, 66–68.

71. Simson, *Flowers of the Year and Other Poems*, 20–22.

72. O'Leary, "Unlocking the Fountains of the Heart." O'Leary follows the lead of Tricia Lootens, who shows the significance of Hemans's circulation among nineteenth-century American women poets; see "Hemans and Her American Heirs."

73. Lootens, *Political Poetess*. See also Prins, *Victorian Sappho*: "The poetess has the implicitly political function of representing public concerns as if they were private" (223).

74. E[liza] H[amilton] D[unlop], "The Aboriginal Mother. (From Myall's Creek.)," *Australian* (13 Dec. 1838): 4 (*Trove*).

75. Keneally, *Australians*, 403.

76. Ibid., 404. See also Wu, "A Vehicle of Private Malice," 891.

77. This is Duncan Wu's primary argument in "A Vehicle of Private Malice," 895.

78. E[liza] H[amilton] D[unlop], "Songs of an Exile—(No.3)," *Australian* (29 Nov. 1838): 3 (*Trove*).

79. M. Richards, *People, Print, and Paper*, 16.

80. Washington Irving, "Dedication" to *Poems by William Cullen Bryant*, v.

81. [John Wilson], "American Poetry," 659.

82. On colonial uses of association, see Carter, *The Road to Botany Bay*.

83. Leakey, *Lyra Australis*, 87. For a more thorough discussion of Leakey's relation to colonial women writers, see my essay with Mary Ellis Gibson, "Colonial and Imperial Writing."

84. Leakey, *Lyra Australis*, 87.

85. Hill, *Poems and Recollections*, 66.

86. Hill, "Preface" to *Poems and Recollections of the Past*, n.p. Hemans's 1812 volume was titled *The Domestic Affections and Other Poems*.

87. Adam Lindsay Gordon, letter to Charley Walker (n.d., ca. 1853), reprinted in *Adam Lindsay Gordon and His Friends in England and Australia*, ed. Humphris and Sladen, 409: "I'm tolerably jolly on the whole at the prospect [of being in Australia], for I shall come back [to England] in two years and sooner if I dislike the place."

88. Douglas Sladen, "The Life of Adam Lindsay Gordon," in *Adam Lindsay Gordon and His Friends*, 28.
89. Ibid., 32.
90. Trollope, *Australia and New Zealand*, 1:383.
91. Mortimer, "The Melbourne Public Library," 376.
92. "Australian Sketches," 79.
93. "The Homes of the South," 301.
94. Hirst, "Empire, State, Nation," 143.
95. Belich, *Replenishing the Earth*, 356.
96. "The Coming Fortunes of Our Colonies in the Pacific," 287.
97. "The University and the Public Library," *Argus* (4 July 1854): 4–5 (*Trove*).
98. "The Melbourne Public Library," *Argus* (20 Feb. 1856): 4 (*Trove*).
99. Serle, *The Golden Age*, 371.
100. "Minute on the Progress and Commerce of Victoria," *Argus* (10 Feb. 1853): 4 (*Trove*).
101. Malouf, "Made in England," 26–27.
102. McCann, *Marcus Clarke's Bohemia*, 25.
103. Ibid., 41.
104. The *South Australian Advertiser* writes in October 1867, "As we said of [Gordon's first volume] so we must say of the book before us, it contains pieces of very unequal merit" (3) (*Trove*). Geoffrey Hutton suggests that Gordon's weak reception had to do with the colonialists' anxiety in thinking themselves authorized to judge literary merit: "The custodians of taste seem to have been too nervous of their own standing to chance their hand on an unknown writer." *Adam Lindsey Gordon*, 124.
105. Marcus Clarke, quoted in the *Argus* (3 Dec. 1868): 5; originally in the *Colonial Monthly Magazine* (*Trove*). Douglas Sladen, "Preface," in Humphris and Sladen, *Adam Lindsay Gordon and His Friends*, xvi.
106. Douglas Sladen, "Gordon as a Poet"; in Humphris and Sladen, *Adam Lindsay Gordon and His Friends*, 284.
107. Hutton, *Adam Lindsay Gordon*, 152.
108. Wright, *Preoccupations in Australian Poetry*, 59, 60.
109. Ibid., 62.
110. Review of *Bush Ballads and Galloping Rhymes*. *South Australian Register* (3 Oct. 1870): 6 (*Trove*).
111. [Wilde], "Adam Lindsay Gordon," 3.
112. Ibid., 3.
113. Browning, *The Poems*, 1:395.
114. Quoted in ibid., 1:1087.
115. Prins, "Robert Browning, Transported by Meter," 206.
116. Gordon, *Poems*, 127. Subsequent citations of this volume are cited in the text by page number.
117. "The Admella," *South Australian Register* (7 Sept. 1859): 3 (*Trove*).
118. [Wilde], "Adam Lindsey Gordon," 3.
119. See C. Levine, *Forms: Whole, Rhythm, Hierarchy, Network*, 6–11.

Chapter 3 • Sounding Colonial: Dialect, Song, and the Scottish Diaspora

1. Fry, *The Scottish Empire*. On Governor Macquarie, see 110–11. For helping to shape the arguments of this chapter, I'd like to thank Kirstie Blair and the participants in Scottish Emigrant Literatures in the Long Nineteenth Century, a daylong (March 2015) seminar at the University of Stirling, Scotland.

2. Magnusson, *Scotland: The Story of a Nation*, 634.

3. Trumpener, *Bardic Nationalism*, 70. Trumpener is here writing specifically of Samuel Johnson's views as expressed in his 1775 *Journey to the Western Islands of Scotland*.

4. Devine, *To the Ends of the Earth*, 11.

5. H. J. M. Johnston, *British Emigration Policy*, 7. According to T. M. Devine, part of the enthusiasm for emigration was necessitated by a steep rise in the Scottish population, which rose 88 percent from the 1750s to 1831. *To the Ends of the Earth*, 63.

6. Devine, *To the Ends of the Earth*, 92.

7. Johnston, *British Emigration Policy*, 37.

8. See Harper, *Adventurers and Exiles*, 44–65.

9. Campey, *After the Hector*, 9–10.

10. Historical accounts of Scottish emigration are substantial. See, in addition to works already cited, Bueltmann, Hinson, and Morton, *The Scottish Diaspora*; Hunter, *Scottish Exodus*; and Tanner, *The Last of the Celts*.

11. B. Porter, *The Absent-Minded Imperialists*, 20.

12. Belich, *Replenishing the Earth*, 127. Belich does note the particular influence of the Scots on the Anglo world: "From about 1750, Scots contributed disproportionately to British politics, philosophy, banking, and medicine, and to military and mercantile activity" (58–59).

13. "Portable property" is John Plotz's term, which he uses to describe "the flow of objects outward from England [that] played a crucial role in exporting a restrictive, distinctive sort of Englishness through a world that stayed distinctly non-English," in particular, the world of nineteenth-century British imperialism. In place of particular objects, I focus on dialect and genre as more abstract possessions for British emigrants. *Portable Property*, 20.

14. Shuttleton, "Nae Hottentots," 40.

15. R. Crawford, *The Bard*, 186.

16. Burns, *Poems, Chiefly in the Scottish Dialect*, iv–v.

17. On the connections between ballads and national cultures, see M. Martin, "Imperfectly Civilized." See also my own "On Cultural Neoformalism, Spasmodic Poetry, and the Victorian Ballad."

18. Mulholland, *Sounding Imperial*, 98.

19. Robson, *Heart Beats*, 74. Robson's work focuses primarily on England and the United States, not Scotland.

20. Motherwell, *Minstrelsy, Ancient and Modern*, 6.

21. See M. Cohen, *The Social Lives of Poems in Nineteenth-Century America*, 29.

22. For an important accounting of Gaelic song on Cape Breton, Nova Scotia, as it persisted into the twentieth century, see Creighton and MacLeod, *Gaelic Songs in Nova Scotia*.

23. Chambers and Trudgill, *Dialectology*, 5.

56. Pringle, *Narrative*, 3.
57. Mill, "What Is Poetry?," 64, 65.
58. See esp. Stewart, "Scandals of the Ballad," in *Crimes of Writing*, 102–31.
59. Similarly, the local particulars of the South African landscape transform into "a generalized landscape of the Romantic sublime dotted with the more celebrated African mammalian fauna." Coetzee, "The Poems of Thomas Pringle," 206.
60. *Descriptive Sketch of the Province of Otago, New Zealand*, 73.
61. Belich, *Paradise Reforged*, 219.
62. Golder, *New Zealand Minstrelsy*, v.
63. Opie, "*The New Zealand Minstrelsy (1852).*"
64. Barr, *Poems and Songs*, n.p.
65. "Burns Dinner," *Otago Daily Times* (16 Feb. 1869): 2 (*Papers Past*).
66. "The Burns Celebration," *North Otago Times* 13 (18 Feb. 1870): 4 (*Papers Past*).
67. "Burns Dinner," 2.
68. Clough, *Selected Poems*, 126. On Clough's politics in the *Bothie*, see I. Armstrong, *Victorian Poetry*, 178–204. Armstrong suggests that "the departure to New Zealand may be an initiation of and into genuine change, or it may be an escape from the hard material realities of a class-bound England, as ideologically suspect, in its movement to a colony, as any colonialist venture" (191).
69. Barr, *Poems and Songs*, 18–19.
70. Moir, *The Poetical Works*, 119.
71. "The Rustic Lad's Lament." *Acadian* (Apr. 1827): 376–77 (Dalhousie University special collections).
72. Blair, "A Very Poetical Town," 102.
73. Helsinger, *Rural Scenes and National Representation*, 7–8.
74. Review of *Poems and Songs, Descriptive and National* [sic], by John Barr, 4.
75. Wilson, "Scots—The Otago settlement."
76. Macaulay, "Minute on Indian Education," 108.
77. Mufti, *Forget English!*, 17.
78. Barr, *Poems and Songs*, 62–63. Translations of dialect from the *Dictionary of the Scots Language* (DSL).
79. Patterson, Brookings, and McAloon, *Unpacking the Kists*, n.p.
80. John Barr, "There's Nae Place Like Otago Yet," *People's Journal* (Dundee, 11 Feb. 1860): 2 (British Library). Great thanks to Kirstie Blair for passing along this amazing find. See too Daniel Tiffany's notion of "a radicalized vernacular" that resists bourgeois "polite conversation," which he locates at the turn of the nineteenth century. *My Silver Planet*, 42.
81. John Barr, "There's Nae Place Like Otago Yet," *Otago Witness* (22 Oct. 1859): 3 (*Papers Past*).
82. Kirstie Blair generously helped me to think through these possible modes of transmission.
83. Trumpener, *Bardic Nationalism*, xiii.
84. "Local Intelligence," *Otago Witness* (19 May 1860): 5; emphasis in original. (*Papers Past*).
85. "Emigration to Otago, New Zealand," *People's Journal* (Dundee, 14 Jan. 1871): 3 (British Library).

24. Finkelstein, "Pringle, Thomas (1789–1834)."
25. Peires, "The British and the Cape, 1814–1834," 474.
26. MacKenzie and Dalziel, *The Scots in South Africa*, 48.
27. Trumpener, *Bardic Nationalism*, 255.
28. Pringle, *Narrative of a Residence in South Africa*, 4.
29. Devine, *To the Ends of the Earth*, 18.
30. B. Anderson, *Imagined Communities*, 145.
31. Crawford, *The Bard*, 191.
32. Burns, *The Poetical Works*, 1.
33. Duncan, *Scott's Shadow*, 48.
34. Gelbart, *The Invention*, 132.
35. A. Campbell, *Albyn's Anthology*, ii.
36. Ibid., ii; McLane, *Balladeering*, 108.
37. A. Campbell, *Albyn's Anthology*, 37; italics in original.
38. Pringle, *The Autumnal Excursion*, 86. Italics in original. Pringle reprinted "The Banks of the Cayle" in *Ephemerides* (1828), but he retitled it "Lament of the Captive Lady," making the connection to "The Scottish Exile's Song" less explicit. The term *little ballad* comes from a footnote in *Ephemerides* (162). Further references are to this edition of *Ephemerides* and appear in the text.
39. Prins, "Break, Break, Break into Song," 132.
40. Pringle, *Ephemerides* 162.
41. Shum, "Improvisations of Empire," 22–23.
42. Pringle, *The Autumnal Excursion*, 115.
43. Shum, "Improvisations of Empire," 23.
44. Mufti, *Forget English!*, 12.
45. MacKenzie and Dalziel, *The Scots in South Africa*, 54.
46. Trumpener points to the distinctions between oral and written cultures in eighteenth-century Scotland: "Scotland's long-standing linguistic complexity also made Scottish intellectuals particularly sensitive to the intricate relationship between oral and written literatures; effectively monolingual (standard English) in its intellectual and official writings, eighteenth-century Scotland remained bilingual in its speech (with large repertoires of poetry and song in Erse/Scots Gaelic and in Scots English) and trilingual (Erse, Scots, and standard English) in its literary life." *Bardic Nationalism*, 73.
47. [Pringle], "An Emigrant's Song." *South African Journal* 1 (Jan.–Feb. 1824): 24.
48. Finkelstein, "Thomas Pringle," para. 6.
49. Pringle, *Ephemerides*, 122.
50. McDowell, "The Art of Printing Was Fatal," 48.
51. McGill, "What Is a Ballad?," 161. See also McDowell, who argues that "eighteenth- and early nineteenth-century ballad critics, responding to the perceived dramatic spread of print in their own time, contributed significantly to the emergence of our modern secular concept of 'oral tradition'" ("The Art of Printing Was Fatal," 39).
52. Pringle, *Ephemerides*, 104–5.
53. Ibid., 108.
54. Davis, Duncan, and Sorenson, *Scotland and the Borders of Romanticism*, 1–2.
55. Boym, *The Future of Nostalgia*, 279.

86. "Scotia's Classic Streams," *Stewart's Literary Quarterly* 2.2 (July 1868): 65–66; and "Moonlight on the Trosachs," *Stewart's Literary Quarterly* 2.3 (Oct. 1868): 129–30 (Dalhousie University Special Collections).

87. Corscadden, "William Murdoch." The title page to *Poems and Songs* spells Murdoch's name "Murdock."

88. Murdock, *Poems and Songs*, 7.

89. Cowan, "Alexander McLachlan," 143. Dates for McLachlan's birth vary from 1817 (according to the *Dictionary of Canadian Biography*) to 1820.

90. Waterston, *Rapt in Plaid*, 24.

91. Edwards, "Alexander McLachlan."

92. J. Rose, *The Intellectual Life of the British Working Classes*, 59.

93. Boos, "Under Physical Siege," 251. See also Sanders, *The Poetry of Chartism*.

94. Boos, "'Spasm' and Class," 573.

95. Stewart, *Poetry and the Fate of the Senses*, 121.

96. "For a brief period Chartist writers evolved a genuinely *public* rhetoric of community which derived from their own traditions—the ballad and refrain, the marching song, the Bunyanesque hymn, biblical imagery." I. Armstrong, *Victorian Poetry*, 193.

97. Wheatley, "Preface," xxxi.

98. The opening poem is titled "The Minstrel," and many ballad-like poems follow, including "Will Elliot. A Border Ballad." McLachlan, *Lyrics*, 65–69.

99. McLachlan, *The Emigrant*. Subsequent citations of this volume are cited in the text by page number.

100. Janowitz, *Lyric and Labour in the Romantic Tradition*, 140.

101. Donaldson, *Popular Literature in Victorian Scotland*, 38–39, 36. Donaldson further shows that "Scots was the dominant medium of spoken communication throughout the Lowlands and this was reflected in the creation of a radical new speech-based vernacular prose" (148).

102. Maidment, *The Poorhouse Fugitives*, 356.

103. Dewart, *Selections from Canadian Poets*, 142.

104. Ballantine, *Chronicle of the Hundredth Birthday of Robert Burns*, 545. On the worldwide phenomenon of the Burns celebration, see Rigney, "Embodied Communities."

105. Burns, *Poetical Works*, 328, 102.

106. Thanks to Kirstie Blair for pointing this out. Her forthcoming monograph "Working Verse" fully explores the connections between Scottish ecological poetry and working-class politics.

107. Quoted in Rigney, "Embodied Communities," 72.

108. Rigney, "Embodied Communities," 79.

109. Waterston, *Rapt in Plaid*, 26, 28.

110. Blakeley, "Andrew Shiels."

111. Review of *The Witch of the Westcot, and Other Poems*, by Andrew Shiels, *Halifax Monthly Magazine* 3 (June 1832): 1 (Dalhousie University Special Collections).

112. Shiels, *The Witch of the Westcot*, title page.

113. Ibid., n.p.

114. [Catherine Helen Spence], "South Australian Lyrics.—No. 1," *South Australian* (22 July 1845): 4 (*Trove*). Spence signs her *South Australian* poems "D.G.," a connection proven by Barbara Wall, "A Guide to Catherine Helen Spence."

115. Spence, *An Autobiography*, 31.
116. Ibid., 56.
117. Lawson, "The Songs They Used to Sing," in *On the Track*, 5–6.
118. Ibid., 7.
119. Ibid., 16.
120. Creighton, *Songs and Ballads from Nova Scotia*, xvii.
121. Ibid., 227.
122. Burton and Ruthven, "Dialect Poetry," 314.

Chapter 4 • Native Poetry: Forms of Indigeneity in the Colonies

1. Bladen, *Historical Records of New South Wales*, 1:135.
2. "Native Flowers," *Sydney Morning Herald* (15 July 1856): 3 (*Trove*).
3. "New Zealand. Concise History of the Present Native Disturbances in Taranaki," *Sydney Morning Herald* (9 May 1855): 3 (*Trove*).
4. "The Native Troops of the Indian Army," *Sydney Morning Herald* (11 Apr. 1854): 3 (*Trove*).
5. Lester, *Imperial Networks*, 16.
6. Kipling, *Complete Verse*, 191.
7. McBratney, "India and Empire," 30.
8. Lootens, "Alien Homelands," 289–90.
9. Kipling, *Complete Verse*, 194. Italics in original.
10. Kipling's experience in India was importantly different from the experiences of second-generation colonialists in Australia, New Zealand, and Canada, so the degree to which we might generalize about the "native-born" is limited. The opening description of Kipling's quasi-autobiographical novel *Kim* (1901) makes these differences explicit: "Though he was burned black as any native; though he spoke the vernacular by preference, and his mother-tongue in a clipped uncertain sing-song; though he consorted on terms of perfect equality with the small boys of the bazar; Kim was white" (1).
11. Ashcroft, Griffith, and Tiffins, *The Empire Writes Back*, 134.
12. John Molony addresses the perception of "native" Australians in *The Native-Born: The First White Australians*.
13. John Darwin suggests that British colonialists more generally were ambivalent about "copying the habits and consuming the products of the industrial British in whose mould they were formed." *The Empire Project*, 15.
14. Goldie, *Fear and Temptation*, 12.
15. Gibson, *Indian Angles*, 268. On the "lone poet" of the South African literary tradition, J. M. Coetzee writes that such figures are "seeking a dialogue with Africa, a reciprocity with Africa, that will allow [them] an identity better than that of visitor, stranger, transient." *White Writing*, 8. Paul Kane identifies what he calls a "thematics of negativity" in the Australian context. *Australian Poetry*, 43–45.
16. Calder, *The Settler's Plot*, 4.
17. Ibid., 5.
18. Atwood, *The Journals of Susanna Moodie*, 11.
19. These various experiences of dislocation were both psychological and physical. Warwick Anderson, for example, writes about the experiences of "previously industrious white men" who, arriving in Australia, found themselves overwhelmed by the new

environment: "They were also becoming unnerved, sometimes showing signs of melancholy and nostalgia, at other times raving incoherently and dancing naked in the bush." *The Cultivation of Whiteness*, 26. Patrick White's novel *Voss* (1957) offers a fictional version of such unnerved incoherence, detailing a group of Europeans who attempt, unsuccessfully, to cross the Australian interior.

20. Abrams, "Structure and Style in the Greater Romantic Lyric," 527.
21. Mill, "What Is Poetry?," 64.
22. A significant body of scholarship has addressed the place of Indigenous peoples in nineteenth-century settler and colonial literature. Both Terry Goldie's *Fear and Temptation* and John O'Leary's *Savage Songs and Wild Romances* document a range of settler poets writing on Indigenous peoples in the middle decades of the nineteenth century. In *The Transatlantic Indian*, Kate Flint demonstrates the crucial symbolic role American Indians played in British, American, and Canadian constructions of cultural identity. Indigenous peoples feature prominently in colonial poetry and occasionally form the subject of full-length works: Alfred Domett's *Ranolf and Amohia, a South-Sea Day-Dream* (1872), for example, and W. A. Cawthorne's *The Legend of Kuperee; or, The Red Kangaroo. An Aboriginal Tradition of the Port Lincoln Tribe* (1858). Scholarship on colonialism, race, and indigeneity has been especially rich. In addition to works cited throughout this chapter, see Hall, *Civilising Subjects*; Hoorn, *Australian Pastoral*; Qureshi, *Peoples on Parade*; Salesa, *Racial Crossings*; Schwarz, *The Expansion of England*; and Wolfe, *Settler Colonialism and the Transformation of Anthropology*.
23. Kendall, "*Verses*, by Henry Kendall (Unpublished)," 394.
24. Ackland, *Henry Kendall*, 8.
25. Sutherland, "Henry Clarence Kendall," 388.
26. On Thomas Kendall's experiences in New Zealand, see Ackland, *Henry Kendall*, 11–30.
27. Ibid., 27.
28. Sutherland, "Henry Clarence Kendall," 390.
29. Townsend, *Rambles and Observations in New South Wales*, 87.
30. Ibid., 87, 88, 90.
31. Karskens, *The Colony*, 12.
32. Clarke, "Preface," ix. Andrew McCann discusses the "Gothic bent" of nineteenth-century Australian poetry; see *Marcus Clarke's Bohemia*, 186.
33. Brantlinger, *Rule of Darkness*, 127.
34. "New Poetry," 236.
35. Letter to Mrs. A. E. Selwyn (25 Mar. 1865). Quoted in Kendall, *Poetry, Prose, and Selected Correspondence*, 213; italics in original. Subsequent citations of Kendall's works refer to this edition and are marked "HK" in the text.
36. R. H. Horne, "The Prize Poem," *Sydney Morning Herald* (7 Jan. 1869): 3 (*Trove*).
37. Ibid., 3.
38. "New Poetry," 237.
39. The poem was reprinted as "The Voice in the Wild Oak" in Kendall's third and final volume of poetry, the 1880 *Songs of the Mountains*. Edmund Clarence Stedman later chose it—under the latter title—for his 1895 *A Victorian Anthology, 1837–1895*; the poem appears in Stedman's section of "Colonial Poets (India—Australasia—Dominion

of Canada)," alongside works by fellow Australian poets Charles Harpur, Adam Lindsay Gordon, and others.

40. [Henry Kendall], "A Colonial Literary Club," *Evening News* (Sydney, 24 Feb. 1871): 3 (*Trove*).

41. Henry Kendall, "Old Manuscripts," *Freeman's Journal* (Sydney, 17 Nov. 1877): 18 (*Trove*).

42. Ibid., 17.

43. Henry Kendall, "Arcadia at Our Gates," *Australian Town and Country Journal* (27 Feb. 1875): 19 (*Trove*).

44. Emerson, "Self-Reliance," 45–46.

45. Henry Kendall, "Arcadia at Our Gates" (concluded), *Australian Town and Country Journal* (6 Mar. 1875): 20 (*Trove*).

46. See Brantlinger, *Dark Vanishings*.

47. Ibid., 130.

48. Horne, "The Prize Poem," 3.

49. A. Meston, "Aboriginal Names," *Sydney Morning Herald* (19 Oct 1921): 11 (*Trove*).

50. Kane, *Australian Poetry*, 67–68. Kane's study frames negativity from a range of perspectives, including the idea of "Australia as the negative of a European positive," "Australia as empty, void," "Australia as the negation of freedom," and Australia as a place of "heroic failure" (44). Simon During makes a related point in arguing that "literary subjectivity failed to blossom in the new colonies," making specific reference to Kendall and Harpur. What During sees as a failure of "literary subjectivity," I instead read in generic terms as a failure of Romantic lyricism. See During, "Out of England," 13.

51. W. Anderson, *The Cultivation of Whiteness*, 13.

52. C. Darwin, *The Voyage of the Beagle*, 320. I am indebted to Eoghan Lewis, a practicing architect in Sydney, for my understanding of that city's geography and development.

53. R. Hughes, *The Fatal Shore*, 107.

54. Keneally, *Australians*, 126.

55. Waterhouse, "Settling the Land," 56.

56. Campey, *After the Hector*, 86–87.

57. Bothwell, *The Penguin History of Canada*, 132.

58. Vincent, "Oliver Goldsmith," 305–6.

59. Goldsmith, *The Rising Village*, 49. Subsequent citations refer to this edition and will be cited by line number.

60. Frye, *The Bush Garden*, 148.

61. Lorenzo Veracini writes of land clearing as one of the "specific rituals and ceremonies" that allowed settlers to assert "sovereignty" over new lands. *Settler Colonialism*, 66.

62. Traill, *The Backwoods of Canada*, 126.

63. T. Mason, "Having Cleared and Embellished the Earth," 21.

64. Coates, "The 'Gentle' Occupation," 148.

65. S. Carter, "Aboriginal People of Canada," 207.

66. See Bentley, *Mnemographia Canadensis*, 47–68.

67. Evans et al., *Equal Subjects, Unequal Rights*, 182.

68. S. Carter, "Aboriginal People of Canada," 205.

69. Quoted in Bentley, *Mnemographia Canadensis*, 82.
70. V. Jackson, "Longfellow's Tradition," 475, 496.
71. Hale, *Isabella Valancy Crawford*, 2.
72. Crawford, *Old Spookses's Pass, Malcolm's Katie, and Other Poems*, 42. Subsequent citations of this poem refer to this edition and are cited by page number.
73. Goldie, *Fear and Temptation*, 59.
74. Flint, *The Transatlantic Indian*, 132.
75. Frye, *The Bush Garden*, 181.
76. Early and Peterman, "Introduction," 43.
77. Crawford, *Winona*, 176. Crawford had composed *Winona* as an entry to a competition organized by the Canadian journal *Hearthstone*, which in 1872 announced a literary "tournament to native talent" with an impressive $500 cash prize "for novels and stories formed on Canadian history, experience and incident—illustrative of back wood life, fishing, lumbering, farming; taking the reader through our industrious cities, floating palaces, steam-driven factories, ship-building yards, lumbering shanties, fishing shacks, &c." Quoted in the "Introduction" to *Winona* (25). As the prize-winning novel, Winona reflects the values associated with Canadian "native talent." Significantly, though the novel's title foregrounds a Native American woman, Winona, the narrative itself focuses primarily on Androsia, Winona's white "foster-sister." Winona serves primarily to facilitate Androsia's happiness, and she dutifully sacrifices herself on Androsia's behalf by the story's end. Equally sacrificial are the Canadian forests, the destruction of which Crawford links to emerging bucolic landscapes: "the great sovereigns of the shady places toppled and crashed to the earth under the blows of their heavy axes" (134). Several chapters later, those fallen trees make way for a domestic interior replete with "a cottage piano ... a sewing-machine, and a neat bookcase.... And the bow-window as full of blossoms and foliage" (212).
78. Baynton, *Bush Studies*, 17.
79. Mulgan, *Man Alone*, 28–29.
80. Evans et al., *Equal Subjects, Unequal Rights*, 89.
81. L. Thompson, *A History of South Africa*, 108.
82. Trollope, *South Africa*, 1:331.
83. Thomson, *Poems, Essays, and Sketches*, xxvi.
84. Ibid., xxv.
85. Ibid., 40–41. On the Frontier Wars, see L. Thompson, *A History of South Africa*, 76–77.
86. L. Thompson, *A History of South Africa*, 108–9.
87. Tompson, "Black Town," 26.
88. Tompson, *Wild Notes*, 30.
89. Kane, *Australian Poetry*, 33.
90. Wilcox, *Verses from Maoriland*, 1. Subsequent references to this volume are cited in the text by page number.
91. Terry Goldie dismisses Wilcox with one sentence, arguing that her poem "simply deems the Maori" a doomed people. *Fear and Temptation*, 154.
92. Stafford and Williams, *Maoriland*, 18.
93. "A Prize Poem," *Colonist* 45 (21 Dec. 1901): 4 (*Papers Past*).
94. Veracini, *Settler Colonialism*, 54.

Chapter 5 • Colonial Laureates: Navigating Settler Culture

1. J. H. M. Abbott, "Yon Blue Mountains," *Sydney Mail* (19 May 1937): 43 (*Trove*).
2. "Caledonian Society of Otago," *Otago Daily Times* (28 Dec. 1872): 2 (*Papers Past*).
3. Pitt, *Tennyson Laureate*, 191, 194.
4. See Cannadine, *Ornamentalism*.
5. R. Hughes, *The Fatal Shore*, 343.
6. David Cannadine writes of "the export, projection and analogization of domestic [British] social structures and social perceptions." *Ornamentalism*, 10.
7. [Michael Massey] Robinson, "Ode: for His Majesty's Birth Day," *Sydney Gazette and New South Wales Advertiser* (9 June 1810): 2 (*Trove*).
8. Lootens, "Victorian Poetry and Patriotism," 256.
9. Newton, "Classical Canadian Poetry and the Public Muse," 16–17.
10. For thorough accounts of Horne's life, see Ann Blainey's biography, *The Farthing Poet*.
11. Richard H. Horne, "Public Works before Fine Arts," *Argus* (31 Jan. 1853): 5 (*Trove*).
12. "The Roads.—No. 7," *Argus* (28 Jan. 1853): 4 (*Trove*).
13. Blainey, *The Farthing Poet*, 233, 231.
14. Richard H. Horne, "The Lights of the World: Public Benefactors and Their Treatment," *Argus* (22 Jan. 1853): 5 (*Trove*).
15. Horne, *Orion, an Epic Poem*, Australian ed., iii.
16. Ibid., xvi.
17. Horne, *Orion* (London, 1843), n.p.
18. Ibid., 106.
19. Blainey, *The Farthing Poet*, 135. Herbert Tucker reads *Orion* as part of a broader project connecting epic poetry to public education. From this perspective, epic poetry "should stay lofty but at the same time should stay open to modern emulation and become accessible to a broadening readership." *Epic*, 350.
20. "Domestic Intelligence," *Argus* (8 Nov. 1854): 5 (*Trove*).
21. "Geelong," *Argus* (3 Mar. 1855): 6 (*Trove*).
22. Horne, *Papers, 1810–1884*, 421.
23. Horne, *Orion, an Epic Poem*, Australian ed., iii, v.
24. Horne, *Prometheus the Fire-Bringer*, v. Subsequent citations refer to this edition and will be marked in text by page number.
25. Aeschylus, *Prometheus Bound*, 139.
26. Shelley, *Prometheus Unbound*, 136.
27. Blainey, *The Farthing Poet*, 230.
28. Horne, *Prometheus the Fire-Bringer*, 7.
29. Horne, *Australian Facts and Prospects*, 93–94.
30. "Belle Lettres," *Westminster Review*, 584.
31. Quoted in *Prometheus*, n.p.
32. Both quoted in ibid.
33. Richard H. Horne, "Australia Explorers," *Sydney Morning Herald* (19 Feb. 1863): 6 (*Trove*). Further references to this poem are all from this one page. For more on the poem's composition, see Elliott, "An R. H. Horne Poem on Burke and Wills."

34. Ibid. Italics in original.
35. See Blainey, *The Farthing Poet*, chap. 18, "Adrift," 208–28.
36. Horne, *The South-Sea Sisters*, 12. Future citations refer to this edition and are cited in text by page number.
37. Horne, *Galatea Secunda*, n.p.
38. "Galatea Secunda," *Argus* (4 Oct. 1867): 5 (*Trove*).
39. "The Musical Association Concert," *Age* (4 Jan. 1868): 6 (*Trove*).
40. Orion: An Epic Poem in Three Books." *Lady Jocelyn Weekly Mail* 14 (25 Sept. 1869): 65.
41. Horne includes a footnote to the chorus indicating that the "rhythm of the Song-dance here adopted, is that of the blacks on the Goulburn River." *The South-Sea Sisters*, 7.
42. "The Duke of Edinburgh in Victoria," *Argus* (4 Jan. 1869): 5 (*Trove*).
43. Ballstadt, "John Wedderburn Dunbar Moodie," 2.
44. Horne, "Canvass Town," 366.
45. Moodie, *Roughing It in the Bush*, 20. Future citations refer to this edition and are marked in text by page number.
46. Ballstadt, "Secure in Conscious Worth," n.p.
47. Bothwell, *The Penguin History of Canada*, 178.
48. W. L. Mackenzie, broadside "Proclamation" from Navy Island, 13 Dec. 1837.
49. Seeley, *The Expansion of England*, 42.
50. On Moodie's relationship with Fothergill, see Michael A. Peterman, "Reconstructing the *Palladium of British America*," reprinted in Moodie, *Roughing It*, 538–59.
51. From 2 Mar. 1833, reprinted in Moodie, *Roughing It*, 95–96.
52. Bumsted, "The Consolidation of British North America," 52–56.
53. Reprinted in Moodie, *Roughing It*, 278.
54. Mackenzie, "Proclamation."
55. Moodie, *Roughing It*, 278, n. 8.
56. Ballstadt, "Secure in Conscious Worth," n.p.
57. Bothwell, *Penguin History of Canada*, 182.
58. *Palladium of British North America* 1 (17 Jan. 1838) (*Canadian Poetry Press*).
59. Armstrong and Stagg, "William Lyon Mackenzie."
60. On Moodie's ambivalence in *Roughing It*, see Thompson, "*Roughing It in the Bush*: Patterns of Emigration and Settlement in Susanna Moodie's Poetry."
61. Butterss, "Fidelia Hill: Finding a Public Voice," 17–18.
62. Spence, *Clara Morison*, 22.
63. Quoted in "Scientific and Literary," 913.
64. Quoted in John Blacket, *The Early History of South Australia*, 258.
65. Spence, *Clara Morison*, 22.
66. Hill, *Poems and Recollections of the Past*, 42. Future references to Hill's poems are from this edition, and will be cited in the text by page number and "FH."
67. Whitelock, *Adelaide*, 28.
68. Wakefield, *A Letter from Sydney*, 18.
69. Ibid., 100.
70. Hall, *Civilising Subjects*, 29.
71. Review of *The New British Province of South Australia*, 179.

72. For a succinct history of Adelaide's founding, including the parliamentary act of colonization, see Whitelock, *Adelaide*, 20–26.

73. Marx, *Capital*, 938–39.

74. Carter, *Road to Botany Bay*, see esp. chap. 2.

75. Philip Butterss suggests that her "laying claim to authorship was no trifle" when one considers "the number of women who chose anonymity or pseudonymity as their strategy for entering the public." "Fidelia Hill: Finding a Public Voice," 20–21.

76. Hemans, "A Tale of the Fourteenth Century"; in *Poems*, 217–18.

77. Barrett Browning, *Aurora Leigh*, 149.

78. Horne, "John Ferncliff," 15.

79. Toye, *The Oxford Companion to Canadian Literature*, 727.

80. Dewart, *Essays for the Times*, 39.

81. Kennedy, *Walt Whitman's Diary in Canada*, 30.

82. Sangster, *The St. Lawrence and the Saguenay*, 50. Future citations to this poem refer to this edition and will be referenced in the text by page number and "CS."

83. Goldsmith, *The Rising Village*, 49.

84. "Minor Minstrels," 465.

85. On the Spasmodic movement, see the special issue of *Victorian Poetry* I co-edited with Charles LaPorte, "Spasmodic Poetry and Poetics."

86. Reviewers identified Barrett Browning herself as "spasmodic"; see Blair, *Victorian Poetry and the Culture of the Heart*, 103–44, and Tucker, *Epic: Britain's Heroic Muse*, 377–84.

87. Spenser, *The Faerie Queene*, 15. The quote is from Spenser's introductory letter to Sir Walter Raleigh.

88. Review of *The St. Lawrence and the Saguenay*, 79.

89. Saunders and Marston, "Recent Poetry," 272. The *National Magazine* reprinted a Sangster poem, "Falls of the Chaudière, Ottawa," in its February 1859 issue.

Chapter 6 • *The Poetry of Greater Britain: Race and Nationhood at Century's End*

1. Plotz, *Portable Property*, 67.

2. Warwick Anderson writes that in turn-of-the-century Australia, the "word 'Australia' had come to presuppose the biological qualified 'white'—the nation was, by then, the apparently predestined place of the working white man" (*Cultivation of Whiteness*, 253). According to Eric Richards, "in 1901 Australia explicitly defined its nationhood in terms of 'Whiteness' within the imperial framework" ("Migrations," 169). James Belich writes of the British Dominions from the 1880s to the 1960s as having "set up and maintained 'great white walls.' . . . The Dominions cherished their racialist immigration barriers because they believed it kept them British, not just white" (*Replenishing the Earth*, 466).

3. Seeley, *The Expansion of England*, 15.

4. Ibid., 15.

5. In *The Idea of Greater Britain*, Duncan Bell examines the nuances of the debates around imperial federation, which included a range of strategies for imagining a globally dispersed and politically united British people. Lauren Goodlad argues that, among midcentury British writers, Trollope was especially invested in "attempt[ing] to root

Englishness in blood and language rather than place, imagining an Anglo-Saxon mastery of space and time independent of British political sovereignty or the cultivation of English institutions on colonial soil." *Geopolitical Aesthetic*, 80.

6. [Stout], "A Colonial View of Imperial Federation," 351.
7. Ibid., 356, 361.
8. Froude, *Oceana*, 12.
9. Martin, *Rise and Fall of Meter*, 37.
10. Gilmour, *Long Recessional*, 146.
11. Kipling, *Complete Verse*, 467. On the "empathy [and] commiseration" that Kipling saw as "inherent in the intimacy of turn-of-the-century combat," see Hoffmann, "Cosmopolitanism and National Identity," 140.
12. Quoted in Gilmour, *Long Recessional*, 149.
13. Ambler, *Ballads of Greater Britain*, 7.
14. Ibid., 13.
15. Martin, *Rise and Fall of Meter*, 118.
16. Butler, *Patriotic and Personal Poems*, 22.
17. On the White Australia policy, see W. Anderson, *The Cultivation of Whiteness*, esp. 89–91.
18. Painter, *The History of White People*, 175.
19. Turner, *The History of the Anglo-Saxons*, 1:179.
20. Knox, *The Races of Men*, 250. Italics in original.
21. Higham, *Strangers in the Land*, 133.
22. Carlyle, *Chartism*, 43.
23. Pike, *The English and Their Origin*, 15.
24. "An Address to Anglo-Saxons," 4.
25. Horsman, *Race and Manifest Destiny*, 77.
26. For a full version of my argument about Sidney Lanier and the poetics of Manifest Destiny, see my "Manifest Prosody."
27. Horsman, *Race and Manifest Destiny*, 5.
28. Lanier, *Centennial Edition*, 4:277. Italics mine.
29. Ibid., 293. Italics mine.
30. As Horsman shows, nineteenth-century British and American writers understood "Anglo-Saxon" in loose terms to mean *the Teutonic race*: "Germans, Norsemen, and Anglo-Saxons, including the English, who had colonized throughout the world" (*Race and Manifest Destiny*, 63). From this perspective, "Anglo-Saxon" means, roughly, white Europeans and their descendants the world over.
31. "The Poetry of Anglo-Saxon America," *Provincial* (Halifax, April 1952): 121–25 and (May 1852): 164–67: 164 (Dalhousie University Special Collections). All italics in original.
32. Ibid., 166.
33. Keneally, *Australians*, 238.
34. H. Irving, "Making the Federal Commonwealth." Connections were especially strong in "defence, trade, international relations, diplomacy and citizenship" (243–44).
35. See W. Anderson, *Cultivation of Whiteness*, 253.
36. McQueen, *A New Britannia*, 42.
37. H. Irving, "Making the Federal Commonwealth," 246. Republican sentiment had grown as Australia approached the centennial anniversary of the First Fleet's 1788

arrival, but it remained unclear how a future Australian nation would negotiate between nationalism and the British Empire. See Hirst, "Empire, State, Nation," 151.

38. "Australian Ballads and Rhymes," *Telegraph* (Brisbane, 11 Apr. 1888): 2 (*Trove*).

39. Sladen, *Australian Ballads and Rhymes*, vi. Future citations from this volume refer to this edition and will be referenced in the text by page number and ABR. With thanks to Tricia Lootens, who knew how thrilled I'd be to receive this book as a gift.

40. Warwick Anderson writes that "the colonial racial crisis was also a gender crisis." *Cultivation of Whiteness*, 27.

41. [J. Steele Robertson], "The Australian Element in Australian Poetry," *Argus* (14 Apr. 1888): 5 (*Trove*).

42. On the evolution of the Australian ballad tradition up through Gordon, see Matthews, *Tradition in Exile*, 160–73.

43. A. G. Stephens, "Henry Lawson's Poems," *Bulletin* (15 Feb. 1896). Reprinted in Roderick, *Henry Lawson Criticism*, 12.

44. Lee, "An Uncultured Rhymer," 89.

45. McQueen, *A New Britannia*, 51.

46. Quoted in Lee, "An Uncultured Rhymer," 89.

47. Ward, *The Australian Legend*, 16.

48. See Carl Bridge's summary of the resistance to Ward's thesis: "Anglo-Australian Attitudes," 189–90.

49. Huggan, *Australian Literature*, 56.

50. See, e.g., "The Cambaroora Star," from Lawson, *In the Days When the World Was Wide*: "There was strife about the Chinamen, who came in days of old/Like a swarm of thieves and loafers when the diggers found the gold" (210–11).

51. Review of *In the Days When the World Was Wide*, by Henry Lawson, *Worker* (9 May 1896): 4 (*Trove*). On Lane's politics, see McQueen, *A New Britannia*, 191–96.

52. Lawson, *In the Days When the World Was Wide*, 216.

53. The early 1890s was a period of "bank collapses and Depression" that was "followed by a severe drought that ran from 1895 to 1903" and "devastated" the nation's wool industry. Hirst, "Nation Building, 1901–14," 15.

54. Lee, "An Uncultured Rhymer," 95.

55. Lawson, *In the Days When the World Was Wide*, 43.

56. Fred J. Broomfield, "A Singer of Big Spaces." *Eclectic* (Sydney, 22 Feb. 1896). Reprinted in Roderick, *Henry Lawson Criticism*, 21.

57. Libra [Victor Daley?], "An Australian Poet." *Age* (Melbourne, 18 Apr. 1896). Reprinted in Roderick, *Henry Lawson Criticism*, 27–28.

58. Lawson, *The Bulletin Story Book*, 78.

59. See Graham Huggan's chapter "Interrogating Whiteness," in *Australian Literature: Postcolonialism, Racism, Transnationalism*, in which he argues that "whiteness" in the Australian context "is routinely invoked to propagate the illusion of stability, cohesion, and homogeneity" (72).

60. Morrison, *Playing in the Dark*, 8.

61. Lawson's explicit racism comes through in a short story he wrote while in New Zealand, "A Daughter of Maoriland." Lawson characterizes a Maori girl in that story as "dog-like," "cow-like," and "like a pig." *Over the Sliprails*, 83, 86, 89.

62. Morrison, *Playing in the Dark*, 13.

63. Semmler, "Paterson, Andrew Barton (Banjo)."
64. Quoted in Ward, *Australian Legend*, 270.
65. Paterson, *The Man from Snowy River*, 9. Future citations refer to this edition and will be referenced by page number and SR.
66. "Man from Snowy River." *Telegraph* (Brisbane, 20 Aug. 1896): 6 (*Trove*).
67. "Australian Poetry. 'The Man from Snowy River,'" (NSW) *Mudgee Guardian and North-Western Representative* (20 Dec. 1895): 25 (*Trove*).
68. Semmler, "Paterson, Andrew Barton (Banjo)."
69. Matthews, *Tradition in Exile*, 177.
70. "Australian Natives' Association," *Argus* (2 July 1871): 6 (*Trove*).
71. As James Jupp has suggested, "Australian national identity developed on the basis of distinguishing the society from England—both aristocratic, snobbish England and poverty-stricken cloth-cap England." *The English in Australia*, 128.
72. J[ames] D. Edgar, *This Canada of Ours*, 5–6. The individual poem discussed here was first published in 1867.
73. See Annmarie Drury's discussion of Welsh culture and its perceived antagonism with Great Britain's Saxon culture. *Translation as Transformation in Victorian Poetry*, 80.
74. Buckner, "The Creation of the Dominion of Canada," 67.
75. E. Johnson, *Canadian Born*, 1.
76. Ibid., v.
77. Mair, *Tecumseh*, 6–7.
78. Flint, *Transatlantic Indian*, 277.
79. Lecker, *Keepers of the Code*, 43.
80. S. Carter, "Aboriginal People of Canada and the British Empire," 214–16.
81. Lighthall, *Songs of the Great Dominion*, xxi. Future citations refer to this volume and will be noted in the text by page number and SGD.
82. Bentley, *The Confederation Group of Canadian Poets*, 40.
83. Lecker, *Keepers of the Code*, 31.
84. Dewart, *Selections from Canadian Poets*, xv.
85. Hogg, *An English Canadian Poetics*, 111.
86. Bentley, *The Confederation Group*, 67.
87. Roberts, *Selected Poetry and Critical Prose*, 258.
88. Roberts, *In Divers Tones*, 3. Future citations from this volume refer to this edition and will be marked in the text by page number and DT. On the dating of both "Canada" and "Collect for Dominion Day," see Bentley, *Confederation Group*, 71–72.
89. Bentley, *The Confederation Group*, 73.
90. "Belles Lettres," 534.
91. Agathocleous, *Urban Realism and the Cosmopolitan Imagination*, 89, 97.
92. Strong, "Charles G. D. Roberts' 'The Tantramar Revisited,'" para 2.
93. A point also noted by many scholars, including W. J. Keith: see *Charles G. D. Roberts*, 48. Lionel Stevenson wrote in 1924 that "something of [Swinburne's] melodies and something of his paganism are permanently incorporated in Canadian poetry." "Overseas Literature," 878.
94. Roberts, *Selected Poetry and Critical Prose*, 258.
95. "Australia," *National Review* 36 (Dec. 1900): 600.

96. A. B. Paterson, "At the Front," *Sydney Morning Herald* (12 May 1900): 10 (*Trove*).

97. A. B. Paterson, "With French to Kimberley," *Sydney Morning Herald* (29 Sept. 1900): 4 (*Trove*).

98. On Scott's reputation among the Confederation group, see Bentley, *The Confederation Group of Canadian Poets*, 254–55.

99. Scott, *A Hymn of Empire*, 9–10.

100. The imagined solidarity of Greater Britain makes partial sense from the perspective of Lauren Berlant's *national symbolic*, a term for the rhetorical and legal mechanisms by which people within a particular "geographical political boundary" are "transform[ed] . . . into subjects of a collectively-held history" (*The Anatomy of National Fantasy*, 20). But the geographical model for Greater Britain is global rather than national, necessitating an even more abstracted sense of collectivity.

Conclusion • *Genres of Belonging*

1. Martín Espada, *Alabanza*, 231.

2. Matthew Arnold, "Dover Beach." *Wallaroo Times and Mining Journal* (9 Feb. 1870): 4 (*Trove*). "Grating" was mistakenly printed "garting."

3. This is, admittedly, a more optimistic reading of Arnold's poem than scholars generally allow. Samuel Baker, for example, writes that "Arnold's poetry works through the ambivalence of a maturing author torn between soulful, local pastoral sociability and the mobile nautical worldliness for which such pastoralism must eventually be renounced" (*Written on the Water*, 227). I agree with Baker's assessment, but my argument here is less concerned with Arnold's poem itself—with the original context of its publication—and more with the poem's circulation among colonial readers. Among those readers, "Dover Beach" may have resonated with the optimism I suggest. My thanks to Jeff Hochstetler for helping me think through this reading.

BIBLIOGRAPHY

All citations for nineteenth-century ship journals and colonial newspapers can be found in the notes. Details on the ship journals may be found in appendix A. Periodical sources below have been accessed via ProQuest's *British Periodicals* online database and Gale's *British Library Newspapers*.

"Aboard an Emigrant Ship." *All the Year Round* 7 (12 Apr. 1862): 111–15. *British Periodicals*.

Abrams, M. H. "Structure and Style in the Greater Romantic Lyric." In *From Sensibility to Romanticism: Essays Presented to Frederick A. Pottle*, edited by Frederick W. Hiller and Harold Bloom, 527–60. New York: Oxford University Press, 1965.

Ackland, Michael. *Henry Kendall: The Man and the Myths*. Carlton, VIC: Melbourne University Press, 1995.

———. *That Shining Band: A Study of Australian Colonial Verse Tradition*. St. Lucia: Queensland University Press, 1994.

Adams, Francis. "Two Australian Writers." *Fortnightly Review* 52 (Sept. 1892): 352–65. *British Periodicals*.

Aeschylus, *Prometheus Bound*. Translated by David Greene. In *Aeschylus II*. Chicago: University of Chicago Press, 1991.

Agathocleous, Tanya. *Urban Realism and the Cosmopolitan Imagination in the Nineteenth Century: Visible City, Invisible World*. New York: Cambridge University Press, 2011.

Ambler, Benjamin George. *Ballads of Greater Britain and Songs of an Anglo-Saxon*. London: Elliot Stock, 1900.

"An Address to Anglo-Saxons." In *The Anglo-Saxon*, 3–8. London: Longman, Brown, Green, 1849.

Anderson, Benedict. "Exodus." *Critical Inquiry* 20 (Winter 1994): 314–27.

———. *Imagined Communities: Reflections on the Origin and Spread of Nationalism*. Rev. ed. London: Verso, 1991.

Anderson, Warwick. *The Cultivation of Whiteness: Science, Health, and Racial Destiny in Australia*. Chapel Hill, NC: Duke University Press, 2006.

Armstrong, Frederick H., and Ronald J. Stagg. "William Lyon Mackenzie." *Dictionary of Canadian Biography*. Vol. 9. Toronto: University of Toronto Press, 1976. Web edition.

Armstrong, Isobel. "The Gush of the Feminine: How Can We Read Women's Poetry of the Romantic Period?" In *Romantic Women Writers: Voices and Countervoices*, edited by Paula Feldman and Theresa Kelley, 13–32. Hanover, NH: University Press of New England, 1995.

———. *Victorian Poetry: Poetry, Poetics, and Politics*. New York: Routledge, 1993.

Ashcroft, Bill, Gareth Griffiths, and Helen Tiffin. *The Empire Writes Back*. 2nd ed. London: Routledge, 1989.

Atwood, Margaret. *The Journals of Susanna Moodie*. Toronto: Oxford University Press, 1970.

Austin, Linda. *Nostalgia in Transition, 1780–1917*. Charlottesville: University of Virginia Press, 2007.

"Australia." *National Review* 36 (Dec. 1900): 599–602. *British Periodicals*.

"Australian Sketches." *Tait's Edinburgh Magazine* (Feb. 1856): 78–84. *British Periodicals*.

Bachelard, Gaston. *The Poetics of Space*. Translated by Maria Jolas. Boston: Beacon Press, 1994.

Baillie, Joanna, ed. *Collection of Poems, Chiefly Manuscript*. London, 1823.

Baker, Samuel. *Written on the Water: British Romanticism and the Maritime Empire of Culture*. Charlottesville: University of Virginia Press, 2010.

Ballantine, James, ed. *Chronicle of the Hundredth Birthday of Robert Burns*. Edinburgh: A. Fullarton, 1859.

Ballstadt, Carl P. "John Wedderburn Dunbar Moodie." *Dictionary of Canadian Biography*. Vol. 9. Toronto: University of Toronto Press, 1976. Web edition.

———. "Secure in Conscious Worth: Susanna Moodie and the Rebellion of 1837." *Canadian Poetry* 18 (Spring/Summer 1986). Reprint available online at *Canadian Poetry Press*.

Barr, John. *Poems and Songs, Descriptive and Satirical*. Edinburgh: John Grieg, 1861.

Barrett Browning, Elizabeth. *Aurora Leigh*. New York: W. W. Norton, 1996 [1856].

Baynton, Barbara. *Bush Studies*. London: Duckworth, 1902.

Belich, James. *Paradise Reforged: A History of the New Zealanders from the 1880s to the Year 2000*. Honolulu: University of Hawai'i Press, 2001.

———. *Replenishing the Earth: The Settler Revolution and the Rise of the Anglo-World, 1783–1939*. New York: Oxford University Press, 2009.

Bell, Bill. "Bound for Australia: Shipboard Reading." In *Journeys through the Market: Travel, Travellers, and the Book Trade*, edited by Robin Myers and Michael Harris, 119–40. New Castle, DE: Oak Knoll Press, 1999.

Bell, Duncan. *The Idea of Greater Britain: Empire and the Future of World Order, 1860–1900*. Princeton, NJ: Princeton University Press, 2007.

"Belles Lettres." *Westminster Review* 28 (Oct. 1865): 568–84. *British Periodicals*.

"Belles Lettres." *Westminster Review* 129 (Jan. 1888): 533–39. *British Periodicals*.

Bentley, D. M. R. *The Confederation Group of Canadian Poets, 1880–1897*. Toronto: University of Toronto Press, 2004.

———. *Mimic Fires: Accounts of Early Long Poems on Canada*. Montreal: McGill-Queens University Press, 1994.

———. *Mnemographia Canadensis: Essays on Memory, Community, and Environment in Canada, with Particular Reference to London, Ontario*. Vol. 1, *Muse and Recall*. London, ON: Canadian Poetry Press, 1999.

Berlant, Lauren. *The Anatomy of National Fantasy: Hawthorne, Utopia, and Everyday Life*. Chicago: University of Chicago Press, 1991.

———. *The Female Complaint: The Unfinished Business of Sentimentality in American Culture*. Durham, NC: Duke University Press, 2008.

Bickers, Robert, ed. *Settlers and Expatriates: Britons over the Seas*. Oxford History of the British Empire. New York: Oxford University Press, 2010.

Bird [Bishop], Isabella L. *The Englishwoman in America*. London: John Murray, 1856. Web: *Canadiana*.

Blacket, John. *The Early History of South Australia: A Romantic Experiment in Colonization, 1836–1857*. Adelaide, SA: Vardon & Sons, 1907.

Bladen, Frank Murcot, ed. *Historical Records of New South Wales*. 7 vols. Sydney: Charles Potter, 1892.

Blainey, Ann. *The Farthing Poet: A Biography of Richard Hengist Horne, 1802–84—A Lesser Literary Lion*. London: Longmans, 1968.

Blair, Kirstie. "'A Very Poetical Town': Newspaper Poetry and the Working-Class Poet in Victorian Dundee." *Victorian Poetry* 52 (Spring 2014): 89–109.

———. ed. *Poets of the People's Journal: Newspaper Poetry in Victorian Scotland*. Glasgow: Association for Scottish Literary Studies, 2016.

———. *Victorian Poetry and the Culture of the Heart*. New York: Oxford University Press, 2006.

Blakeley, Phyllis R. "Andrew Shiels." *Dictionary of Canadian Biography*. Vol. 10. Toronto: University of Toronto Press, 1972. Web edition.

Blum, Hester. *The View from the Masthead: Maritime Imagination and Antebellum American Sea Narratives*. Chapel Hill: University of North Carolina Press, 2008.

Boehmer, Elleke. *Colonial and Postcolonial Literature: Migrant Metaphors*. 2nd ed. Oxford: Oxford University Press, 2005.

Boos, Florence Boos. "'Spasm' and Class: W. E. Aytoun, George Gilfillan, Sydney Dobell, and Alexander Smith." *Victorian Poetry* 42 (Winter 2004): 553–83.

———. "Under Physical Siege: Early Victorian Autobiographies of Working-Class Women." *Philological Quarterly* 92.2 (2013): 251–69.

Bothwell, Robert Bothwell. *The Penguin History of Canada*. New York: Penguin, 2006.

Boym, Svetlana. *The Future of Nostalgia*. New York: Basic Books, 2001.

Brantlinger, Patrick. *Dark Vanishings: Discourses on the Extinction of Primitive Races, 1800–1930*. Ithaca, NY: Cornell University Press, 2003.

———. *Rule of Darkness: British Literature and Imperialism, 1830–1914*. Ithaca, NY: Cornell University Press, 1988.

Bratton, J. S. *The Victorian Popular Ballad*. London: Macmillan Press, 1975.

Bridge, Carl. "Anglo-Australian Attitudes: Remembering and Re-reading Russel Ward." *Journal of Australian Colonial History* 10.2 (2008): 187–200.

Bright, James Wilson. *Elements of English Versification*. Boston: Ginn, 1910.

Browning, Robert. *Robert Browning: The Poems*, edited by John Pettigrew. 2 vols. New York: Penguin, 1996.

Buckner, Phillip, ed. *Canada and the British Empire*. Oxford History of the British Empire. New York: Oxford University Press, 2010.

Buckner, Phillip. "The Creation of the Dominion of Canada, 1860-1901." In Buckner, *Canada and the British Empire*, 66-86.

Bueltmann, Tanya, Andrew Hinson, and Graeme Morton. *The Scottish Diaspora*. Edinburgh: University of Edinburgh Press, 2013.

Bumsted, J. M. "The Consolidation of British North America, 1783-1860." In Buckner, *Canada and the British Empire*, 43-65.

Burns, Robert. *Poems, Chiefly in the Scottish Dialect*. Kilmarnock: John Wilson, 1786.

——. *The Poetical Works of Robert Burns*. Edited by J. Logie Robertson. London: Oxford University Press, 1963.

Burton, Antoinette, and Isabel Hofmeyr, eds. *Ten Books That Shaped the British Empire: Creating an Imperial Commons*. Durham, NC: Duke University Press, 2014.

Burton, T. L., and K. K. Ruthven. "Dialect Poetry, William Barnes, and the Literary Canon." *ELH* 76.2 (2009), 309-41.

Butler, Martin. *Patriotic and Personal Poems*. Fredericton, NB: Journal Office, 1898.

Butterss, Philip. "Fidelia Hill: Finding a Public Voice." In Butterss, *Southwards: Essays on South Australian Writing*, 16-26. Kent Town, SA: Wakefield Press, 1995.

Calder, Alex. *The Settler's Plot: How Stories Take Place in New Zealand*. Auckland: Auckland University Press, 2011.

Campbell, Alexander, ed. *Albyn's Anthology; or, A Select Collection of the Melodies and Vocal Poetry Peculiar to Scotland and the Isles: Hitherto Unpublished*. Edinburgh: Oliver & Boyd, 1816.

Campbell, John. *Travels in South Africa*. Andover, MA: Flagg & Gould, 1816 [1815].

Campey, Lucille H. *After the Hector: The Scottish Pioneers of Nova Scotia and Cape Breton, 1773-1852*. Toronto: Natural Heritage Books, 2007.

Cannadine, David. *Ornamentalism: How the British Saw Their Empire*. New York: Oxford University Press, 2002.

Carlyle, Thomas. *Chartism. Past and Present*. London: Chapman & Hall, 1858.

Carter, Paul. *The Road to Botany Bay*. New York: Knopf, 1988.

Carter, Sarah. "Aboriginal People of Canada." In Buckner, *Canada and the British Empire*, 200-219.

Cavitch, Max. *American Elegy: The Poetry of Mourning from the Puritans to Whitman*. Minneapolis: University of Minnesota Press, 2007.

Chakrabarty, Dipesh. *Provincializing Europe: Postcolonial Thought and Historical Difference*. Princeton, NJ: Princeton University Press, 2008.

Chambers, J. K., and Peter Trudgill. *Dialectology*. Cambridge: Cambridge University Press, 2004.

Chapman, Alison. *Networking the Nation: British and American Women's Poetry and Italy, 1840-1870*. Oxford: Oxford University Press, 2015.

Charlwood, Don. *The Long Farewell*. New York: Penguin, 1983.

Clarke, Marcus. "Preface" to Adam Lindsay Gordon, *Poems*, vii-xi. London: Robert A. Thompson, 1905.

Clough, Arthur Hugh. *Selected Poems*. Edited by Shirley Chew. New York: Routledge, 2003.

Coates, Ken. "The 'Gentle' Occupation: The Settlement of Canada and the Dispossession of the First Nations." In *Indigenous Peoples' Right in Australia, Canada, and New Zealand*, edited by Paul Havemann, 141–61. New York: Oxford University Press, 1999.

Coetzee, J. M. "The Poems of Thomas Pringle." In *Stranger Shores: Literary Essays, 1986–1999*. New York: Viking, 2001: 203–7.

———. *White Writing: On the Culture of Letters in South Africa*. New Haven, CT: Yale University Press, 1988.

Cohen, Lara Langer. *The Fabrication of American Literature: Fraudulence and Antebellum Print Culture*. Philadelphia: University of Pennsylvania Press, 2012.

Cohen, Margaret. *The Novel and the Sea*. Princeton, NJ: Princeton University Press, 2010.

Cohen, Michael. *The Social Lives of Poems in Nineteenth-Century America*. Philadelphia: University of Pennsylvania Press, 2015.

"The Coming Fortunes of Our Colonies in the Pacific." *Blackwood's Edinburgh Magazine* 76 (Sept. 1854): 268–87. British Periodicals.

Corsacadden, Laura M. "William Murdoch." *New Brunswick Literary Encyclopedia*. Winter 2011. Web edition.

Cowan, Edward J. "Alexander McLachlan: The 'Robert Burns' of Canada." *Studies in Scottish Literature* 37 (Aug. 2012): 131–49.

Crawford, Isabella Valancy. *Old Spookses's Pass, Malcolm's Katie, and Other Poems*. Toronto: Bain, 1884.

———. *Winona; or, The Foster-Sisters*. Edited by Len Early and Michael A. Peterman. Peterborough, ON: Broadview, 2007 [1873].

Crawford, Robert. *The Bard: Robert Burns, A Biography*. Princeton, NJ: Princeton University Press, 2009.

Creighton, Helen. *Songs and Ballads from Nova Scotia*. New York: Dover, 1966 [1932].

Creighton, Helen, and Calum MacLeod. *Gaelic Songs in Nova Scotia*. Ottawa: National Museums of Canada, 1979.

Dames, Nicholas. *Amnesiac Selves: Nostalgia, Forgetting, and British Fiction, 1810–1870*. New York: Oxford University Press, 2003.

Darwin, Charles. *The Voyage of the Beagle*. New York: Penguin, 1989.

Darwin, John. *The Empire Project: The Rise and Fall of the British World-System, 1830–1970*. Cambridge: Cambridge University Press, 2009.

Davis, Leith, Ian Duncan, and Janet Sorenson. *Scotland and the Borders of Romanticism*. Cambridge: Cambridge University Press, 2004.

De Schmidt, Johanna. "'This Strange Little Floating World of Ours': Shipboard Periodicals and Community-Building in the 'Global' Nineteenth Century." *Journal of Global History* 11 (2016): 229–50.

Descriptive Sketch of the Province of Otago, New Zealand. Edinburgh: Bell & Bradfute, 1862.

Devine, T. M. *To the Ends of the Earth: Scotland's Global Diaspora, 1750–2010*. Washington, DC: Smithsonian Books, 2011.

Dewart, Edward Hartley. *Essays for the Times: Studies of Eminent Men and Important Living Questions*. Toronto: William Briggs, 1898.

———. *Selections from Canadian Poets*. Montreal: John Lovell, 1864.

Donaldson, William. *Popular Literature in Victorian Scotland: Language, Fiction, and the Press.* Aberdeen: Aberdeen University Press, 1986.

Drury, Annmarie. *Translation as Transformation in Victorian Poetry.* Cambridge: Cambridge University Press, 2015.

Duncan, Ian. *Scott's Shadow: The Novel in Romantic Edinburgh.* Princeton, NJ: Princeton University Press, 2007.

During, Simon. "Out of England: Literary Subjectivity in the Australian Colonies, 1788–1867." In *Imagining Australia: Literature and Culture in the New New World,* edited by Judith Ryan and Chris Wallace-Crabbe, 3–21. Cambridge, MA: Harvard University Press, 2004.

Early, Len, and Michael A. Peterman. "Introduction" to Isabella Valency Crawford, *Winona; or, The Foster-Sisters,* 9–61.

Edgar, J[ames] D. *This Canada of Ours, and Other Poems.* Toronto: William Briggs, 1893.

Edwards, Mary Jane. "Alexander McLachlan." *Dictionary of Canadian Biography.* Vol. 12. Toronto: University of Toronto Press, 1990. Web edition.

Elliott, Brian. "An R. H. Horne Poem on Burke and Wills." *Australian Literary Studies* 1 (Dec. 1963): 122–33.

Emerson, Ralph Waldo. *The Complete Works of Ralph Waldo Emerson: Essays, First Series.* Boston: Houghton Mifflin, 1903.

"Emigrant Voices from New Zealand." *Chambers' Edinburgh Journal* (2 Dec. 1848): 353–58. *British Periodicals.*

"English Birds in New Zealand." *Saturday Review* 104 (19 Aug. 1907): 168–69. *British Periodicals.*

Espada, Martín. *Alabanza: New and Selected Poems, 1982–2002.* New York: W. W. Norton, 2003.

Evans, Julie, Patricia Grimshaw, David Philips, and Shurlee Swain. *Equal Subjects, Unequal Rights: Indigenous Peoples in British Settler Colonies, 1830–1910.* Manchester, UK: Manchester University Press, 2003.

Finkelstein, David. "Thomas Pringle (1789–1834)." *Oxford Dictionary of National Biography.* Oxford University Press, 2004. Web edition, 2009.

Fitzpatrick, David. *Oceans of Consolation: Personal Accounts of Irish Migration to Australia.* Ithaca, NY: Cornell University Press, 1994.

Flint, Kate. *The Transatlantic Indian, 1776–1930.* Princeton: Princeton University Press, 2009.

Froude, James Anthony. *Oceana; or, England and Her Colonies.* London: Longmans, Green, 1886.

Fry, Michael. *The Scottish Empire.* East Lothian, UK: Tuckwell Press, 2001.

Frye, Northrop. *The Bush Garden: Essays on the Canadian Imagination.* Concord, ON: House of Anansi Press, 1995 [1971].

Gandhi, Leela. *Affective Communities: Anticolonial Thought, Fin-de-Siècle Radicalism, and the Politics of Friendship.* Durham, NC: Duke University Press, 2006.

Garlick, Barbara. "Colonial Canons: The Case of James Brunton Stephens." *Victorian Poetry* 40 (Spring 2002): 55–70.

Gelbart, Matthew. *The Invention of "Folk Music" and "Art Music": Emerging Categories from Ossian to Wagner.* Cambridge: Cambridge University Press, 2011.

Gibson, Mary Ellis. *Indian Angles: English Verse in Colonial India from Jones to Tagore.* Athens: Ohio University Press, 2011.

Gibson, Mary Ellis, and Jason R. Rudy. "Colonial and Imperial Writing." In *The Cambridge Companion to Victorian Women's Writing*, edited by Linda Peterson, 189–205. Cambridge: Cambridge University Press, 2015.

Gikandi, Simon. *Maps of Englishness: Writing Identity in the Culture of Colonialism.* New York: Columbia University Press, 1996.

Gilmour, David. *The Long Recessional: The Imperial Life of Rudyard Kipling.* New York: Farrar, Straus & Giroux, 2002.

Golder, William. *New Zealand Minstrelsy, Containing Songs and Poems on Colonial Subjects.* Wellington, NZ: R. Stokes & W. Lyon, 1852. Web edition: *New Zealand Electronic Text Collection.*

Goldie, Terry. *Fear and Temptation: The Image of the Indigene in Canadian, Australian, and New Zealand Literatures.* Kingston, ON: McGill-Queens University Press, 1989.

Goldsmith, Oliver. *The Rising Village.* In *Canadian Poetry from the Beginnings through the First World War*, edited by Carole Gerson and Gwendolyn Davies, 47–66. Toronto: New Canadian Library, 1996.

Goodlad, Lauren. *The Victorian Geopolitical Aesthetic: Realism, Sovereignty, and Transnational Experience.* Oxford: Oxford University Press, 2015.

Gordon, Adam Lindsay. *Poems of Adam Lindsay Gordon.* Oxford: Oxford University Press, 1913.

Hale, Katherine. *Isabella Valancy Crawford.* Toronto: Ryerson, 1923.

Hall, Catherine. *Civilising Subjects: Metropole and Colony in the English Imagination, 1830–1867.* Chicago: University of Chicago Press, 2002.

Hamilton, Walter. *Parodies of the Works of English and American Authors.* London, 1884.

Harper, Marjory. *Adventurers and Exiles: The Great Scottish Exile.* London: Profile, 2003.

———. "British Migration and the Peopling of the Empire." In *The Nineteenth Century*, Oxford History of the British Empire, edited by Andrew Porter, 75–87. New York: Oxford University Press, 1999.

Harper, Marjory, and Stephen Constantine. *Migration and Empire.* Oxford History of the British Empire. New York: Oxford University Press, 2010.

Hazlitt, W. Carew. "Introduction." In Thomas Griffiths Wainewright, *Essays and Criticisms*, ix–lxxxi. London: Reeves & Turner, 1880.

Heidegger, Martin. "Poetically Man Dwells" In *Rethinking Architecture: A Reader in Cultural Theory*, edited by Neil Leach, 109–18. New York: Routledge, 1997.

Helsinger, Elizabeth K. *Rural Scenes and National Representation: Britain, 1815–1850.* Princeton, NJ: Princeton University Press, 1997.

Hemans, Felicia. "The Homes of England." *Blackwood's Edinburgh Magazine* 21 (Apr. 1827): 392. *British Periodicals.*

———. *Poems.* London: William P. Nimmo, 1878.

Higham, John. *Strangers in the Land: Patterns of American Nativism, 1860–1925.* New York: Antheneum, 1963 [1955].

Hill, Fidelia. *Poems and Recollections of the Past.* Sydney: T. Trood, 1840. British Library Rare Books.

Hirst, John. "Empire, State, Nation." In Schreuder and Ward, *Australia's Empire*, 141–62.

———. "Nation Building, 1901–14." In *The Cambridge History of Australia*. Vol. 2, *The Commonwealth of Australia*, edited by Alison Bashford and Stuart Macintyre, 15–38. New York: Cambridge University Press, 2013.

Hoffmann, Natalie Phillips. "Cosmopolitanism and National Identity: English-Language Poetry, 1820–1920." PhD diss., University of Maryland, College Park, 2015.

Hogan, James Francis. *The Irish in Australia*. Australian ed., Melbourne, 1888.

Hogg, Robert, ed. *An English Canadian Poetics*. Vol. 1, *The Confederation Poets*. Vancouver, BC: Talon Books, 2009.

"The Homes of the South." *Dublin University Magazine* 53 (Sept. 1858): 298–312. British Periodicals.

Hood, Thomas. *The Complete Poetical Works of Thomas Hood*. Edited by Walter Jerrold. London: Oxford University Press, 1920.

Hoorn, Jeanette. *Australian Pastoral: The Making of a White Landscape*. Fremantle, WA: Fremantle Press, 2007.

Horne, Richard H. "Canvass Town." *Household Words* 7 (18 June 1853): 361–67. British Periodicals.

———. *Galatea Secunda: An Odaic Cantata*. Melbourne: Printed for Private Circulation, 1867. National Library of Australia, Canberra.

———. "John Ferncliff: An Australian Narrative Poem." Manuscript dated 1866. State Library of New South Wales, Sydney. ML MSS 2410/13, CY Reel 3425.

———. *Orion, an Epic Poem*. London: J. Miller, 1843.

———. *Orion, an Epic Poem*. Australian ed., Melbourne: Blundell, 1854.

———. *Papers, 1810–1884; with associated papers, 1798–1932*. Print manuscript, State Library of New South Wales, Sydney. MS. MLMSS 2410/14.

———. *Prometheus the Fire-Bringer*. Edinburgh: Edmonston & Douglas, 1864.

———. *The South-Sea Sisters, A Lyric Masque*. Melbourne: H. T. Dwight, 1866.

Horsman, Reginald. *Race and Manifest Destiny: The Origins of American Racial Anglo-Saxonism*. Cambridge, MA: Harvard University Press, 1981.

Houston, Natalie M. "Newspaper Poems: Material Texts in the Public Sphere." *Victorian Studies* 50 (Winter 2008): 233–42.

Huggan, Graham. *Australian Literature: Postcolonialism, Racism, Transnationalism*. New York: Oxford University Press, 2007.

Hughes, Linda K. "What the Wellesley Index Left Out: Why Poetry Matters to Periodical Studies." *Victorian Periodicals Review* 40 (Summer 2007): 91–125.

Hughes, Robert. *The Fatal Shore: The Epic of Australia's Founding*. New York: Vintage, 1986.

Humphris, Edith, and Douglas Sladen, eds. *Adam Lindsay Gordon and His Friends in England and Australia*. London: Constable, 1912.

Hunter, James. *Scottish Exodus: Travels among a Worldwide Clan*. Edinburgh: Mainstream Publishing, 2007.

Hutton, Geoffrey. *Adam Lindsay Gordon: The Man and the Myth*. London: Faber & Faber, 1978.

Irving, Helen. "Making the Federal Commonwealth, 1890–1901." In *The Cambridge History of Australia*. Vol. 1, *Indigenous and Colonial Australia*, edited by Alison

Bashford and Stuart Macintyre, 242–66. New York: Cambridge University Press, 2013.
Irving, Washington. "Dedication" to *Poems by William Cullen Bryant, an American*. London: J. Andrews, 1832.
Jackson, MacD. P. "Poetry: Beginnings to 1945." In *The Oxford History of New Zealand Literature in English*, edited by Terry Sturm, 335–84. Auckland: Oxford University Press, 1991.
Jackson, Virginia. *Dickinson's Misery: A Theory of Lyric Reading*. Princeton, NJ: Princeton University Press, 2005.
———. "Longfellow's Tradition; or, Picture-Writing a Nation." *MLQ* 59 (Dec. 1998): 471–96.
Jameson, R. G. *New Zealand, South Australia, and New South Wales: A Record of Recent Travels in These Colonies*. London: Smith, Elder, 1842.
Janowitz, Anne. *Lyric and Labour in the Romantic Tradition*. Cambridge: Cambridge University Press, 1998.
Johnson, Anna, and Alan Lawson, "Settler Colonies." In *A Companion to Postcolonial Studies*, edited by Henry Schwarz and Sangeeta Ray, 360–76. Malden, MA: Blackwell, 2000.
Johnson, E. Pauline. *Canadian Born*. Toronto: George N. Morang, 1903.
Johnston, H. J. M. *British Emigration Policy, 1815–1830: "Shoveling Out Paupers."* London: Oxford University Press, 1972.
Jupp, James. *The English in Australia*. Cambridge: Cambridge University Press, 2004.
Kane, Paul. *Australian Poetry: Romanticism and Negativity*. Cambridge: Cambridge University Press, 1996.
Karskens, Grace. *The Colony: A History of Early Sydney*. Crows Nest, NSW: Allen & Unwin, 2009.
Keith, W. J. *Charles G. D. Roberts*. Toronto: Copp Clark, 1969.
Kendall, Henry. *Poetry, Prose, and Selected Correspondence*. Edited by Michael Ackland. St. Lucia: University of Queensland Press, 1993.
———. "Verses. By Henry Kendall. (Unpublished.)" *Athenaeum* (27 Sept. 1862): 394. *British Periodicals*.
Keneally, Thomas. *Australians: Eureka to the Diggers*. Crows Nest, NSW: Allen & Unwin, 2011.
———. *Australians: Origins to Eureka*. Crows Nest, NSW: Allen & Unwin, 2009.
Kennedy, William Sloane, ed. *Walt Whitman's Diary in Canada*. Boston: Small, Maynard, 1904.
Kipling, Rudyard. *Complete Verse*. New York: Anchor, 1989.
———. *Kim*. New York: Doubleday, 1922 [1901].
Knox, Robert. *The Races of Men: A Fragment*. Philadelphia: Lea & Blanchard, 1850.
Krebs, Paula. *Gender, Race, and the Writing of Empire: Public Discourse and the Boer War*. Cambridge: Cambridge University Press, 2004.
Kuduk Weiner, Stephanie. *Republican Politics and English Poetry, 1789–1874*. New York: Palgrave, 2005.
Lanier, Sidney. *Centennial Edition of the Works of Sidney Lanier*, edited by Charles R. Anderson. 10 vols. Baltimore: Johns Hopkins University Press, 1945.
LaPorte, Charles, and Jason R. Rudy, eds. *Spasmodic Poetry and Poetics*. Special issue of *Victorian Poetry* 42 (Winter 2004).

Lawson, Henry. *The Bulletin Story Book*. 2nd ed. Sydney: Bulletin Newspaper, 1901.
——. *In the Days When the World Was Wide and Other Verses*. Sydney: Angus & Robertson, 1903 [1896].
——. *On the Track*. Sydney: Angus & Robertson, 1900.
——. *Over the Sliprails*. Sydney: Angus & Robertson, 1900.
Leakey, Caroline W. *Lyra Australis; or, Attempts to Sing in a Strange Land*. London: Bickers & Bush, 1854.
Lecker, Robert. *Keepers of the Code: English-Canadian Literary Anthologies and the Representation of Nation*. Toronto: University of Toronto Press, 2013.
Lee, Christopher. "An Uncultured Rhymer and His Cultural Critics: Henry Lawson, Class Politics, and Colonial Literature." *Victorian Poetry* 40 (Spring 2002): 87–104.
Le Page, John. *The Island Minstrel: A Collection*. Charlottestown, PEI: William H. Bremner, 1867.
Lester, Alan. *Imperial Networks: Creating Identities in Nineteenth-Century South Africa and Britain*. London: Routledge, 2001.
Levine, Caroline. *Forms: Whole, Rhythm, Hierarchy, Network*. Princeton, NJ: Princeton University Press, 2015.
Levine, Philippa, ed. *Gender and Empire*. Oxford History of the British Empire. New York: Oxford University Press, 2004.
Lighthall, William Douw, ed. *Songs of the Great Dominion: Voices from the Forests and Waters, the Settlements and Cities of Canada*. London: Walter Scott, 1889.
Longfellow, Henry Wadsworth. *Poems and Other Writings*. New York: Library of America, 2000.
Lootens, Tricia. "Alien Homelands: Rudyard Kipling, Toru Dutt, and the Poetry of Empire." In *The Fin-de-Siècle Poem: English Literary Culture and the 1890s*, edited by Joseph Bristow, 285–310. Athens: Ohio University Press, 2005.
——. "Hemans and Her American Heirs: Nineteenth-Century Women's Poetry and National Identity." In *Women's Poetry, Late Romantic to Late Victorian: Gender and Genre, 1830–1900*, edited by Isobel Armstrong and Virginia Blain, 243–60. London: Macmillan, 1999.
——. "Hemans and Home: Victorianism, Feminine 'Internal Enemies,' and the Domestication of National Identity." *PMLA* 109 (Mar. 1994): 238–53.
——. *The Political Poetess: Victorian Femininity, Race, and the Legacy of Separate Spheres*. Princeton, NJ: Princeton University Press, 2016.
——. "Victorian Poetry and Patriotism." In *The Cambridge Companion to Victorian Poetry*, edited by Joseph Bristow, 255–79. New York: Cambridge University Press, 2000.
Macaulay, Thomas Babington. "Minute on Indian Education." In *Minutes on Education in India*, edited by H. Woodrow, 104–16. Calcutta: C. B. Lewis, 1861.
Mackail, John William. *Latin Literature*. New York: C. Scribner's Sons, 1895.
MacKenzie, John M., with Nigel R. Dalziel. *The Scots in South Africa: Ethnicity, Identity, Gender and Race, 1772–1914*. Manchester, UK: Manchester University Press, 2007.
Mackenzie, William Lyon. Broadside "Proclamation" from Navy Island, 13 Dec. 1837. Web: *Toronto Public Library*.

Painter, Nell Irwin. *The History of White People*. New York: W. W. Norton, 2010.
Paterson, Andrew Barton. *The Man from Snowy River and Other Verses*. Sydney: Angus & Robertson, 1896 [1895].
Patterson, Brad, Tom Brookings, and Jim McAloon. *Unpacking the Kists: The Scots in New Zealand*. Montreal: McGill-Queens University Press, 2013.
Paz, Denis G. *Popular Anti-Catholicism in Mid-Victorian England*. Stanford: Stanford University Press, 1992.
Peires, J. B. "The British and the Cape, 1814–1834." In *The Shaping of South African Society, 1652–1840*, edited by Richard Elphick and Herman Giliomee, 472–517. Middletown, CT: Wesleyan University Press, 1988.
Peterman, Michael A. "Reconstructing the *Palladium of British America*: How the Rebellion of 1837 and Charles Fothergill Helped to Establish Susanna Moodie as a Writer in Canada." Reprinted in Moodie, *Roughing It*, 538–59.
Piesse, Jude. *British Settler Emigration in Print, 1832–1877*. Oxford: Oxford University Press, 2016.
Pike, Luke Owen. *The English and Their Origin: A Prologue to Authentic English History*. London: Longmans, Green, 1866.
Pitt, Valerie. *Tennyson Laureate*. Toronto: University of Toronto Press, 1962.
Pitts, Jennifer. *A Turn to Empire: The Rise of Imperial Liberalism in Britain and France*. Princeton, NJ: Princeton University Press, 2005.
Plotz, John. *Portable Property: Victorian Culture on the Move*. Princeton, NJ: Princeton University Press, 2008.
"Poetry under a Cloud." *Irish Quarterly Review* 6 (Mar. 1856): 1–30. *British Periodicals*.
Porter, A. N., ed. *Atlas of British Overseas Expansion*. New York: Simon & Schuster, 1991.
Porter, Bernard. *The Absent-Minded Imperialists: Empire, Society, and Culture in Britain*. New York: Oxford University Press, 2004.
"The Press at Sea." *Chambers's Journal of Popular Literature, Science and Arts* 188 (Aug. 1867): 488–91. *British Periodicals*.
Price, Leah. *The Anthology and the Rise of the Novel from Richardson to George Eliot*. Cambridge: Cambridge University Press, 2000.
Price, Richard. *Making Empire: Colonial Encounters and the Creation of Imperial Rule in Nineteenth-Century Africa*. Cambridge: Cambridge University Press, 2008.
Pringle, Thomas. *The Autumnal Excursion; or, Sketches in Teviotdale: with Other Poems*. Edinburgh: Archibald Constable, 1819.
———. *Ephemerides; or Occasional Poems Written in Scotland and South Africa*. London: Smith, Elder, 1828.
———. *Narrative of a Residence in South Africa*. A new edition. London: Edward Moxon, 1840 [1834].
Prins, Yopie. "Break, Break, Break into Song." In *Meter Matters: Verse Cultures of the Long Nineteenth Century*, edited by Jason David Hall, 105–34. Athens: Ohio University Press, 2011.
———. *Ladies' Greek: Victorian Translations of Tragedy*. Princeton, NJ: Princeton University Press, 2017.
———. "Robert Browning, Transported by Meter." In McGill, *The Traffic in Poems*, 205–30.

———. *Victorian Sappho*. Princeton, NJ: Princeton University Press, 1999.

———. "What Is Historical Poetics?" *Modern Language Quarterly* 77 (Mar. 2016): 13–40.

Qureshi, Sadiah. *Peoples on Parade: Exhibitions, Empire, and Anthropology in Nineteenth-Century Britain*. Chicago: University of Chicago Press, 2011.

Ramazani, Jahan. *A Transnational Poetics*. Chicago: University of Chicago Press, 2009.

Review of *Poems and Songs, Descriptive and National* [sic], by John Barr. *Dundee Courier and Daily Argus* (2 Nov. 1861): 4. British Library Newspapers.

Review of *The Song of Hiawatha*. *Athenaeum* (10 Nov. 1855): 1295–96. British Periodicals.

Review of *The Song of Hiawatha*. *Chambers's Edinburgh Journal* 105 (5 Jan. 1856): 7–9. British Periodicals.

Review of *The St. Lawrence and the Saguenay; and Other Poems*. *Athenaeum* (17 Jan. 1857): 79. British Periodicals.

Richards, Eliza. "Correspondent Lines: Poetry, Journalism, and the U.S. Civil War." *ESQ* 54 (2008): 145–70.

Richards, Eric. "Migrations: The Career of British White Australia." In *Australia's Empire*, edited by Deryck M. Schreuder and Stuart Ward, 163–85. Oxford: Oxford University Press, 2008.

Richards, Michael. *People, Print, and Paper*. Canberra: National Library of Australia, 1988.

Rigney, Ann. "Embodied Communities: Commemorating Robert Burns, 1859." *Representations* 115 (Summer 2011): 71–101.

Roberts, Charles G. D. "The Beginnings of a Canadian Literature." In *Selected Poetry and Critical Prose*, edited by W. J. Keith, 243–59. Toronto: University of Toronto Press, 1974.

———. *In Divers Tones*. Boston: D. Lothrop, 1886.

Robson, Catherine. *Heart Beats: Everyday Life and the Memorized Poem*. Princeton, NJ: Princeton University Press, 2012.

Roderick, Colin, ed. *Henry Lawson Criticism, 1894–1971*. Sydney: Angus & Robertson, 1972.

Rose, Jonathan. *The Intellectual Life of the British Working Classes*. New Haven, CT: Yale University Press, 2002.

Rose, Margaret. A. *Parody: Ancient, Modern, and Post-Modern*. Cambridge: Cambridge University Press, 1993.

Rudy, Jason R. *Electric Meters: Victorian Physiological Poetics*. Athens: Ohio University Press, 2009.

———. "Hemans' Passion." *Studies in Romanticism* 45 (Winter 2006): 543–62.

———. "Manifest Prosody." *Victorian Poetry* 49 (Summer 2011): 253–66.

———. "On Cultural Neoformalism, Spasmodic Poetry, and the Victorian Ballad." *Victorian Poetry* 41 (Winter 2003): 590–96.

Rushdie, Salmon. *Imaginary Homelands: Essays and Criticism 1981–1991*. New York: Penguin, 1991.

Said, Edward. *Culture and Imperialism*. New York: Vintage, 1994.

Salesa, Damon Ieremia. *Racial Crossings: Race, Intermarriage, and the Victorian British Empire*. New York: Oxford University Press, 2011.

Sanders, Mike. *The Poetry of Chartism: Aesthetics, Politics, History*. Cambridge: Cambridge University Press, 2009.

Sangster, Charles. *The St. Lawrence and the Sanguenay*. In *Nineteenth-Century Narrative Poems*, edited by David Sinclair, 43–80. Toronto: McClelland & Stewart, 1972.

Saunders, John, and John Westland Marston, eds. "Recent Poetry." *National Magazine* 4 (Sept. 1858): 267–72. British Periodicals.

Schreuder, Deryck M., and Stuart Ward, eds. *Australia's Empire*. Oxford History of the British Empire. New York: Oxford University Press, 2008.

Schwarz, Bill, ed. *The Expansion of England: Race, Ethnicity, and Cultural History*. New York: Routledge, 1996.

"Scientific and Literary." *Athenaeum* (16 Dec. 1837): 913. British Periodicals.

Scott, Frederick George. *A Hymn of Empire, and Other Poems*. Toronto: William Briggs, 1906.

Seeley, John. *The Expansion of England*. Chicago: University of Chicago Press, 1971 [1883].

Semmler, Clement. "Paterson, Andrew Barton (Banjo)." *Australian Dictionary of Biography*, Vol. 11. Carlton, VIC: Melbourne University Press, 1988. Web edition.

Serle, Geoffrey. *The Golden Age: A History of the Colony of Victoria, 1851–1861*. Carlton, VIC: Melbourne University Press, 1977 [1963].

Shaikh, Fariha. "The Alfred and the Open Sea: Periodical Culture and Nineteenth-Century Settler Emigration at Sea." *English Studies in Africa* 57 (2014): 21–32.

Shelley, Percy. *Poetry and Prose*, edited by Donald H. Reiman and Sharon B. Powers. New York: W. W. Norton, 1977.

Shiels, Andrew. *The Witch of the Westcot; A Tale of Nova-Scotia, in three cantos; and other Waste Leaves of Literature*. Halifax: Joseph Howe, 1831.

Shum, Matthew. "Improvisations of Empire: Thomas Pringle in Scotland, the Cape Colony and London, 1789–1834." PhD diss., University of KwaZulu-Natal, Durban, 2008.

Shuttleton, David E. "'Nae Hottentots': Thomas Blacklock, Robert Burns, and the Scottish Vernacular Revival." *Eighteenth-Century Life* 37.1 (2013): 21–50.

Simson, Letitia F. *Flowers of the Year and Other Poems*. Saint John, NB: J. & A. MacMillan, 1869). Rare books collection at the Killam Memorial Library, Dalhousie University, Halifax.

Sladen, Douglas B. W., ed. *Australian Ballads and Rhymes: Poems Inspired by Life and Scenery in Australia and New Zealand*. London: Walter Scott, 1888.

Smeaton, Oliphant. "A Gallery of Australasian Singers." *Westminster Review* 144 (July 1895): 477–503. British Periodicals.

Socarides, Alex, *Dickinson Unbound: Paper, Process, Poetics*. New York: Oxford University Press, 2012.

"The Song of the Chaffinch on the Continent." *Penny Magazine* 7 (7 July 1838): 260. British Periodicals.

Spence, Catherine Helen. *An Autobiography*. Middletown, DE: Create Space Independent Publishing Platform, 2015.

———. *Clara Morison: A Tale of South Australia during the Gold Fever.* 2 vols. London: John W. Parker, 1854.

Spenser, Edmund. *The Faerie Queene.* New York: Penguin, 1978 [1590–96].

Stafford, Jane. "'No cloud to hide their dear resplendencies': The Uses of Poetry in 1840s New Zealand." *Journal of New Zealand Literature* 28 (2010): 12–34.

Stafford, Jane, and Mark Williams. *Maoriland: New Zealand Literature, 1872–1914.* Wellington, NZ: Victoria University Press, 2006.

Stapleton, R. J., ed. *Poetry of the Cape of Good Hope. Selected from the Periodical Journals of the Colony.* Cape Town, 1828.

Stedman, Edmund Clarence. *A Victorian Anthology, 1837–1895.* Boston: Houghton Mifflin, 1895. *Hathi Trust.*

Stevenson, Lionel. "Overseas Literature: From a Canadian Point of View." *English Review* (Dec. 1924): 876–86. *British Periodicals.*

Stewart, Susan. *Crimes of Writing: Problems in the Containment of Representation.* Durham, NC: Duke University Press, 1994.

———. *Poetry and the Fate of the Senses.* Chicago: University of Chicago Press, 2002.

[Stout, Robert]. "A Colonial View of Imperial Federation." *Nineteenth Century and After* 121 (Mar. 1887): 351–61. *British Periodicals.*

Strong, William. "Charles G. D. Roberts' 'The Tantramar Revisited.'" *Canadian Poetry* 3 (Fall/Winter 1978). Web: *Canadian Poetry Press.*

Sutherland, Alexander. "Henry Clarence Kendall." *Melbourne Review* 28 (Oct. 1882): 388–410.

Syron, Gordon. "Invasion Day" (2012). Artist's statement. Coo-ee Aboriginal Art Gallery, New South Wales.

Tanner, Marcus. *The Last of the Celts.* New Haven, CT: Yale University Press, 2004.

Tasker, Meg, ed. *Nineteenth-Century Australian Poetry.* Special issue of *Victorian Poetry* 40 (Spring 2002).

Tennyson, Alfred. *The Poems of Tennyson.* 3 vols. Edited by Christopher Ricks. Berkeley: University of California Press, 1987.

Thompson, Elizabeth. "*Roughing It in the Bush*: Patterns of Emigration and Settlement in Susanna Moodie's Poetry." *Canadian Poetry* 40 (Spring/Summer 1997). Reprint available online at *Canadian Poetry Press.*

Thompson, Leonard. *A History of South Africa.* New Haven, CT: Yale University Press, 2000.

Thomson, William Roger. *Poems, Essays, and Sketches, with a Memoir.* Cape Town: J. C. Juta, 1868.

Tiffany, Daniel. *My Silver Planet: A Secret History of Poetry and Kitsch.* Baltimore, MD: Johns Hopkins University Press, 2015.

Tompson, Charles. "Black Town." In *Bards in the Wilderness: Australia Colonial Poetry to 1920*, edited by Brian Elliott and Adrian Mitchell, 25–27. Hong Kong: Thomas Nelson, 1970.

———. *Wild Notes: From the Lyre of a Native Minstrel.* Sydney: University of Sydney Library, 2002 [1826]. Web edition: *Australian Literature Electronic Gateway.*

Townsend, Joseph Phipps. *Rambles and Observations in New South Wales.* London: Chapman & Hall, 1849.

Toye, William, ed. *The Oxford Companion to Canadian Literature*. Toronto: Oxford University Press, 1983.

Trachtenberg, Alan. *Shades of Hiawatha: Staging Indians, Making Americans, 1880–1930*. New York: Hill & Wang, 2004.

Traill, Catherine Parr. *The Backwoods of Canada: Being Letters from the Wife of an Emigrant Officer, Illustrative of the Domestic Economy of British North America*. London: Charles Knight, 1836.

Trollope, Anthony. *Australia and New Zealand*. 2 vols. 2nd ed. London: Dawsons of Pall Mall, 1968 [1873].

——. *John Caldigate*. New York: Dodd, Mead, 1911 [1879].

——. *South Africa*. 2 vols. London: Dawsons of Pall Mall, 1968 [1878].

Trumpener, Katie. *Bardic Nationalism: The Romantic Novel and the British Empire*. Princeton, NJ: Princeton University Press, 1997.

Tucker, Herbert. *Epic: Britain's Heroic Muse, 1790–1910*. New York: Oxford University Press, 2008.

Turner, Sharon. *The History of the Anglo-Saxons, from the Earliest Period to the Normal Conquest*. 2 vols. Philadelphia: Carey & Hart, 1841.

Veracini, Lorenzo. *Settler Colonialism: A Theoretical Overview*. New York: Palgrave, 2010.

Vincent, Tom. "Oliver Goldsmith." In *The Oxford Companion to Canadian Literature*, edited by William Toye, 305–6. Toronto: Oxford University Press, 1983.

"Visitants of Ships at Sea." *Chambers's Edinburgh Journal* 260 (25 Dec. 1858): 408–11. *British Periodicals*.

"A Voice on Emigration to Australia." *Chambers's Edinburgh Journal* 483 (2 Apr. 1853): 210–12. *British Periodicals*.

Wagner, Tamara S., ed. *Domestic Fiction in Colonial Australia and New Zealand*. London: Pickering & Chatto, 2014.

Wakefield, Edward Gilbbon. *A Letter from Sydney, the Principal Town of Australia, and Other Writings on Colonization*. London: J. M. Dent, 1929.

Wall, Barbara. "A Guide to Catherine Helen Spence." State Library of South Australia, Adelaide. Web: http://guides.slsa.sa.gov.au/spence.

Ward, Russel. *The Australian Legend*. Melbourne: Oxford University Press, 1978 [1958].

Waterhouse, Richard. "Settling the Land." In Schreuder and Ward, *Australia's Empire*, 54–77.

Waterston, Elizabeth. *Rapt in Plaid: Canadian Literature and Scottish Tradition*. Toronto: University of Toronto Press, 2003.

Webby, Elizabeth. "Literature and the Reading Public in Australia, 1800–1850: A Study of the Growth and Differentiation of a Colonial Literary Culture during the Earlier Nineteenth Century." PhD diss., University of Sydney, 1971.

"What to Take to Australia." *Household Words* (3 July 1852): 364–66. *British Periodicals*.

Wheatley, Henry B. "Preface" to *Reliques of Ancient English Poetry*, by Thomas Percy, ix–xi. London: Bickers & Son, 1876.

Whitelock, Derek. *Adelaide: From Colony to Jubilee, A Sense of Difference*. Adelaide, SA: Savvas, 1985.

Wilcox, Dora. *Verses from Maoriland*. London: George Allen, 1905.
Wilde, Oscar. "Adam Lindsay Gordon." *Pall Mall Gazette* (London, 25 Mar. 1889): 3. *British Library Newspapers*.
———. "Pen, Pencil and Poison." In *The Complete Works of Oscar Wilde*, 993–1008. New York: Harper & Row, 1989.
Williams, Carolyn. *Gilbert and Sullivan: Gender, Genre, Parody*. New York: Columbia University Press, 2010.
———. "Parodies of the Pre-Raphaelite Ballad Refrain." *Nineteenth-Century Literature* 71 (Fall 2016): 227–55.
———. "Poetry and Poetic Tradition: Gilbert and Sullivan's Patience." *Victorian Poetry* 46 (Winter 2008): 375–403.
[Wilson, John]. "American Poetry. William Cullen Bryant." *Blackwood's Edinburgh Magazine* 31 (Apr.1832): 646–64. *British Periodicals*.
Wilson, John. "Scots—The Otago settlement." Web: *Te Ara—The Encyclopedia of New Zealand*.
Wolfe, Patrick. *Settler Colonialism and the Transformation of Anthropology: The Politics and Poetics of an Ethnographic Event*. London: Cassell, 1999.
Wright, Judith. *Preoccupations in Australian Poetry*. Melbourne: Oxford University Press, 1965.
Wu, Duncan. "'A Vehicle of Private Malice': Eliza Hamilton Dunlop and the *Sydney Herald*." *Review of English Studies* 65 (2014): 888–903.

INDEX

The letter *f* following a page number denotes a figure

Abrams, M. H., 110, 114
accent. *See* dialect
Ackland, Michael, 111, 199n37
Adelaide, Australia, 10, 44–45, 103, 152f; early settlement, 65–66, 151–57; economic boom, 60
Agathocleous, Tanya, 182
Ambler, Benjamin George, 165
Anderson, Benedict, 22, 37, 136; and unisonality, 81, 97, 105
Anderson, Warwick, 119, 212n19, 218n2, 220n40
Anglo-Saxonism, 33, 163–70, 219n30; in Australia, 67, 166, 169–70, 172, 174, 177; in Canada, 178–81, 185; and colonialism, 144, 219n5, 219n30; myth of racial unity, 17, 220n59; and poetics, 164–65, 167–69, 183, 188
animals: antelope, 88; birds, 38, 40–41, 50, 131–32, 203n87, 203n88; cattle, 70, 120, 176; dingos, 107, 117; gazelle, 88; kangaroos, 50; sheep, 19, 70, 120, 186
anthologies (of colonial poetry): in Australia, 169–72, 174, 176, 180; in Canada, 100, 158, 179–81, 185–86; in South Africa, 15, 46, 48–55, 73
Argus (Melbourne), 67, 137–38, 140, 145, 171
Armstrong, Isobel, 17, 205n58, 210n68, 211n96
Arnold, Matthew, 69; "Dover Beach," 191–92, 222n3
Atwood, Margaret, 109–10

Auckland, New Zealand, 22, 46
Australia: agriculture in, 120; colonial poetry of, 3, 9, 59–60, 62–74, 103–4, 111–19, 130, 134–46, 151–57, 169–78; landscape of, 29, 71–72, 107, 112–20, 126–27, 130, 152, 155, 171, 174, 177; outback, 2, 7, 10, 66, 70–73, 126, 127, 172, 176–77, 185, 187; perceived lack of culture, 39, 41; preference for British goods, 63. *See also* First Fleet; gold digging (Australia); nationalism; transportation (of convicts)
Australian Federation, 146, 162, 166, 169
authenticity (of colonial culture), 43–74

ballad, 10, 14, 35, 89, 104–5, 202n65; bush-ballads, 69, 176–77; and nationalism, 78, 81–82, 202n65; and nostalgia, 36; Scottish, 87–88, 98
Barr, John, 90–95, 97, 105, 134, 190; advocate for New Zealand emigration, 94–95; as laborer, 90–91; as laureate, 134; and Scottish dialect, 90, 92–94, 109
Baynton, Barbara, 127
Belich, James, 4, 67, 77, 89, 198n36; and "cloning system," 44, 136; and race, 218n5
Bentley, D. M. R., 123, 180–81, 199n37
Berlant, Lauren, 58, 63, 222n100
Bird, Isabella L., 56–58, 63
Blair, Kirstie, 92, 211n106
Botany Bay, 107, 120
Boym, Svetlana, 25, 88

Brantlinger, Patrick, 113, 118
British Empire: colonial loyalty to, 108, 178, 180–81; and literary circulation, 7; and poetry, 12, 13, 108, 144, 178, 180, 186–88; and Scottish emigrants, 76–77
Browning, Elizabeth Barrett, 12, 17, 157–58, 160, 218n86
Browning, Robert, 11, 12, 15, 59, 137, 146; "How They Brought the Good News from Ghent to Aix," 70–73
Bryant, William Cullen, 15, 54; as colonial poet, 48–49; as generic, 50–51, 64–65; "Indian Girl's Lament," 64; "To a Water Fowl," 48, 49f, 50–51, 57, 63–65
Bulletin (Sydney), 172, 173, 175, 177
Bulletin School (Australia), 17, 166, 172–78
Burn, Henry, "Swanston Street from the Bridge," 67, 68f
Burns, Robert, 75, 90–91, 95, 97–103, 190; "Auld Lang Syne," 100–101, 104; and dialect, 78, 92; "Elegy on Capt. Matthew Henderson," 101; as Scottish national poet, 81; "Tom O'Shanter," 81
Burton, Antoinette, 7, 153
Butler, Martin, 165
Byron, George Gordon, 70, 199n41; *Childe Harold's Pilgrimage*, 159, 160

Calder, Alex, 109–10, 123
Campbell, Alexander, *Albyn's Anthology*, 82, 84, 85, 89
Campbell, John, 9–10, 11f, 55
Canada: colonial poetry of, 3, 60–62, 95–103, 119–28, 146–51, 158–61, 178–86; landscape, 109, 120–28, 150–51, 159–61, 182–86, 215n77; Scottish culture in, 95–103. *See also* Canadian Confederation; Confederation Poets (Canada); nationalism
Canadian Confederation, 7, 96, 123, 148, 162, 164, 178; poetry of, 158
Cape Town, South Africa, 2, 48–56, 129; colonial politics of, 52–53; early periodical press of, 15, 48, 54, 85
Carlyle, Thomas, 146, 167
Carter, Paul, 1, 29–30, 155, 197n5
Charlottestown, Prince Edward Island, 96
Chartism, 97–99, 102; and revision of Felicia Hemans, 60

circulation (of poetry), 7, 35, 46, 79, 89–90, 109
Clarke, Marcus, 69, 113, 115
class (social): and conditions for emigrants, 19, 22–23, 29; and education, 67, 97; and literary culture, 52–53, 97, 99, 102, 160; mobility between classes, 8, 78, 93, 104; and politics, 76, 94–95, 98; structure of, 7, 59, 77, 105, 140, 146–47, 154, 172, 177, 191; and working-class culture, 29–30, 91–92, 99, 173–74. *See also* dialect
Clough, Arthur Hugh, 12, 91, 210n68
Coetzee, J. M., 55–56, 212n15
Cohen, Michael, 79
Coleridge, Samuel Taylor, 23, 205n47
colonial culture, 2, 39, 46, 67–69, 161, 176, 190–91, 199n41; anxiety regarding, 25–26, 41–42, 108, 116, 207n104; as diverse, 93; and Indigenous cultures, 109, 113–19, 124–26, 131–32; as innovative, 15, 17, 71–73, 109, 158–61; marginalization of, 3–4. *See also* derivativeness (of colonial literature, perceived); plagiarism, and colonial culture
colonialists: and education, 38, 67, 108, 137, 141–42, 147, 149; and political identification, 20, 53, 108–11, 116–17, 132, 135, 148–49; and race, 108, 163–66, 169–88; relation to landscape, 29–30, 120–24, 126, 131–32, 151, 159–61; and violence, 6, 117–19, 127. *See also* colonial culture; communal feeling
colonial laureate, 6, 17, 134–61
communal feeling, 2, 8, 13, 15; on board ships, 22, 34; among emigrants, 97–102, 114, 132, 151; and genre, 51, 110, 132–33; and nationality, 81; and poetry, 54, 78, 90, 104, 110, 128, 135, 191; and war, 187–88
Confederation Poets (Canada), 17, 166, 181–86, 188
convicts. *See* transportation (of convicts)
Crawford, Isabella Valancy: and Canadian land-clearing, 124–25; *Malcolm's Katie*, 124–28; and Native American tropes, 125–26, 128, 132; *Winona*, 126, 215n77

Darwin, Charles, 120
Deakin, Alfred, 169, 177
derivativeness (of colonial literature, perceived), 4, 15, 44–46; in Australia, 39–40, 41, 64, 70; in South Africa, 54

Dewart, Edward Hartley, *Selections from Canadian Poets*, 100, 158, 180–81
dialect, 6, 15–16, 95, 147, 189; and nostalgia, 78, 105; Scottish, 77–81, 85, 88–89, 94, 97–101; "second-rateness" of, 105
Dickens, Charles, 137, 146
Dunedin, New Zealand, 90, 93–94
Dunlop, Eliza Hamilton, 62–64, 65, 73, 128; and massacre at Myall Creek, 62

economics, 76, 167, 181; of colonies, 60, 120, 144; and emigration, 22, 94, 154–55, 198n21
Edgar, James, 178–79
Edinburgh, Scotland, 79, 92, 94, 102, 140
education, 57, 108, 146, 149, 216n19
egalitarianism, 102; in Australia, 67, 173, 177; in Canada, 179; in New Zealand, 94
Emerson, Ralph Waldo, 117, 199n46
emigrant ships: life on board, 19–20, 23, 29–30, 200n18; poetry on board, 20–42, 110
emigration: conditions of, 23, 45; encouraged by poetry, 95, 97; socioeconomic reasons for, 76, 80, 154, 198n21; statistics for, 22, 89, 197n6, 200n13, 208n5
epic, 17, 31, 40, 137–40, 216n19
Espada, Martín, 189–90
exile, 2, 16, 21, 88; and colonial poets, 141–42, 144; and Ovid, 36–37; poems about, 40, 51–52, 59, 63, 86–89, 98, 114, 157

Field, Barron, 50, 139
First Fleet, 107, 120, 219n37
Flint, Kate, 32, 213n22
folk tradition, 98, 99, 104–5
Froude, James Anthony, 164, 188
Frye, Northrop, 121, 125, 199n37

Gaelic (language), 78, 79, 81, 94, 208n22, 209n46
genre: and circulation, 7, 14, 58, 73, 89, 166, 189; and colonialism, 6, 54, 73, 105, 124, 176, 192; and literary reproduction, 46, 73, 128, 135. *See also* ballad; epic; lyric poetry; ode
Gibson, Mary Ellis, 12, 109
Glasgow, Scotland, 76, 90, 97, 101–2, 105
gold digging (Australia), 22, 25, 66–67, 104, 137–39, 220n50

Golder, William, *New Zealand Minstrelsy*, 89–90
Goldie, Terry, 109, 125, 213n22, 215n91
Goldsmith, Oliver (Canadian), 120–24, 125, 128, 130, 132, 158, 184; and land-clearing, 120–24
Goldsmith, Oliver (English), *Deserted Village*, 120, 130
Goodlad, Lauren, 13, 218n5
Gordon, Adam Lindsay, 10, 15, 66–73, 111, 115; "From the Wreck," 70–73; and other colonial poets, 169, 176; and plagiarism accusations, 70, 72–73
Greater Britain, 17, 163–66, 168–69, 171, 178, 184, 218n5, 222n100

Halifax, Nova Scotia, 15, 45, 102–5, 168
Harpur, Charles, 9, 39, 114, 116
Hemans, Felicia, 6, 15, 45–46, 58, 63; Australian periodical press and, 59; colonial versions of, 56–66, 156–57; "Homes of England," 6–8, 59–62; "Indian Woman's Death Song," 62; sentimental tradition and, 15, 58–66, 79, 205n58; "The Traveller at the Source of the Nile," 56–58
Higham, John, 167
Highlanders (Scottish), 76, 80–82, 85, 88–89, 98–99, 105
Hill, Fidelia, 73, 139, 151–57, 161, 218n75; "Adelaide," 10, 153–55, 182; arrival in Adelaide, 151–53; first woman to publish a poetic volume in Australia, 10, 65, 151; and poetic tradition, 155–57; "Recollections," 65–66, 155–57
historical poetics, 6–8, 198n23
Hofmeyr, Isabel, 7, 153
Holford, Margaret, 54; "The Emigrant's Song of Memory," 51–52
homeland: as British, 25, 34, 38; colonial, 5–6, 8, 44, 133, 184–86, 192; dislocation from, 51; and nostalgia, 8, 78, 86; Scottish, 90, 93, 97, 101, 103
Hood, Thomas, "The Song of the Shirt," 14, 29–30
Horne, Richard H., 17, 25, 45, 137–46, 147, 158, 161; "Australian Explorers," 143; first volume of poetry published in Victoria, 17, 139–40; *Galatea Secunda*, 145–46; and

Horne, Richard H. (*continued*)
    Henry Kendall, 113, 119; *John Ferncliff*, 40;
    as Melbourne's poet laureate, 137–38,
    143–46; *Orion*, 137–41, 142; *Prometheus the
    Fire-Bringer*, 140–42; return to England,
    146; *South-Sea Sisters*, 144, 146, 190
Household Words (London), 23, 137, 147
Huggan, Graham, 173, 220n59
Hughes, Linda K., 24
Hughes, Robert, 44, 200n13
Hume, David, 76

imitation. *See* derivativeness (of colonial
    literature, perceived)
imperialism, 1, 21, 53, 108, 172, 198n21, 198n36,
    218n2; and Canada, 179, 180, 185; and
    ceremony, 135; and Imperial Federation, 17,
    164–70, 186, 188, 218n5; and India, 12, 34, 67,
    93, 107; and Ireland, 33; and literary
    circulation, 7, 13, 208n13; and Scotland, 75
India, 34, 53, 107–8; poetry of, 12, 13
indigeneity (of emigrants, imagined), 6, 16,
    108–33
Indigenous peoples: of Australia, 1, 62, 107,
    112, 126, 128, 130, 175; of Canada, 8, 121–28,
    179–80; displacement of, 1, 6, 8, 116, 128–29,
    190; and *Hiawatha*, 31–33, 124–25, 126,
    201n47; and land-rights, 122–23, 180; Maori,
    107, 109–11, 131–32; and music, 146, 217n41;
    poetic depictions of, 54–55, 114–15, 125, 128;
    trope of the dying Indian, 32, 118–19, 122,
    125; violence against, 113, 117–18, 129;
    Xhosa, 53, 128–29
Ireland, 62–63, 92, 179–80; emigration from,
    33–34, 36, 124, 147, 198n21, 202n51, 202n56

Jackson, Virginia, 3, 58, 124, 203n88
Johnson, E. Pauline, 179–80, 185

Kane, Paul, 70, 119, 130, 199n37, 212n15,
    214n50
Karskens, Grace, 112, 197n5
Kendall, Henry, 16, 39, 69, 111–20, 121, 124, 161;
    "Arcadia at Our Gates," 116–18; and colonial
    ambivalence, 113, 115–16, 118–19, 127; and
    emasculation, 170–71; *Leaves from
    Australian Forests*, 113–14, 118–19; as "Native
    Australian Poet," 111, 116–19; and other
    colonial poets, 129, 131–32, 144, 184; "Voice
    in the Native Oak," 115–16; "Wail in the
    Native Oak," 114–15, 118, 126, 127
Kendall, Thomas, 111–12
Kipling, Rudyard, 108, 164–65, 176; *Kim*,
    212n10; "The Native-Born," 108; in South
    Africa, 186–87
Knox, Robert, 166, 172

Lane, William, 173–74
Lanier, Sidney, 168, 184–85
laureate poetry, 6, 17, 134–61
Lawson, Henry, 104; "The Drover's Wife," 175;
    In the Days When the World Was Wide,
    173–75; racism of, 220n50, 220n61
Lawson, Louisa, 173
Leakey, Caroline, 65, 73, 128
Lee, Christopher, 172, 174
Le Page, John, 96
Levine, Caroline, 72
libraries, 2, 53, 103; National Library of
    Australia (Canberra), 14, 63; State Library of
    New South Wales, 1, 14, 17; State Library of
    Victoria (Melbourne), 67, 69, 140
Lighthall, William Douw, 179–80, 181, 185
literacy, 67, 87
London, England: Anti-Slavery Society of, 129,
    147; emigrant memories of, 10, 107; literary
    culture of, 66, 76, 102, 111, 113, 180;
    panorama of, 182; relation to colonies,
    67–68, 144, 147, 153, 155
Longfellow, Henry Wadsworth: *Evangeline*,
    182–84; *Hiawatha*, 14, 30–33, 124–26,
    201n47
Lootens, Tricia, 59, 62, 108, 136, 206n72
Loyalists, 135, 147–51
lyric poetry, 3, 41; and colonial culture, 54,
    124, 133; as generic, 50; "greater Romantic,"
    110, 114, 127; as overheard, 115, 119; as
    sentimental, 63, 128, 157, 189; as universal-
    izing, 58

Macaulay, Thomas Babington, 53; *Lays of
    Ancient Rome*, 66; "Minute on Indian
    Education," 93
Mackenzie, William Lyon, 148–50
Macquarie, Lachlan, 75–76, 134
Mair, Charles, 179–80

Manifest Destiny, 168, 185
Maori. *See* Indigenous peoples
Martin, Meredith, 136, 164–65, 199n43, 202n65, 208n17; and the "ballad theory of civilization," 3
Marx, Karl, 154
Matthews, John Pengwerne, 177, 199n38, 220n42
McGill, Meredith, 46, 52, 87, 202n65
McLachlin, Alexander, 9, 97–102, 105, 134, 158, 184; *The Emigrant*, 98–100; and the Scottish Gathering, 100–102, 190
McQueen, Humphrey, 169
Melbourne, Australia, 2, 15, 40, 102, 115, 158, 169; 1850s rise of, 66–69; class distinctions in, 147; colonial life in, 45, 147; Intercolonial Exhibition, 143–44, 145f, 158, 190; literary culture of, 17, 25, 46, 115, 137–46, 171; public library, 67, 69, 140
memorization (of poetry), 14, 57, 78–79, 136
meter, 28, 164; common meter, 35, 63; cultural work of, 10, 30, 136, 164, 171; elegiac couplet, 37, 42, 203n70; heroic couplet, 121, 124; hexameter, 182; of *Hiawatha*, 31; and nostalgia, 28, 35; and parody, 30–33; and poetic transmission, 71; sonnet, 168, 184; Spenserian stanzas, 159–61; tetrameter couplets, 10, 24. *See also* ballad
Mill, John Stuart: and imperialism, 53; on poetry, 2–3, 53, 88–89, 110
Milton, John, 156–57
Moir, David Macbeth, 92
Moodie, Susanna, 109–10, 146–51, 158, 217n50; and Anti-Slavery Society, 147; and British loyalty, 147–51; distaste for colonial culture, 147, 150, 159, 217n60; as laureate-like poet, 148–51, 161
Morris, William, 1, 5
Morrison, Toni, 175–76
Mufti, Aamir, 84, 93
Mulgan, John, 127
Murdoch, William, 96
music, 83, 141, 144, 190; Indigenous, 146, 217n41; as metaphor, 116, 126, 159; and Scotland, 82–83, 87, 89, 97. *See also* oral culture; song
Myall Creek, massacre at, 62

nationalism, 6, 12, 17, 25, 162, 188; Australian, 163, 166, 169–78, 181, 188, 201n29, 220n37; Canadian, 60–62, 128, 163, 166, 178–86, 188; Irish, 33; in New Zealand, 90, 163; Scottish, 76, 82
Native Americans. *See* Indigenous peoples
native. *See* colonialists; Indigenous peoples
newspapers: Australian, 2, 9, 25, 62–64, 69, 137–40, 191–92; British, 39, 44, 92, 94; Canadian, 149; on emigrant ships, 2, 6, 8, 16, 19–42, 146, 190; Irish, 33, 63; in New Zealand, 46, 90, 95; South African, 48, 56; in the United States, 46, 48
New Zealand: bookseller advertisements in, 46, 47f; colonial poetry of, 89–95, 130–32; feeling of belonging in, 109–10; landscape of, 94, 131–32; missionary work in, 111–12; and nationalism, 90; public recitation of Hemans in, 59; Scottish culture in, 89–95
nostalgia: and dialect, 78, 99; and emigration, 16, 25, 41, 213n19; and Indigenous culture, 125, 131; for original homelands, 5, 8, 60, 117–18, 184; and parody, 25; and poetry, 28–29, 35–38, 45–46, 203n75; for the rural, 92, 177; for Scotland, 83, 86–88, 90, 92, 99, 101, 103–5

ode, 134–37, 144–46
oral culture, 15, 76, 95, 209n46; and ballads, 78, 87, 89, 104–5, 209n51; and dialect, 85, 97, 102; and nostalgia, 90
Otago, New Zealand, 74, 79, 89–95, 96f, 103, 105, 134
Ovid, 36–38, 66, 70

Painter, Nell Irvin, 166
Pakeha turangawaewae, 109–10, 113, 123, 132
parody, 6, 25, 26–35, 42, 70, 110, 201n26
Paterson, Andrew Barton "Banjo," 69, 173, 182, 185–88; *Man from Snowy River*, 176–77; as poet of Australian nationalism, 172, 176–78; *Rio Grande*, 187–88
patriotism, 136, 151, 164, 189; Australian, 166; British, 147–50; Canadian, 123, 165–66, 181–82; in New Zealand, 90; Scottish, 101–2
performance (of poetry), 2, 78, 99–102, 179
Peterloo massacre, 76, 80
Phillip, Arthur, 1, 107

Pike, Luke Owen, 167
plagiarism, and colonial culture, 43–44, 70–74
Plotz, John, 163; idea of portable property, 77, 88, 97, 208n13
poetry: and Anglo-Saxonism, 164–65, 167–69, 183, 185; of the British Empire, 12, 13, 108, 144, 178, 180, 186–88; and communal feeling, 54, 78, 90, 104, 110, 128, 135, 191; on emigrant ships, 20–42, 110; about exile, 40, 51–52, 59, 63, 86–89, 98, 114, 157; about Indigenous peoples, 54–55, 114–15, 125, 128; and nostalgia, 28–29, 35–38, 45–46; and portability, 7, 78, 88; as ubiquitous, 2, 8–10, 14. *See also* poetry of individual countries
politics: and British poetry, 29, 59, 197n13; colonial independence from Britain, 12, 25, 76, 148–50, 164–66, 168, 177, 187; and colonial poetry, 2–3, 8, 13, 61–63, 86, 90, 96–102, 149–51, 165; and parody, 32–33, 35; and settler colonialism, 52–53, 76–77, 128, 134, 137, 148–51, 165–69, 187–88, 189; and ship newspapers, 34–35. *See also* class (social); egalitarianism
Prince, Mary, 147
Pringle, Thomas, 15, 79–89, 90, 95, 97, 106, 184; "Afar in the Desert," 54–56, 57, 128; *African Sketches*, 86; and Anti-Slavery Society, 129, 147; *Autumnal Excursion*, 80, 83–84; "The Banks of Cayle," 82–83, 84f, 87; "The Bechuana Boy," 128; and the Cape Colony, 54–56, 80–81, 85–89, 204n31; "The Emigrant's Song," 85–86; *Ephemerides*, 86, 87; as laureate-like poet, 134; *Narrative of a Residence*, 80, 84–85
Prins, Yopie, 7, 71, 83, 206n73

race: and health, 119, 170–71, 212n19; mixed, 128–29; and national identity, 17, 163–88; and sentimentality, 62–63. *See also* Anglo-Saxonism; Indigenous peoples; White Australia (policy)
railroad, 8, 177, 181
rhyme, 28, 98, 164, 165, 188
rhythm (poetic), 165, 177, 183; as cultural, 7, 136, 164, 188, 217n41; galloping, 10, 69, 71, 172
Roberts, Charles G. D., 181–85, 188; as cosmopolitan nationalist, 181, 185–86;
panoramic view, 182–84; "Tantramar Revisited," 182–84
Robinson, Michael Massey, 134–37
Robson, Catherine, 57, 78, 136
Romanticism, 55, 180; and breezes, 55; and harps, 38; and interiority, 53; and lyric, 40, 54, 110, 114, 127, 214n50; and nostalgia, 184; and the sublime, 210n59
Rushdie, Salman, 5–6, 8

Saint John, New Brunswick, 6, 7–8, 60, 96, 181
Sangster, Charles, 17, 151, 158–61; and Canadian landscape, 159–61; as laureate-like poet, 159, 161; and romance, 159–61
Scotland, 75–106; ballad culture of, 78; and colonialism, 75–77, 80; emigration from, 75–79, 102–4; as homeland, 78, 88, 128, 184; landscape of, 83, 87–88, 101, 103; and working-class culture, 97, 99. *See also* dialect; Gaelic (language); Highlanders (Scottish)
Scott, Frederick George, 188, 222n98
Scott, Walter, 46, 80, 82, 88; *Minstrelsy of the Scottish Border*, 89; and Scottish solidarity, 76
Seeley, John, 148, 163–64, 177, 188
sentimentality, 2, 58, 62–65, 79, 110, 157, 166
settler colonialism. *See* colonialists
Shakespeare, William, 156–57, 167, 184
Shelley, Percy, 40, 141–42, 184
Shiels, Andrew, 102–4
ship newspapers. *See* newspapers
Simson, Letitia F., 7–8, 60–62, 72, 73
Sladen, Douglas, 69; *Australian Ballads and Rhymes*, 169, 170f, 171–72, 174, 180
Smith, Adam, 76
Smith, Alexander, 97, 160
song: and ballads, 14, 82–83, 78, 87, 98; of birds, 40–41, 203n87, 203n88; communal, 88–89, 101, 104–5, 174, 211n96; and dialect, 16, 77, 85–87, 97, 104, 208n22, 209n46; Indigenous, 146, 180, 217n41; and national culture, 78, 81–82, 88, 148, 150, 178, 185, 189; of nature, 115–16, 159; and nostalgia, 35, 81, 87–88, 92, 99; parodic, 21, 201n26. *See also* music; oral culture
South Africa: "1820 settlers," 76–77, 80–81, 86, 129; colonial poetry of, 9–10, 48–56, 79–89,

128–30; landscape of, 9–10, 54–56, 86–89, 129, 210n59
Spasmodic poets, 160
Spence, Catherine Helen, 103–4; *Autobiography*, 19, 45, 104; *Clara Morison*, 19, 104, 152–53; first woman to run for political office in Australia, 104; newspaper poetry, 103–4
Stafford, Jane, 131, 199n37
Stapleton, R. J., *Poetry of the Cape of Good Hope*, 48, 49f, 50–56
Stedman, Edmund Clarence 3, 213n39
Stout, Robert, 164
Swinburne, Algernon Charles, 183, 221n93
Sydney, Australia, 1, 6, 14, 62, 177, 197n5; colonial architecture of, 75; convicts transported to, 43–44, 130, 134–35; and Federation, 169; Indigenous peoples in, 112; as industrialized, 117, 118; literary culture in, 9, 51, 59, 63–64, 134–35, 143, 172–77
Sydney Morning Herald, 2, 107, 111, 113, 119, 143, 186
sympathy, poetic evocations of, 62, 64, 86. *See also* communal feeling
Syron, Gordon, 1

Tennyson, Alfred, 12, 59, 69, 134, 146, 160; "Break, Break, Break," 30; and colonial book sales, 59, 69; colonial performances of, 2; *Maud*, 14, 27–29; "The May Queen," 2; parodied, 27–29; as Poet Laureate, 134
Thomson, William Roger, 129–30
Tompson, Charles, 130
Toronto, Canada, 100, 102, 148–50
Traill, Catherine Parr, 121, 122f
transportation (of convicts), 22, 43–44, 120, 130, 134–35, 154, 200n13
Trollope, Anthony, 13, 19; on Cape Town, 55–56, 129; on Melbourne, 66
Trumpener, Katie, 33, 76, 80, 209n46; and "transcolonial consciousness," 95, 101
Turner, Sharon, 166

United States, 57, 67, 69, 76, 91, 113, 149; literary culture of, 44, 46, 52, 64–65, 128, 181–85; poetry of, 15, 31–33, 39, 48–51, 54, 64, 73, 136; and race, 175. *See also* Manifest Destiny

Veracini, Lorenzo, 2, 132, 214n61

Wainewright, Thomas Griffiths, 43–44, 204n1
Wakefield, Edward Gibbon, 153–54
Wales, 92, 105, 179, 221n73
Ward, Russel, 172–73
wars and conflicts: American War of Independence, 76, 120; Boer Wars (South Africa), 164–65, 186–88; Canadian Rebellion (1837), 148–50, 158; Frontier Wars (South Africa), 129; Indian Rebellion (1857), 34; War for Mexican Independence, 137
Wellington, New Zealand, 45, 90
White Australia (policy), 166, 169. *See also* Anglo-Saxonism; Indigenous peoples; race
Whitman, Walt, 159, 184
Wilcox, Dora, 130–32, 215n91
Wilde, Oscar: "Pen, Pencil and Poison," 43–44; review of Adam Lindsay Gordon, 70, 72
Williams, Carolyn, 25, 35
Williams, Mark, 131, 199n37
women: on emigrant ships, 23, 29–30; and emigration, 65; and literacy, 67; poets, 7–8, 12, 51–52, 56–66, 73, 124–32, 146–57, 179–80, 206n72, 206n83, 218n75; and political advocacy, 173–74; and social mobility, 104
Wordsworth, William, 48, 89, 146; colonial revisions of, 100, 155–56, 182
Wright, Judith, 9, 70, 199n37

Xhosa. *See* Indigenous peoples

Young Canada (movement), 180–81